'Joy ... in the Morning'
FAVORITES™

Selected Inspirational Columns

Written, Re-edited, Compiled
by
Dotty Moore

Wings of Joy Publishers ™

579B Paperdale Rd.   Stillwater, Pennsylvania 17878-9351

'Joy...in the Morning' FAVORITES by Dotty Moore
Selected Inspirational Columns, re-edited,
which first ran in the Press Enterprise.
Copyright © 2003 by Dotty Moore. All rights reserved.
First Edition. First Printing.

To purchase additional copies of this book, write or call:
Wings of Joy Publishers ™
579B Paperdale Rd., Stillwater, PA 17878
Phone: (570) 925-2555 or (570) 925-6888 E-mail: dotty@bwkip.com

Cover Design and Photos: © 2003 Jim Moore
Book Design and Layout: Jim Moore

ISBN 0-9744581-0-4

Printed in the U.S.A.

Dedicated to the Lord
as an offering
of
praise and thanksgiving
for every time
He
has touched, blessed
and sustained
me...
when
I needed
joy.

Blessings of Joy!
Dottye Moore
Isaiah 35:10

Meet the author...

Dotty Moore, with a Bachelor of Science degree in elementary education, never taught fulltime, but her easy-to-read style of writing reveals a teacher at heart.

Author of a popular, weekly inspirational newspaper column " 'Joy...in the Morning,' " appearing since 1985 in the *Press Enterprise* out of Bloomsburg, Pennsylvania, Dotty has had pieces published in *Pathways To God; The Christian Writer; The* (Shippensburg, Pa.) *News-Chronicle*; and *The* (Sweet Valley, Pa.) *Suburban News.* Her very first publication credit came in grade four when one of her poems ran in a professional teachers' journal.

From March 1988 to December 1993, Dotty was religion editor at the *Press Enterprise,* writing church announcements and numerous feature articles for the paper's religion pages.

With more than 900 columns to date, and still producing a new one each week, Dotty insists she is first of all a wife, a mother, a grandmother and a friend. A love for the Lord and her family defines her life. Husband Jim is a Christian counselor, and with both he and Dotty working out of their rural home near Stillwater, Pennsylvania, Dotty is called upon to wear a variety of hats, daily. Grown-daughters April and Lori; and granddaughters Dallas and Lily live not far away.

As a guest speaker, Dotty has been well-received in churches and women's groups in her home state; in New York State; and out of the country in the Grand Cayman Islands. In 1986, for a column about "Milk Carton Kids," Dotty placed fourth in a national writing competition sponsored by the Amy Foundation Writing Awards.

After two years of undergraduate studies in Anderson, Indiana, at Anderson College (now University), Dotty transferred to Shippensburg State College (now University) in Pennsylvania, where, in 1967, she earned a bachelor's degree.

With Gratitude

It is with grateful acknowledgment and sincere appreciation I thank God for:

Paul "Pete" Eyerly III, publisher of the *Press Enterprise* daily newspaper, and his family for their tireless commitment to producing an awarding-winning publication while maintaining high standards of community service and involvement;

Editors Carl Beck (former) and Jim Sachetti (present) who welcomed me and the " 'Joy...in the Morning' " column to be a part of the religion pages in the *Press Enterprise* each Saturday since February 2, 1985;

Faithful readers, church families and friends who have prayed for me, written to me, called me and spurred me on through many a dark night and fearsome storms. Scores of you have become precious to me, even though, in many instances, we have not yet met face to face;

The Billy Graham Evangelistic Association, Minneapolis, Minnesota, for sponsoring schools of Christian writing and schools of evangelism where I found direction, encouragement and courage to pursue writing opportunities. In particular I value Roger C. Palms, former editor of BGEA's *Decision* magazine, who directed the School of Christian Writing I attended for the first time in Toronto, 1978, and again in Minneapolis, 1987;

My husband Jim for his devotion and good humor whenever he is stopped on the street and addressed as "Mr. Joy in the Morning." He and the rest of our family, especially daughters April and Lori, and granddaughters Dallas and Lily, have willingly "volunteered" themselves as material for my writing and speaking. I covet your prayers, your love and your support. You guys are my life.

'JOY...in the MORNING' FAVORITES
is a compilation of inspirational newspaper columns
written by freelance columnist Dotty Moore.
Originally published in the *Press Enterprise*, the 138
columns selected for this book are
re-edited, rewritten or revised.

Contents

'JOY...in the MORNING' FAVORITES is one volume
consisting of two parts:

FIRST PART — thought-provoking, yet conversational
perspectives on *Daily Life* topics and issues categorized,
alphabetically, from "acceptance" and "attitude" to "work" and
"worry." The goal is to equip you with a renewed outlook along
life's journey, one step at a time, often with a smile.

SECOND PART — reflections and insights surrounding
celebrations of *Seasonal & Holiday Life*. See how your approach
to the changing seasons and special events in your life become
landmarks of who you really are, not only on extraordinary days,
but also year in and year out.

A date appears with each reading as a point of reference to
when the original piece ran in the *Press Enterprise*.

———

FIRST PART

Daily Life

SECOND PART

Seasonal & Holiday Life

FOREWORD

Dotty Moore talks to us. She doesn't lecture or sermonize, she visits. That's what I like about her writing.

We first met 25 years ago. That was before she started writing her weekly column " 'Joy...in the Morning.' " She has been writing her column for 18 years. Now she has compiled a collection of favorite columns in this volume.

There will be a lot of exclamations of "I remember this column." Many readers will say, "This one really spoke to me right at the time I needed it," and still others are going to say, "Good, I've been telling my friends in other states about Dotty's writing. Now I can send them a copy of her book."

I'm glad she's putting this volume together. Her down-to-earth honesty; her right-where-we-live way of looking at things makes these visits with Dotty special. But then, you already know that.

Roger C. Palms

...editor of Billy Graham Evangelistic Association's Decision *magazine from 1976 to 1998*

BY WAY OF INTRODUCTION...

'Joy...in the morning' is a promise

March 2, 1985

Every last one of us has headaches and heartaches, problems and worries ranging from the kids driving us crazy on a Saturday morning to life-or-death wars waged against cancer; from a flat tire to someone contemplating suicide.

During our time of being burdened with whatever problem comes our way, things appear hopeless, dark, like the night. During the night, we weep. Sometimes it seems like the weeping and the night will never end. Quite possibly the night has already been many hours, many months or many years long, and it's not over yet.

Someone knows about our nights and our weeping. Someone cares. This Someone is God and He has something to say in His Word about our situation. Psalm 30:5 reassures us that "...weeping may endure for a night, but joy cometh in the morning" (KJV).

There is no getting around it: weeping and night come to all of us. But (and there *is* a "but") *joy cometh in the morning.*

That's a promise.

It's not my promise. It's God's promise.

It's not my word. It's His.

God doesn't say how long or how deep our nights will be. But He does say that there will be joy in the morning.

When is morning?

Morning is when the light of day begins to push the night away.

Morning is when there is a breakthrough, however slight, concerning the dark situation through which we have been weeping.

In these pages, it's a privilege to try to help lighten the load of some of the problems that accompany daily living. None of us is free of responsibilities and concerns. None of us can escape the nights of weeping. But together, sometimes through laughter and sometimes through tears, you and I can look for and expect to find the "joy...in the morning." □

Living within reach of God's storehouse

February 3, 2001

The " 'Joy...in the Morning' " column began running in the *Press Enterprise* on the first Saturday in February 1985. Prior to the column's debut, yours truly was somewhat concerned there might come a time, perhaps after six months or so, when I might encounter a shortage of ideas. What if there was nothing to share? Not even an inspirational thought or two?

To be honest, "the concern" was actually a fear. A fear so gripping I contemplated backing out a few weeks before the first column appeared. But something occurred to me; I credit the Lord with tapping me on the shoulder of practicality. It was nothing more than a humorous little analogy, but it made all the difference in the world. It gave me courage to take the step, and here we are, all these years later, still going strong.

The tapping I sensed was an unspoken flash-of-a-thought question that didn't really need an answer, and yet the answer was clear: *The day you got married, Dotty, you weren't afraid you would run out of ideas about what to cook for you and Jim for supper each day for the rest of your lives, were you?*

When I "heard" that question, I smiled. One of the things Jim and I enjoyed right from the beginning of our marriage in 1965 was grocery shopping together. Although, like most newlyweds, we had a tight budget — he was just starting a teaching career and I was still in college — we took pleasure in figuring out what to eat. Naturally, we didn't plan detailed menus for the next 75 years or so in advance. We took it a day or a week at a time. The same would hold true for " 'Joy...in the Morning.' " And it has.

Perhaps you, right now, are facing a task or a decision that calls for resources you fear you might not have. You might be concerned you lack the energy, the drive, the vision or a myriad of other necessary ingredients for success.

The most important issue, however, is not the resources at *your* disposal, but the resources that God holds in His storehouse. When He calls you or me to take a specific action, He is the One we can repeatedly trust to replenish our supply of whatever is needed to accomplish what He has directed us to do.

No one can tell you or me in advance exactly how the Lord will grant us the strength, the wisdom or the wherewithal to carry out whatever commitment He has lead us into. But one thing is certain: He will not expect more of us than He plans to provide.

In all these years, I have faced countless deadlines when it appeared I had nothing to write, nothing to offer, nothing to share. But the Lord met the need with a word here or a comment there; a song or a story that came across my path; a phone call; a note that came in the mail; or a variety of circumstances so diverse that I am both continually and vividly reminded of God's unlimited provisions.

Ingredients for " 'Joy...in the Morning' " come from so many different sources that I have no choice but to acknowledge God's hand, time and time again. I thank Him for not letting me quit before I got started. I thank Him for the prayers of so many people, behind the scenes, who continue to participate in the long life of this column.

Since 1993, I've tried to compile a book of " 'Joy...in the Morning' " favorites. One thing or another always slows the progress of fulfilling this dream, but it's still alive. Perhaps this will be the year!

It's no coincidence this very column is dedicated to anyone who might be questioning whether or not to accept a particular assignment or to persevere toward completion of an unseen end. Hang in there! You can do it if the Lord is the One nudging you onward.

A few month's ago, someone asked me, regarding "my project," if I could see the light at the end of the tunnel. My response was, "No, but I think I have finally located the tunnel!"

My prayer for anyone in a similar predicament is that you, too, with the Lord's help, might keep looking for *your* tunnel. Who, but God, knows what any of us might accomplish this very week, this very day, if we don't lose heart. Lord willing, we *will* make it!

P.S.:

When the above column was written in 2001, it turned out that wasn't the year, after all, for me to publish a book. Only in hindsight does it make sense it should be now, instead. I never wanted to say this, but I do see the advantage of all those delays.

FIRST PART

'Joy ... in the Morning' Favorites

Daily Life

Trust in the LORD with all your heart,
And lean not on your own understanding;
In all your ways acknowledge Him,
And He shall direct your paths.
Proverbs 3:5-6 (NKJV)

CHAPTER ONE

Acceptance

Reflecting on gains and losses

March 18, 1989

Thirteen years ago yesterday, my husband Jim and I fell in love with a piece of land. We had been looking for the right place to build our dream house, and when we saw this particular forest with its panoramic view a mile outside of Benton, we knew it was perfect.

There was only one catch: The land wasn't for sale.

Even so, Henry and Ruth Babb, the man and his wife who owned the farm on which "our land" was located, decided to sell us the seven-and-a half acres that had caught our eye.

The whole adventure of owning that land had begun with Jim's giving me a surprise gift on March 17, 1976, my thirty-first birthday. The present was his cooking lunch for the two of us and then taking me for a drive anywhere I wanted to go.

Seeing as how we had lived in the area slightly more than six months, I chose a road we had never been on before. It was when that road climbed a hill above the Benton Cemetery and rounded a bend that we saw it: the land and the view.

As we gasped at the snow-covered mountains and hills beyond, little did we know what joy and what heartbreak were to come from that moment.

During the next couple of years, it was to be on that land, standing on a stump, that I fell in love with the Lord.

It was there in the peaceful atmosphere that I began to take my dream of writing seriously.

It was also on that land many family memories were created with camp outs, wiener roasts, kite flying, tobogganing and work. We cleared out brush and cut down trees, leaving all the right ones in place to frame the soon-to-be-built (or so we thought) log house.

But before the house was ever built anywhere other than in our dreams, we had to say good-bye to the dream and to the land.

During the three years that the land was ours, we couldn't afford to start building the log house until we sold our house in Benton.

"What will you do if your house doesn't sell?" a friend had asked us.

"It'll sell. It's just a matter of time," we responded, never guessing we were wrong.

The house didn't sell. And after Jim's job as administrator of the Benton Area Health Center was eliminated due to cutbacks in federal funding, we had to sell the land. Since Jim was unemployed for more than a year, the profit from the sale of the land helped to see us through the crunch.

That was in 1978 and 1979. We had no way of knowing, then, that history would repeat itself, and that in 1986, we would face a similar jobless situation — again.

We learned a lot from all of this.

We learned that sometimes dreams are meant to be spent — and that's what we had to do to survive.

It took a few years to "almost recover" from the death-of-a-dream ordeal, but eventually we experienced the birth of new dreams. Through it all, as hard as it was (and believe me, it was) we gained more than we lost:

We lost energy but gained a deeper dependency on the Lord

for His strength to sustain us; we lost our savings, including our daughters' future college funds, but gained compassion for others going through trials of their own; we lost sleep but learned how to rest in the Lord (not always, but most of the time); we lost a dream but gained a desire to focus on the Lord's plan for us more than on our plans for ourselves.

For me personally, falling in love with the land we eventually lost was worth more than the land itself, because as I said earlier, it was there I fell in love with the Lord. Although I had "known" Him and had been a Christian most of my life, I had missed out on the joy, the thrill of truly loving Him and absorbing His Presence. The land afforded me the setting and the space I needed to "converse" aloud with a God Who meets every need in His own divine way.

Reflecting on all of this, this week, as I once again celebrated another birthday, I realized that some dreams are eternal. And because Christ bought me with His life, I have already gained more than I'll ever lose.   □

Hand-me-down ideas, and one ideal, worth pondering

June 21, 2003

Hand-me-downs are among life's most prized possessions. Hand-me-down clothes. Hand-me-down trinkets. Hand-me-down stories or memories. Even hand-me-down ideas and ideals bear fruit, both bitter and sweet, from generation to generation.

Most recently I've been taking a long look at a hand-me-down concept that, as far as I know, remains timeless in its

application: There is something to be learned from every experience, otherwise life is in vain.

You've probably heard it as often as I have, stated and restated in many different ways. Yes, there is a purpose, not only
for living, but also for everything that happens to us in the
course of our lives.

We might not always receive it with an open mind, but we
do know it's true. If we believe that there is a purpose for everything that happens, then we are also affirming the stance
that there's a reason things go wrong. A reason for tears. A
reason for pain. A reason for sorrow. For brokenness. For heartache. For detours and delays.

Too often, however, we assume we must move quickly from
the hurtful things we encounter rather than linger near their
shadow for the sole purpose of understanding "the purpose."
If only we can get on with life after grief we might spare ourselves more pain, we reason, so we pooh-pooh the need to stand
still for a while under the guise we're moving on.

But whoever authored the notion that standing still is a bad
thing, especially when we've suffered a loss that only time,
and rest, will heal? A hand-me-down theory holds true: Rushing away from the "scene" of our hurts often only prolongs a
deeper recovery. Much like a physical wound can fester if it
scabs over too readily, an injured spirit deprived of adequate
time to weep harbors the risk of a worse hurt building up beneath the surface.

Unfortunately, society and even well-meaning friends un-
consciously assign a schedule to our getting on with life after
a tragedy or devastating loss. This is one hand-me-down not
worth hanging on to. Whenever you or I listen to others who
are not walking in our shoes, we can be setting ourselves up
for added bitterness later on. Honesty really *is* best. Instead of
avoiding being honest with others or self, we're better off to
separate our tendency to comply with expectations from our
deep need to dissect, understand, accept, cope with and then
live with reality.

One of the reasons I've been thinking a great deal lately about there being a time-tested redeeming quality for everything that happens, is because all around I see heartbreak. There is so much grief that so many of us are struggling to overcome, and if there is no purpose for it, then who has failed? Us or God?

Obviously, God has not failed. For God to fail is an impossibility. But in most cases we haven't failed either. We're merely victims of hurts that are common to the human race. Nonetheless, no matter how common, the hurts are real. The questions are bold. The hunger for answers is insatiable. Yet we're afraid to admit it. We try to hide behind a façade of what's expected of us — a hand-me-down Stoicism — rather than stand our ground and say, "I don't understand, world, but please bear with me until I can at least accept that I'll probably never understand!"

Amazingly, "never understanding" doesn't negate the age-old concept that there is something to be learned from every experience. Often what we learn is that, although there is a reason for everything that happens, we might have to live the rest of our lives without ever knowing "the reason" for some of the things that matter most to us.

That's why there is more than good reason for leaning on a hand-me-down faith in the Lord. Not a worn-out, hand-me-down faith, however, but a fresh, decisive, active belief steeped in acceptance, at last. Many, many, many times it's the only ideal that makes any sense at all. It's a fruit born of the very essence of God's handing down a plan for us to relinquish into His grasp what we can never totally comprehend.   ☐

CHAPTER TWO

Attitude

Spiritual care just can't be neglected

January 13, 2001

It's a fact of life: Some things you just gotta' do because not doing them shows! Recalling this recently helped me not to let discouragement get the best of me.

It was one of those cold January mornings with wind-chill temperatures whistling around the vicinity of zero degrees. If it hadn't been garbage-pick-up day, you couldn't have dragged me more than 10 feet away from a warm cup of tea and my cozy reading corner.

But garbage day it was! Everything we had piled up since Christmas needed bagged up and boxed up to be thrown away. Then it had to be pushed and pulled out our lane on our hauling cart through a few inches of snow. (Ordinarily my husband would have done this part, but he had to leave before I had the garbage assembled.)

After two trips out the lane I was cold and tired, but not yet exhausted nor frozen, so I decided to do the composting. Seeing as how I was already bundled up with extra layers, boots, head-band, hood and insulated gloves, it made sense not to have to bundle up again later.

By the time I made a path through the drifted snow to our compost bin, freed the frozen-shut lid and carried out three buckets' worth of organic scraps and peelings, *then* I was exhausted. My frozen toes were on fire; my socks were soggy from the snow that had wedged its way inside my not-high-enough boot tops. Even so, I felt like I had really accomplished something. Two big jobs were done. So was the morning. Now it was time for lunch.

Inside the warm house, my pleased-with-myself attitude endured just long enough for me to peel off my wet gloves, boots and socks. It was at that moment I made the mistake of glancing around the kitchen and the living room. Heaving a sigh nearly equal to the size of the tasks I had just completed, I dropped my head.

"You can't see one thing I've done," I whined out loud. "I've been up since 5:30 and the house looks like I never crawled out of bed!"

That's when I knew: It's times like this you can't let discouragement get the best of you! I have a feeling many of you readers know what I mean. You work, you overwork, you get exhausted and still you can't see a thing you've done. Yet deep down you know things would be worse if you stopped trying.

This brings to mind other areas of life where neither you nor I can allow ourselves to give up. Places that don't *show* per se, but places that *do* show if we do nothing. On a regular basis we have to give some time and effort to "cleaning up" our attitudes, our outlooks, our thoughts and our neglected spiritual corners.

Effort. Work. Discipline. It takes all of that and often more to sort out why we do some of the things we do; what we're feeling, and why. On a good day or a bad day we can let little annoyances get out of hand or we can try to keep everything in perspective. Chances are no one but ourselves — and of course, the Lord — will ever know how hard we work at maintaining a pleasant personality. But if we don't, it shows.

It shows if we grumble and complain at every turn. It shows if we snap at everything everyone says or does. It shows if we don't spend time nurturing a relationship with the Lord. It shows if we don't work at seeking His guidance and wisdom in solving life's problems and carrying life's burdens.

There's no way around it. Keeping things in order, especially in our hearts, our minds and our souls, involves a faithfulness devoid of fanfare and drama. Calling it a sense of accomplishment is an understatement. Perhaps the rewards aren't clearly visible. But, oh, the mess we create if we spend our days and our lives shirking our responsibilities in these areas. These are the places, these are the things, these are the issues that matter more than anything else.

Help us, Lord, to work hard at putting order in our lives where it counts the most. In Jesus' Name. Amen. □

What are you waiting for?
November 2, 1985

Is there something you have always wanted to do? Write a book? Fly a plane? Sing in the choir? Bake homemade bread? Be a Sunday school teacher or a youth leader? Learn to swim?

Well, what are you waiting for?

If you're like me, you're waiting for the whole house to be cleaned (and to stay that way) before tackling anything new.

Well, that just "ain't never gonna be." I'm sure you already know that, but it has taken me nearly 20 years to figure it out. I think I finally see that if I wait for everything to be perfect before I try to do the thing I've always wanted to do, I'll never do it.

The writer of Ecclesiastes 11:4 puts it this way: "If you wait for perfect conditions, you will never get anything done" (TLB).

If I'm waiting to know everything there is to know about gardening before I plant any seeds, then there'll never be any flowers or trees or bushes around my house. It's true that sometimes getting something done requires a certain degree of foreknowledge and preparation. But on the other hand, there are some things that can be better accomplished by diving in and learning as you go. (Swimming, however, may not be one of them.)

Take parenting for instance. If my husband and I would have waited until we knew how to change diapers blindfolded; how to answer all the questions of a four-year-old; how to teach a six-year-old to ride a two-wheeler; how to handle a 16-year-old dating and driving in the same year; and how to get a senior in high school into college next year, we would still be waiting to become parents.

It's a challenge to solve all these things as they surface. Often it is fun besides — well, maybe not the diapers or the driving, but there is joy in answering questions and in seeing kids beaming over riding a bicycle. The point is not what is enjoyable and what is not, but rather that we are blessed by having children without waiting until we have all the answers.

What is that thing that *you've* always wanted to do?

What are you waiting for?

If you wait for perfect conditions, you will never get anything done.

Why not pray for God's help and take that first step — TODAY.   ☐

CHAPTER THREE

Commitment

Small efforts can make a difference

November 3, 2001

"It ain't over till it's over" applies to a lot of circumstances. It can also be said of life in general. As long as we're still alive, it isn't over. The point is, it's what we do while we can that makes the difference. We stand at a time in history when the concept of "making a difference" is being revisited. Since September 11, 2001, Americans have a renewed interest in the meaning of "the difference."

For one thing, *the difference* is better illustrated than defined.

By illustration we all know there's a difference between right and wrong. A difference between up and down, cold and hot, slow and fast. But when you think about it, there is also a point where opposites meet. Right and wrong at extreme ends of a continuum are easy to identify, but when you travel toward the center on that same line, the differences begin to lose their distinctiveness. It's like when hot and cold properties of a substance are blended to produce a lukewarm result. At some point "the difference" we try to make by the life we live is hard to spot. Still, like an acorn, we can try to make an impact.

"Today's mighty oak is just yesterday's little nut that held its ground."

The author of this earthy gem is unknown, but that doesn't alter the illustration of encouragement it offers. It's an encouragement suggesting perseverance. And perseverance doesn't just happen. It's a deliberate act, an act of the will.

"The will to persevere is often the difference between failure and success," said David Sarnoff (quoted in *Topical Encyclopedia of Living Quotations,* edited by Sherwood Wirt and Kersten Beckstrom, 1982, Bethany House Publishers).

Perseverance sounds noble, but where does the will to persevere come from? Often it is simply birthed by duty, concern or love. Another word for this is service. These days in America we are seeing more people involved in giving service than in expecting to be served. "Little" people are doing big things.

Acts of selfless service we witness via news reports around our nation are reminiscent of an old story about a young girl who, years ago, helped "to build" Milan Cathedral.

As the story goes (in *Knight's Master Book of New Illustrations* compiled by Walter B. Knight, 1956, Wm. B. Eerdmans Publishing Company), when work on the cathedral was completed and vast numbers of people gathered for the dedication, a little girl in the crowd pointed to the majestic structure and cried out in childish glee, "I helped to build that!"

" 'What!' exclaimed one of the guards who was standing in brilliant uniform. 'Show me what you did,' " the story relates.

"I carried the dinner pail for my father while he worked up yonder," the young girl explained. Her humble participation played a part in the completion of the architect's plan.

How often is it in life, that without many behind-the-scenes acts of service by who knows how many "little people," big plans, like a towering cathedral, would never get off the ground? Before success can be realized, many individuals must be dedicated to serve.

Success, unlike turning over a new leaf on the calendar, doesn't just happen. At whatever endeavor you and I are led to participate in, it will make all the difference if we persevere until the job is done. At this time in our nation, in our world, a resurgence of commitment to making a difference is more than an expression of putting this thought to the test.

Dear Lord, while there is yet time for us to make a differ-ence in the world around us, we ask You to guide us toward the center of Your will. There we trust You to teach us perse-verance in the midst of all sizes, shapes and degrees of ser-vice. Instruct us in the best way to put our time, energies and resources to work where it matters. Help us all to do our part. In Jesus' Name. Amen.   ☐

Evangelists can be anyone, anywhere

June 23, 1990

BACKGROUND NOTE: In the spring of 1990, Dotty Moore and her husband Jim attended the Billy Graham School of Evangelism in Montreal, Quebec, Canada.

Mission Quebec, an evangelistic crusade of the Billy Gra-ham Evangelistic Association, was also taking place there. The following is a behind-the-scenes look at a crusade from Dotty Moore's perspective as a guest of the Billy Graham Crusade News Media Team.

Early in the evening of June 7, while people swarmed into the stadium at The Forum in downtown Montreal for Mission Quebec — a Billy Graham Crusade with Leighton Ford — I was one of six or eight people sitting in a bar on the second floor of The Forum's complex.

The bar, converted to a prayer room specifically for the duration of the crusade, later became abuzz with the petitions of 25 or 30 pray-ers before the evening ended. The framed liquor license (written in French) displayed on a corner wall seemed out of place in a room where only intercessory prayer was on tap.

That night and throughout the week of Mission Quebec there was no alcohol flowing in that bar, only prayers:

Prayers for the unsaved people in the audience downstairs. Prayers for the speakers on the platform. Prayers for the 2,400-member choir. Prayers for the singers and special guests sharing their testimonies. Prayers for Leighton Ford to speak the words God would have him speak. Prayers for the interpreters so that both English and French would be clearly understood.

As I sat alone under the liquor license reflecting on where I was and why I was there, a small, soft-spoken, white-haired lady entered the room and sat down beside me in a circle of six chairs, four of them remaining empty.

As she and I quietly chatted for a few minutes, I learned her name was Betty, she was from London, England, and she was now living in Montreal.

When I spoke her name as we conversed, she gently corrected my pronunciation.

"It's 'Bet-tee'," she said, "pronounced with the 'tts' sounding like 'tts' and not 'dds' like Americans say it."

I loved her instantly. She was special and precious, partly because of her British accent, partly because of her sweetness and elderly glow, but mostly because of her love for the Lord and her willingness to do whatever He asks.

She didn't express that love and willingness in those words, but it was boldly evident in the story she told me before the two of us prayed aloud together.

Betty said that although this was the first time a Billy Graham Crusade had come to Montreal, it was not her first crusade experience.

"In 1954, I was visiting London with a friend," Betty began. "She and I were there on holiday — known as a vacation to Americans — expecting to tour the city. When we arrived there, we learned that the first service of a Billy Graham Crusade was being held that evening. So we went.

"While there, it was announced that crusade volunteers were desperately needed. We signed up, and that's how we spent our entire vacation. It was wonderful. We did volunteer work during the days and attended the services every night," Betty told me in her matter-of-fact manner.

Eventually, I slipped out of the prayer room and entered the stadium in time for the opening part of the service. Midway through the service, I left the stadium and returned to the prayer room.

Betty was gone.

I'll likely not see her again on this earth, but I know any time I watch a Billy Graham Crusade on television from now on, I'll think of her and that prayer room.

With pray-ers and workers behind the scenes like Betty, it's no wonder hundreds of people come to know the Lord when large crowds are gathered for such an event as took place that night in The Forum.

It's the Bettys of the world as well as the Billy Grahams and Leighton Fords that are called to be evangelists.

Dear Lord, bless our efforts for You, no matter how small we are and no matter how small our efforts. In Jesus' Name. Amen. □

Awakening one's heart takes more than an alarm clock

February 15, 1992

Labour to awaken your own hearts, ...that you may be fit to awaken the hearts of (others)... ." — Richard Baxter in The Reformed Pastor (1656); abridged edition (1829), quoted in Christianity Today, Feb. 10, 1992.

Sometimes the hardest thing I have to do is stay awake in order to accomplish what needs done. But is merely being awake enough?

In spite of getting lots of practice keeping my eyes open when I'd rather be napping (about the only time I treat myself to the luxury is on a Sunday afternoon), when the sleepies hit I have to do something pretty quick to fight them off.

One morning this week, the urge to sleep hits me the moment I wake up around 7:15. Instead of allowing myself to go back to sleep, I slowly crawl out of bed and get dressed, fixing my hair right away so I am less tempted to lay back down.

Drinking orange juice and eating a bowl of shredded wheat doesn't help. I am still sleepy. I read the paper, run up and down the stairs a couple of times, drink a cup of tea and put on a pair of earrings. It's useless, but I continue the fight.

Going to the basement, I check on Licorice our cat who is nearly 13 years old. In cat years I guess that makes her about 91 which probably explains why she is no more interested in waking up than I was a short while earlier. And yet I coax her awake by scratching her neck and petting her head. She follows me up to the kitchen where I give her a breakfast of canned cat food (the equivalent of orange juice and shredded wheat, I suppose), after which she goes in and sits looking at the front door. I know this is her way of telling me she wants out, so out she goes.

Licorice is up and at 'em; and I'm still thinking I can't stay awake. But I do. I have too much to do not to stay awake, so I muddle through the morning, researching and clipping articles to file or pass on, all the while thinking, "I can't stay awake... I can't stay awake... I can't stay awake."

By lunch time, it's no better. The fight itself is making me sleepy. Determination and hunger drive me to eat a bowl of soup while reading more of the newspaper.

"It must be because of a lack of exercise," I reason to myself. "After all, it's the middle of February, and since it's so cold, I'm not out walking like I do in nice weather. If I exercise, surely I'll get wide awake."

Not to be outdone by a cat, I bundle up and go outside. After sweeping a dusting of snow off the sidewalks, I tie my hood tighter and start walking. "I'm awake...I'm awake...I'm awake," the rhythm of my stride seems to say. But the cold and the wind get the best of me, and after walking for no more than 10 or 12 minutes, I'm back inside, sleepier than ever, probably from the wind.

A piece of jelly bread and a Red Delicious apple later, I'm at the computer keyboard in my upstairs writing office, making notations about some of the things I'm researching. Suddenly I realize, that although it's nearly four o'clock in the afternoon and I'm still fighting being drowsy, I haven't yet drawn on the best wake-up source I know. I haven't yet asked the Lord (even though I did pray about other things) to help me wake up completely and get me going.

There's no doubt in my mind what triggers this realization. I am typing a notation concerning something I had underlined from *Christianity Today* magazine. It's a quote from Richard Baxter, gleaned from *The Reformed Pastor,* referencing more than 300 years ago as Baxter is speaking to pastors about the urgency of being awakened:

"Oh sirs, how plainly, how closely, how earnestly, should we deliver a message of such [a] moment as ours, when the everlasting life or everlasting death of our fellow men is involved in it!

"...There [is] nothing more unsuitable to such a business, than to be slight and dull. What! speak coldly for God, and for men's salvation? Can we believe that our people must be converted or condemned, and yet speak in a drowsy tone?

"In the name of God, brethren, labour to awaken your own hearts, before you go to the pulpit, that you may be fit to awaken the hearts of sinners ... ."

At that, Baxter's exhortation makes it clear to me what's missing in my day, probably in many of my days: Although I'm not a pastor, because I am a Christian, I need my heart awakened more than my body. For it's through my heart the Lord helps me see and feel what matters most. And so I pray:

Dear Lord, I've worked most of the day at waking up. I've tried to wake up my mind and my body, and without patting myself on the back, I feel justified in emphasizing I have really worked at it. But suddenly I feel more awake than I have all day. Now I see, that while I was concentrating on simply waking up, You wanted to awaken my heart. I had it backwards, but You kept working on me. Thank You. Show me how, each day, Lord, to labor at awakening my heart at least half as hard as I try to awaken the rest of me. In Jesus' Name. Amen. ☐

CHAPTER FOUR

Coping with life

It's wise to live near 'The Church'

August 20, 1988

How far away from your church do you live? One of my friends is glad she lives practically next door to hers. In addition to being a Sunday-morning convenience, it's a nearby retreat when life's hassles "just about drive a person up a wall," she told me not long ago.

On one recent occasion, being the mother of a four-year-old and a two-year-old (need I elaborate?), my friend knew she had to get out of the house for a while. Since her husband was home to be with the kids, she went for a walk, determined to go however far she needed until her tolerance level returned to the safety zone.

Oddly, her walk was much shorter than she had expected, because she found herself going into the church instead. There, in the peace and quiet, she sat down at the piano and played one hymn after another for at least a half-hour. Without any further agonizing or walking, she returned home, refreshed, perfectly calm and ready to go back to being an in-control-of-herself mother.

When she told me about this experience, I commented, "Too bad more people don't live near a church, huh?"

Obviously, we can't all live next door to a church, but if we live close to Jesus, we won't have far to run when we're in the midst of a crisis situation. There's one catch, however. If we only approach Him when we're in big trouble, it might take us a while to feel His Presence. Not because He has distanced Himself *from us,* but because we have drifted farther and farther away *from Him.*

Although we can't all build our houses near a church, we owe it to ourselves to take a look at where we're building our lives. Are we living next door to temptations that could gain control of our thinking and influence our decisions and priorities? Or are we living close to the One Who will "lead us not into temptation," but Who will "deliver us from evil" (Matthew 6:13, KJV).

The Lord never promised us that we can do anything we want and still expect Him to be right next door whenever we need Him. Instead, the promise we can count on, is this: "Draw near to God, and He will draw near to you" (James 4:8, NKJV).

We're all going to need help and at times experience desperate situations, simply because we live in a world full of difficulties and not-so-easy choices. The Lord knows that. That's why He made provision for us to live *in* the world without being *of* the world.

That's why He sent His Son to provide a way of escape from the temptation that could destroy us or those we love. That's why it's smart to live so close to Jesus that it won't take us long to find Him when we need Him. Needing Him, for many of us, including me, is all the time. He is "The Church."

□

Finding a favorite vacation spot

June 25, 1988

Ah, to be a kid again in the summertime. Grass was greener then, and mowing it was fun, not work. Thunderstorms were nature's videos, and the grape-arbor swing flew nonstop to anywhere in the world.

Strawberries, blueberries, corn on the cob, tomato-and-onion sandwiches, lightning bugs, new kittens, mud puddles and homemade lemonade. All there was to do was pick them, eat them, catch them, pet them, play in them or drink the lemonade.

The smells, the tastes, the colors, the memories, all were part of a world that was uncomplicated and carefree. There was no responsibility beyond getting the most out of the moment. Even when jobs and chores were assigned, there was no weight of worry about the next task, and the next and the next. At times it would be nice to go back for a day or so, but of course, that's not possible.

That's why we need vacations. We need refreshed by cool, ocean breezes or sparkling mountain streams. But needing a vacation and getting one are two different things. It's not always possible to get away when we most need to do so.

However, there is at least one vacation spot that we can go to often, no matter where we are or what we're doing. It's called Psalm 23, and there we can "lie down in green pastures" or stroll "beside the still waters" (v.2, KJV).

It may sound corny, but I go there often.

Throughout my adult years, I've been there on numerous occasions. While awaiting major surgery. While waiting to hear that a loved one is safe and sound. While burdened over finances. While sick and tired of responsibilities that simply won't go away.

I've also been there when all I wanted was to spend time with the Lord, for no other reason than to be near Him.

A long time ago, someone made a life-changing suggestion concerning the Twenty-third Psalm. I don't remember who it was, so I can't say thank you or give credit, but I *can* pass it on. Perhaps you've heard the same suggestion and have benefited from it. If you haven't, or simply need reminded, here it is.

Turn to Psalm 23 in your Bible or in your memory and read or recite it like this:

"Lord, You are my shepherd; I shall not want. You maketh me to lie down in green pastures: You leadeth me beside the still waters. You restoreth my soul: You leadeth me in the paths of righteousness for Your name's sake. ..."

And so on.

The key is speaking *to* the Lord instead of *about* Him.

When I've taken this kind of a walk with the Lord, I've often found it to be a vacation from the burdens and worries of life.

Try it. Maybe it will become *your* favorite get-away spot. A place where "goodness and mercy shall follow (you) all the days of (your) life."

See you there.   ☐

Is God 'working at home' in our hearts?

May 14, 1994

Ah-h-h, working at home — there's nothing like it!

If you haven't yet become one of the 32 million "SoHo"·(small office/home office) workers in this country, let me tell you what you're missing...but first, please hold on a minute. I'll be right back as soon as I throw a load of clothes in the dryer.

OK, that's done...now back to how wonderful it is to be part of the So/Ho trend.

First things first, when you work at home (unless you have hours open to the public), you can wear anything you want: bathrobe, sweat suit, pajamas, old shoes, no shoes, curlers, no make-up...oh, no...there's someone at the door. If I answer it dressed like this they'll think I just crawled out of bed...and here it is nearly 3:30 in the afternoon and I've been at the computer since dawn!

Well, that was a close call. Young kids out selling candy don't care how anyone looks. Now, where was I?

Oh yes, secondly, you can cram two or three days into one by working 'round the clock, then taking the next day off, assuming you don't mind sleeping all day on your day off or the risk of looking worse than on the day you worked three shifts and forgot about combing your hair and brushing your teeth until midnight.

Trust me, I do plan to draw a spiritual parallel from all of this, and I'll try to do that right after I check the pot roast and throw in the potatoes and carrots.

I'm back...please forgive me for taking so long...but while I was in the kitchen I unloaded and loaded the dishwasher and wiped off the stove and refrigerator. Then, deciding against vacuuming the floor, I measured the window for new curtains.

My, oh, my, it's like I said before — there's nothing like working at home!

Now, for the best part, hopefully.

The benefits of working at home are a lot like coming before the Lord at any time, dressed up or dressed down, looking good or completely shabby. No matter what, we're always welcome in His sight and looked upon with love.

However, as with any benefit, comes responsibility. Even though we can do some jobs at home, coping with all sorts of distractions, we have to be disciplined enough to get the job done and keep the right focus at the appropriate times: this block of time for home and family and this one for "the job."

The same is true of our relationship with the Lord. Distractions come while we're studying the Bible, praying, praising or simply enjoying quiet times in His Presence. And although we are free to approach Him with or without attention to our outward appearance, we are wise not to neglect our inner condition. Our inner condition is worth working at, any time of the day or night, whether on the road, in a home office, behind a plow, at a teller's window, climbing a high tower, digging a tunnel or fixing a weary traveler's lunch in a local diner.

No job, no station in life, no talent or lack of such need keep us from devoting time and space within our hearts to a God who wants to work at home there, teaching us, leading us and cultivating us in line with what He hopes we will one day become.   ☐

'Oh, well, some days are like that'

October 6, 1990

No sooner had I gotten the house all warmed up one chilly morning recently, than I had to turn around and open windows and doors to let out the smoke. Burnt-toast smoke, that is. While I was basking in the warm kitchen, reading the newspaper, my toast got a little over-heated.

Scraping the burnt part into the sink (a trick mothers pass on despite moans and groans from the one who has to eat the toast — this time, "The Mom" herself), I sighed, "Oh, well, some days are like that."

Funny thing is, the day before was like that, too.

That was the day I accidentally got hit on the ankle bone with a "one by six." That's a board six inches wide, one inch thick, and this one was eight feet long.

Later that same day, my husband, who felt really bad about the mishap, because he was the one moving the board when my ankle got in the way, also had his own mishap. He turned his ankle in a dip in the back yard and, that night, together, we limped into bed.

Oh, well, some days are like that.

At least our ankle injuries, although painful at the time, were not severe and did not slow us down a whole lot.

Some days are like that, too. The worst that could have happened, didn't happen.

On those days, while we ouch and complain, we also say "thank you."

Thank You, Lord, that the house didn't burn down from a piece of toast stuck in the toaster. Thank You that a couple of ankles are only bruised and not broken. Thank You, Lord, that on the days when some things go wrong, there are still plenty of things to be thankful for.

Even on the days when everything does go wrong and the worst that could happen, happens, remind us that You are there. That You are here. That You know what's going on and You're in it with us. Thank You for the good days and thank You for the good that You bring out of the bad days, even when it takes a while for us to see it. In Jesus' Name. Amen. □

Walking through a memory, or something like that...

October 28, 1989

The Lord shall preserve thy going out and thy coming in from this time forth, and even for evermore (Psalm 121:8, KJV).

The woman had to get out of the house for a while, so she went for a walk. However, as she walked, she carried the house in her mind and thus on her shoulders. Step after step, after step, as though walking in lead-filled shoes, she trudged on, still seeing all the things in the house that needed done.

Step after step, after step, she tried to look at the blue sky, but all she saw were dust balls under furniture, piles and piles of dirty clothes, stacks of magazines waiting to be read and cluttered closets bulging behind closed doors.

Step after step, she carried the piles of clothes, the stacks of magazines and all the frustration that had driven her out of the house—the frustration that echoed in her mind, "There's not enough time or energy to do everything that needs done, but do it anyway...do it anyway...do it anyway!"

She tried to see beauty in the autumn-colored hills surrounding the valley where she walked, but the heavy, dark shadows cast by her thoughts obstructed the view. Minute after minute, step after step dragged by until the woman stooped down along the edge of a cornfield to pick up a small, smooth stone.

It was in this lower-to-the-ground-than-usual crouching position the woman noticed beside her a little girl at eye level— a little girl standing, staring, listening to the rustling sounds of dry, soon-to-be-harvested cornstalks as they gently quivered against each other in the wind. Neither the woman nor the little girl counted the moments, but one of them listened for a long time. By then the woman was gone, and the little girl continued the walk.

Step after step, after step, the little girl stopped and listened, stopped and listened.

She was still fascinated by the sounds of scratching and scraping, scratching and scraping coming from the field of cornstalks that to her looked like a tired, broken and torn army of soldiers standing in line after line waiting for a hot bowl of soup, a bandage or a bed to lie down in forever.

Standing perfectly still, the little girl heard another sound: Pop, pip...pop, pip.

Kneeling in the grass, she smiled as she watched an acrobatic leap-and-land, leap-and-land grasshopper attempting to move an upside-down, brittle-looking insect—an insect whose dry, delicate, transparent wings would never again know the delight of flight.

Eventually, the little girl walked on, stopping to look at this or to poke at that, losing track of time until she began to feel hungry. Although her stomach and her head agreed it was time to go home for lunch—a late one at that—her feet were in no hurry. It was such a pretty day with so many things to see...her eyes, her heart, her feet didn't want it to end.

When she at long last reached her house, instead of staying on the sidewalk, the little girl shuffled and crunched through the leaves covering her front yard. It was then she realized she wasn't a little girl any longer, but a woman, who earlier, had had to get out of the house.

But what do you suppose she did then?

Instead of rushing back into instant reality, she shuffled around the front yard a little longer. The crunch, crunch, crunch of the leaves reminded her of when she *was* a little girl, raking and piling and hiding in the piles until her mother called, "Dotty ...where are you? It's time for supper!"

Not quite ready to let go of that memory, the woman, who by now was sitting on her porch swing, listened to the rattle and squeak, rattle and squeak of the swing's chains taking her back and forth, back and forth. Decisively she went back one last time before accepting it was now time to go forth.

Leaving the swing behind, she gave Licorice the family cat (sunning itself on the porch) a pat on the head, stepped inside to her living room and walked through the hallway into the kitchen. Things didn't look so bad after all.

Lord, although not all of life's memories are pleasant, thank You for the ones that are, especially the memories of pleasant yesterdays that help us get through unpleasant todays. Amen. ☐

Next time you're overwhelmed, think 'spaghetti sauce on the wall'

March 13, 1993

It's late Thursday night and I feel like the mother in the "spaghetti sauce on the wall" story. If you don't know the story, you're in for a treat. Mark my words, one of these days you'll feel like the story was written just for you. The story came to my attention about 15 years ago in a paperback book called *I Need You Now, God, While the Grape Juice is Running All Over the Floor*. Dotsey Welliver is the author of the book (1975, Light and Life Press).

I've told and retold Dotsey's story often. It's so powerful, you, too, will soon be retelling it. That's a pretty lofty lead for any story, but you'll not be disappointed. I guarantee it!

Dotsey, the mother of three young boys, writes, "God is not afraid of messy kitchens. He walks right in and blesses. He knows who slopped spaghetti sauce all over the wall last night. He knows who was too tired to clean it."

That's about all Dotsey says on the subject of the spaghetti sauce, but her words, nevertheless, paint a vivid picture in our imaginations. At least they do in mine. Can you see it? Here she is, a wife, a mother, a homemaker, a referee, a maid, a cook and more-than-ready to fall into bed one night when, out of the corner of her eye, orange-red splatters on the kitchen wall remind her of what she had intended to do after supper: Wipe down the spaghetti-sauce mess smeared on the wall by delicious little fingers.

Now, here it is, bedtime, and the mess will have to wait. Dotsey is too tired to drag herself through the motions of performing a gold-medal-winning domestic feat. To me, what she *doesn't* do this night, is worth even more than a gold medal: her decision to *not* scrub the wall is priceless.

Ever since I first read her book, I've often feasted on Dotsey's brief mentioning of the spaghetti-sauce episode. Time after time, I've paraphrased her words to form a personal prayer: *Lord, You know why things are as they are; and You know why there's nothing I can do about any of it right now.*

With that, I, too, have often gone straight to bed. I've often put troublesome things out of my mind. I've often stepped over clutter and kept right on going. And I've thanked God over and over for Dotsey's story.

As I sit, tonight, here and now, why is the story once again "my salvation?"

Well, it's been one of those days. Actually, it's been one of those days, end-over-end, for several weeks running. As a result, my mind is mush; my whole being is shrieking, "No way!" to the slightest suggestion I ought to press myself to be the perfect housekeeper, the perfect woman, the perfect anything. So, right now, I'm affording myself the luxury of following the trail of the mother in the "spaghetti sauce on the wall" story.

Happy dreams and good night.   □

Tale of dog and his tail show God's healing touch

October 30, 1993

One fall day in my childhood stands out. I don't know what year it was, so I can't say how old I was. But I can tell you this: The leaves were never brighter, the air was never crisper, and before the day was over, none of that mattered. Yet it did. Otherwise, why would I remember such details?

Even so, the day would not have been memorable, at least the unexpected, happy-ending part, had not Skip been by my side. Skip was part collie, part beagle and all un-purebred mutt. Mostly, he was my best friend in the truest sense. He kept every one of the secrets I whispered in his ear. He was always there when I needed him, and he never complained. Skip was perfect, except for his tail and his limp.

Skip had "inherited" a knot of a tail when his mother's owner snipped the tails off all the pups in the litter. But, as Skip grew, a long, hairy, feather-duster-type plume emerged from his tail stub. It was the result of his determination to have something to wag, I'm sure. And Skip was a wagger all right, but his tail had more of a swish than a wag. Without the usual support, that's all the tail-less plume could do: swish, swish, swish.

The only time Skip's tail didn't swish was the day Dad accidentally backed over him with his red pickup truck. That was the day I forgot about the bright leaves and crisp fall air. That was the day Skip looked like he wouldn't make it. Dad felt terrible, and I thought my whole world had just ended.

That was the day Dad, Mum, Skip and I paid our first and only visit to a veterinarian. (We never had money for trips to the vet back then. But, then, I never had a pet dog before. And Dad never before had run over his only child's only pet dog.) That was the day Skip got a cast on his broken hind leg and, only a day or two later, he started to limp around. Even when the cast eventually came off, the limp was as permanent as his swish.

I could not have cared less. Skip was well, and that's all that mattered. Bright leaves turned to snowflakes, and my best friend was back in action. Together we traipsed through the fields behind our house, through the forest beyond the fields and shared more secrets and more memories.

Speaking of memories—now that I think of it—I'm not certain the leaves that fall day were so bright at all. The air may have been crisp, but perhaps it wasn't. Perhaps the only reason I think I remember those things is because a happy ending can turn any old day into the most beautiful day of the season.

Dear Lord, we all have good and bad memories . We wouldn't be who we are without both kinds. Whether our memories are of limping dogs or broken dreams, Your touch can heal. If a tail-less dog can adjust to swishing instead of wagging, help us to expect Your touch on our lives to accomplish even more. In Jesus' Name. Amen. ☐

When the end is out of sight
October 13, 1990

Did you ever work so long on one project that you felt like it would never end? Not long ago, that's exactly how I felt while spackling and sanding and painting, and spackling and sanding and painting and spackling and sanding and painting. Half in desperation, half in prayer, I said aloud to myself and to the Lord: "I can't see the end of all this work. All I see in front of me is more to do!"

Almost immediately, it was as though the Lord responded, "I know you can't see the end, Dotty, but I can. Remember I'm taller than you are, and I can see a lot farther down the road than you can. Trust Me. You're going to make it."

Since then, I'm still spackling and sanding and painting, but I'm not quite so overwhelmed. Oh, I'm tired of the spackling, sanding and painting, but I feel better knowing My Father can see past where I'm at today.

It's like being a little kid, not knowing what's up ahead, but confident there's nothing to worry about because your dad has you by the hand. He's big and strong and can see all the way down the street. You know, when the time is right, he'll pick you up, put you on his shoulders, and you'll see it all, too.

Thank You, Lord, for tasks that make us dependent upon You. If we never had to call on You for strength and encouragement, we might be deceived into thinking we can handle everything on our own. Whether painting or witnessing about Jesus, doing dishes or visiting the sick, some things are better done with You by our side. Come to think of it, aren't all things better done with You than without You? Help me remember that, today, and even tomorrow. In Jesus' Name. Amen. □

When there's nothing to do but...
March 10, 1990

What do you do when there are no leftovers in the refrigerator? I don't know about you, but I complain. To me, having leftovers is the next best thing to eating out. Leftovers mean there's something to eat without cooking.

It's not that I don't like to cook; it's just that I don't like to cook every day. When I do create something in the kitchen, I like to make enough for several days. But alas, there are those times when the several days are up, the leftovers are all gone, and although it's time to eat, there's no time to cook up a new batch of anything.

Such was the circumstance one day this week when, alone in the house, I saw it as an ideal time to write. However, it was also time for a bite to eat and the refrigerator was bare. Well, not exactly bare, but what can you do with a handful of spaghetti (but no sauce), a couple of hunks of cheese, milk, mustard, catsup, mayonnaise and the usual in-the-door ingredients like soy sauce, Worcestershire sauce and a jar of pickle juice with nothing more than a pickle stem in it?

After opening and closing the refrigerator door twice (ever notice how once is never enough?), I glanced around the kitchen. It was then I spotted a can of soup I had set on the counter several days earlier in case someone needed a quick eat-and-run lunch. When I spied that can of soup, I sighed out loud, "There's nothing to eat except…soup."

Then it hit me: So? Eat soup.

While I did, I thought about how often we use the phrase, "There's nothing to do but."

There's nothing to do but make the best of things.

There's nothing to do but go on.

There's nothing to do but pray.

There's nothing to do but wait.

I came to the conclusion, that if and when "there is nothing to do but," then we probably had better do it. It often means the choice of what to do is already made for us and we can save ourselves a lot of time and effort by going with that choice. Like it or not, even in waiting, we *are* doing something.

A few nights ago I was scanning the stations on the car radio when I heard a Christian speaker mention "the prayer for patience." It went something like this: "Lord, give me patience and give it to me now!"

We laugh at that because it's so real. It's so like us not to want to wait for what's best for us. Interestingly enough, waiting can make us stronger and thus more likely to accomplish whatever comes next, even if it's another "nothing to do but."

When we find ourselves at a loss to know what to do, and we eventually throw up our hands and say, "There's nothing to do but get someone else's opinion," there's the cue to do just that. Or if there's nothing to do but think it through, you've got it, we've got to start thinking. Thinking, praying, asking, waiting. Any or all of these can be just the right thing to do, and perhaps right now is the best time to do them.

"But they that wait upon the Lord shall renew their strength; they shall mount up with wings as eagles; they shall run, and not be weary; and they shall walk, and not faint" *(Isaiah 40:31, KJV).*   □

Life: Sometimes there are tangled strings attached

April 17, 1993

When I tossed my off-white winter jacket (with three drawstrings attached) and my white spring jacket (with two drawstrings attached) into the washing machine this week, I didn't know I was soon to become a cold-water, underwater surgeon of sorts. At least that's what I felt like a short while later with both hands and forearms submerged in the icy, sudsy waters inside the tub of my Maytag.

Luckily, I had dashed out to the utility room and lifted the lid to check the progress of my jackets halfway through the spin-out segment of the 10-minute agitation cycle. Gasping at the twisted, tangled mess created by the drawstrings (remember, each of the five drawstrings has two ends), I hit the off button. Only then did I plunge my hands into what was about to become one or more lessons on life.

The first thing I learned was why the Hunters Run winter jacket was labeled, "Dry Clean Only." Not because the fabric, the lining or the insulating material might not withstand home laundering, but because multiple drawstrings and washing machine cycles (even on gentle) are obviously notorious challenge producers.

Naturally, I didn't learn that at the precise moment my hands first entered the cold water. It took a while for the impact of the lesson to sink in, but then, it took even longer for my hands to thaw out, 20 or 30 minutes later, after the last string was untangled and the freed sleeves and hoods of the jackets began to look like sleeves and hoods once again.

(For those of you who might be wondering why I didn't just let the rest of the water spin out and make my job a little less cold, I couldn't risk ripping the jackets because the drawstrings were not only wrapped and twisted around each other and the extremities of the jackets, but also they were looped, knotted and caught around and under and between the blades of the agitator. Believe me, the next time I wash these jackets, it won't be together. And it won't be without somehow securing the drawstrings.)

But later, while cupping my hands around a hot bowl of micro-waved oatmeal, the early-morning episode at the washing machine reminded me that life is sometimes a lot like that twisted, tangled mess. At those times—and usually they appear without warning—we can grumble or complain loudly (as I began to do at the sight of my wet, mangled-looking jackets), or we can attempt to untangle and straighten things out.

If we ask the Lord to help us (which I finally did when my hands began to hurt from the cold and especially from the awkward positions required to get the job done), the task may not be as impossible as we first imagine.

Furthermore, after the mess is no longer a mess, we might even harvest something from the experience we can pass on to someone else. When that happens, the strings attached to our troubles help to bind us together.   □

Jesus' yoke is custom-fitted

September 8, 2001

There's nothing much worse than walking in the wrong pair of shoes. If the shoes hurt your feet you can't very well run the race of life. That's why most of us are careful to select shoes that fit well. Shoes that are comfortable. Shoes that don't pinch. Shoes that are not too short. Shoes that allow us to look good, feel good and let us get on with our day without giving our feet a second thought.

Wouldn't it be great if the rest of life "fit us" like a pair of well-designed, priced-right, perfectly-made-just-for-us pair of shoes? Well, there's a place in the Bible where Jesus talks about this. He invites us to wear, not shoes, but a yoke — His yoke — and He speaks of our getting the kind of rest we need even when we work hard beneath a heavy burden.

"Come unto Me all ye that labor and are heavy laden," Jesus says in Matthew 11:28-30, "and I will give you rest. Take My yoke upon you, and learn of Me; for I am meek and lowly in heart: and ye shall find rest unto your souls. For My yoke is easy, and My burden is light" (KJV).

Many people spend a lifetime wearing a yoke that doesn't fit. Carrying a burden that could be lightened. People turn to philosophies, codes of conduct, ancient rituals, humanistic ideas, world religions and yet never "try on" the yoke of Christ.

What is the yoke of Christ, and what can it do for us besides being a perfect fit? The yoke of Christ, if you will, is the presence of His hands on our shoulders. With His touch He leads us. Directs us. Steers us. You and I don't need to go it alone. We don't need to carry the weight of the baggage we've picked up along the journey of life. But even more than a weightless steering mechanism on our shoulders, Christ's yoke revives our heart and restores our soul. His yoke is His perfect will for each of us.

What is His will for you? For me? His will is that we invite Him into our life. Ask Him to forgive us, cleanse us and take control. Then we can walk as confidently as walking in the right pair of shoes.

Dear Lord, help me to believe that there is a tailor-made, custom-fitted yoke that You have created and selected just for me.   □

Life's realities can be faced with God

October 13, 2001

Each year when the wild geese go south I look up with a bittersweet lump in my throat. Coming and going, leaving and arriving, this is life. Life is bitter. Life is sweet. Life is uncertain in its certainty and vice versa.

Fretting about life, and its ills versus thrills, serves little purpose unless our frustrations draw us closer to God. We can't expect to fly away from the harsh winters of our lives, but we can draw strength and comfort from the fire of God's power to sustain us.

Everywhere we look since the unthinkable terrorism of September 11, 2001, there is either another tragic story or an act of heroism being reported. On one hand we are touched and impressed; on the other we have to admit that life is really like this all the time. It's just that, now, we're more aware.

We don't like hearing it, but life isn't meant to be easy.

Recently, while preparing for a sizeable gathering of people in our home, I verbalized a concern. In regard to vacuuming, cleaning and rearranging furniture to accommodate extra seating, I uttered, "Oh, Lord, will I ever be done?"

No, you won't, I sensed God's reply.

It was the jolt I needed. No way was I going to accomplish everything. It was the turning point between sheer panic and acceptance. Either I had to accept that some areas of the house and yard would have to remain just as they were at that moment or I would fall apart right then and there. I opted, by the Grace of God, to stay in one piece.

Among those of you who are reading these words right now, there are some who surely feel that life is expecting too much of you. You can't do it all. You can't be everything to everyone. You would like to fly away with the wild geese, but you can't. You would like things to get better, but in all likelihood they won't. What has to change is you. You must either accept and pray for strength to endure or crumble in a heap. The latter is not an option. Crumbled heaps don't travel far along the road of finding God's will and plan for each life, for each circumstance.

Nothing is much worse than having someone insensitively trivialize your unique heartaches. This is why it is my sincere hope that this column addresses reality with a promise, not with a discouraging word. In this world we now wake up to each day, there is bittersweet realism to face. The best part is, God is Lord over this, too.

Realistically God is the Only One Who is qualified to see us through. If nothing else comes of life and its trials, the decision to turn to God makes it all worthwhile. What happens beyond this is all in His hands anyway. When we invite the Lord to dwell within our heart, He can be trusted to show us the way.   □

Why must life be so hard?

May 19, 2001

I, for one, sometimes question why life has to be so hard. Why certain struggles repeat themselves. Why God doesn't just give us a lifetime supply of all we'll ever need from the first moment we are born into His Kingdom by believing on His Son as our Savior.

Are you with me? Do you, too, long for an easier time of it? Do you wish that struggling to get ahead would become extinct? Do you wonder why you are asked to trust God for "daily bread" when you'd much prefer a full larder?

As much as we might think we know how God should best dish out life and blessings, the truth is, we don't. We are ill-equipped to have all the answers and solutions as to how our lives ought to be run.

For one thing, if we needed only one-big-event-blessing per lifetime, how quickly we would forget that moment. The thrill and the joy would fade. We would begin to doubt God's very existence if we had no need to seek His gracious provisions on an ongoing basis. Our once-grateful spirits would begin to take for granted all that we have, and we would soon forget how to express thankfulness and appreciation. We would begin to view our "endless supply" of all we'll ever need as a self-sufficiency. It wouldn't be long before shallow faithfulness turned into hollow faith-less-ness.

Despite our cries of why can't life be easier, there is reason to believe we don't completely mean it. Deep down we know it's better to be reliant on the Lord each day than to not need Him. It's better to witness His love and His grace again and again than to experience His mercy only once in a lifetime.

The Apostle Paul wrote in 2 Corinthians 1:5: "You can be sure that the more we undergo sufferings for Christ, the more He will shower us with His comfort and encouragement" (TLB).

In all honesty, I relish the thought of being showered with God's comfort and encouragement. Not that I look forward to the hard things that happen prior to the Lord's comfort and encouragement, but that I know the inevitable pain and suffering will be soothed and I will be bathed with compassion by God's healing nature. Do you feel this way, too?

In order to partake of God's graciousness repeatedly throughout a lifetime, you and I must also grow to expect and accept rough times, failures, regrets and seemingly hopelessness. Ah, but the wonder of it all is, as we grow to understand the reality of suffering and disappointment, we become grounded in the unexplainable expectation that God will show His hand at the precise moment His hand is needed. Not a moment too early and not a moment too late.

That's the way God works. With precision. Not with reckless thoughtlessness, but rather with profound wisdom, love and flawless timing.

Why does life have to be so hard? Why do certain struggles repeat themselves? Why doesn't God give us a lifetime supply of all we'll ever need from the very moment we are born into His Kingdom by believing on His Son as our Savior?

If you and I truly think about these things, we know the answers. We know God works in mysterious ways His wonders to perform, and we know we'd rather be the recipients of His ways and His wonders than to be without.   □

How can I go on when I'm empty?

The very first 'Joy ... in the Morning' column, February 2, 1985

Do you ever feel empty? I mean totally drained? I do.

As a matter of fact, I've felt that way for several days. Last night I was so tired that I almost dumped a scoop of cat food, instead of Tide, into the washing machine.

What's making me feel this way?

Could it be giving, doing, listening, sharing, going, coming, working, preparing, fixing, helping, holding...living?

Yes, that's what life is all about. But how do I go on when I'm empty?

Well, how does a car run when it's out of gas? You're right, it doesn't. However, it *can* be filled again.

Being empty doesn't have to be a dead end. Instead, it can qualify you or me as the perfect vessel for being filled.

Whenever we need refueled, we can ask God to fill us with His love, His presence, His purpose. Any of us can pray, any time:

Fill me, Lord, with a desire to seek Your guidance for the next stretch of the road.

Fill me with patience for the slow-movers ahead of me and with tolerance for the horn-beepers behind.

Fill me with energy for the long hauls between rest stops. Fill me with the drive to keep on going. Fill me with assurance that I'm on the right road.

Fill me with the ability to discern dangers and obstacles. Fill me with the wisdom to know when to put on the brakes and when to step on the gas; when to move ahead with caution and when to detour.

Fill me, Lord, with peace that yesterday is miles behind me. And fill me with confidence that today will get me closer to my destination.

Most of all, Lord, fill me with the conviction that the race is worth running.

Help me expect to be empty, so I can be filled again.

Amen.   □

Facing life during 'one of those days'

November 12, 1988

One day last week I ran away. Not from my husband or my kids, but from responsibility. I had a job to do that I didn't feel like doing, so I "hid out" at the new Columbia Mall for a while. After looking around and finding a couple of inexpensive things I needed, I felt more like facing what had to be done.

Please don't get me wrong. I'm not suggesting that it's appropriate to run off to the mall or go downtown shopping every time life gets difficult. I, for one, couldn't afford to do so, and wouldn't, even if I could. But I do think what I did that day was not uncommon, because, over the years, I've heard a lot of people say they went shopping "to get away from it all."

In many cases, it's good therapy. It gets us out of the house, puts our mind on other things besides our problems and can bring us home feeling like a new person. But is it the kind of behavior we adult, mature Christians are expected to exhibit on every occasion when we're faced with difficult choices and decisions?

I don't think so, and I don't suspect you do either.

However, my reason for sharing this incident with you is to illustrate that sometimes, especially when we feel tired and overloaded, it's easy to want to run away from the things needing our attention.

On that particular day last week, I hadn't wanted to confront the responsibility of writing something that was going to take a lot of prayer, personal effort and energy. Instead, I wanted to turn my back on it, hoping that that responsibility might disappear while I became one of the crowd at the mall.

Of course the task waiting to be done didn't vanish, and to

be honest, I'm thankful it didn't. In the end, I wrote the article I was trying to avoid, and I felt good about it when it was done.

Could I have come to the same conclusion without having gone shopping that day? I know I could have, because I have before. But I'm glad it worked out this way this time, because I think I deserved the break that those couple of hours gave me. I think many of us are often too hard on ourselves and we push ourselves beyond the limits of what we can take. Then we explode.

Blowing up hurts us and those we love and it certainly doesn't do our Christian witness any good either. Sometimes we can head off the explosive situation by doing something for ourselves that will make it easier to then face reality.

Naturally, we need to be sensible and moderate when it comes to doing something for ourselves, but the Lord can give us wisdom even in this area if we but ask Him.

On the day after my personal, mental-health trip to the mall, the following poem ended up on my desk. It's from Gail Harter of Paperdale Road, Stillwater, Pennsylvania, a woman who writes poetry as one of her ways of dealing with difficult situations.

Thank you, Gail, for the poem and for your permission to share it:

One of Those Days

Father, I've just had one of those days
That has tried my patience sore;
I've done my best and nothing's gone right
And I just don't care anymore.

I feel so tense and I can't relax,
I'm glad that this day is thru;
My problems today seemed endless,
That's why I'm talking to You.

I've told You all of my troubles, Lord,
And given You each one to keep;
Please smooth my ruffled feathers
While I lay me down to sleep.

And if I awake to the morning light,
The light of a brand-new day—
Remind me, dear Lord, that You're still in control
And send me on my way.

                              —by *Gail Hampton Harter*   ☐

CHAPTER FIVE

Encouragement

Words can be 'apples of gold'

August 25, 2001

"You can do it, Dotty," our friend Sue Lewis once said after she and her husband Tom ate supper with us. "You can get one more plate in the dishwasher. I know you can. I've seen you do it before." She was right. When it appears not one more thing will fit on those racks, I can find a way to shove in one more plate, one more cereal bowl and at least another saucer or two.

But today's encouraging word isn't about me and my dishwasher-stacking prowess. More to the point, it's about all of us encouraging each other in general. Just as Sue had no idea a few years ago, when she lightheartedly spurred me on, how long-term her influence would be, you and I have no clue how our own words might help or hinder someone else.

Often I recall Sue's confidence-building comment. True, it was directly made concerning her helping me load the dishwasher, but it springs to mind many times in my life whenever I'm ready to call it quits with the dishes or with other demands that ring impossible.

You can do it. I know you can.

How often do you and I speak these words to a loved one, a neighbor, a friend or a co-worker? If only we could all respond,

"Oh, I do that all the time!" life would surely be more pleasant if more of us instilled confidence in those around us.

Can we do it? Of course we can. If we don't already make it a practice to sincerely encourage others, we can start, today. You and I won't have to look far for someone who needs a kind word, a vote of confidence or a reassuring statement of affirmation.

It might be a check-out clerk at a discount store who has been on her feet way too long, or a son or daughter who is fearful of going off to trade school or college. We can make a difference in her day, perhaps in his life, by praising him or her with a word or two fitly spoken.

"A word fitly spoken," the Bible tells us in Proverbs 25:11, "is like apples of gold in pictures of silver" (KJV).

We don't ordinarily think of words being like silver and gold. Perhaps we should. If we did, we might realize anew the value of being considerate. The value of being polite when the inclination is to be rude. We, ourselves, might treasure each other more if we more fully realized our potential either to lift up or tear down another human being.

A word fitly spoken can change someone's outlook. You and I need to be on the lookout for opportunities to do just that. We can even pray along these lines:

Dear Lord, I've been curt with too many people lately. Help me to be more thoughtful before I speak. When I do speak, touch my heart and give a polished shine to my smile, so that those I compliment will know I'm sincere. In Jesus' Name. Amen.   □

God is always watching

November 9, 1985

Recently, while parked at the corner of a busy intersection in Danville where I waited in the car during my daughter's ballet class, I watched as car after car went by. Since I'm used to living on a quiet street in the small town of Benton, the noise of the traffic began to bother me.

The constant flow of someone coming and going made me think of one of the Psalms that says something about the Lord watching over us as we come and go. "How does He stand it?" I wondered. There is never any time when the whole world is still and quiet. Someone is always *coming from* or *going to* somewhere.

How does God keep His eyes on each of us as we go back and forth through life? Does He ever tire of seeing us make the same mistakes over and over, day in and day out? He must surely wish that we would look for ways to serve Him, when, instead, we seem content to travel the same highway of self-centered living day after day.

And what about our complaining and our moaning and groaning? God must hear a nonstop barrage of, "Why, Lord?" "Why me?" "Why did You ever allow this to happen?"

How does He put up with our never-ceasing demands? Always there is someone, somewhere, saying, "Gimme, Lord, gimme."

The longer I sat in my parking space, the more the traffic got to me. I finally pulled out and found a less busy spot. I wondered why God doesn't do the same. Why does He endure watching over us and listening to us constantly? Could it be because He loves us so much? Could that be why He never takes His eyes off us?

It must be. I could think of no other reason why God would maintain a continual surveillance of our lives.

When I got home I looked up the Scripture that had come to my mind earlier. It was Psalm 121: 4 and 8: "[God] is always watching, never sleeping;" and "He keeps His eye upon you as you come and go, and always guards you" (TLB, brackets added).

We don't know how You do it, Lord, but we're glad You do. Thanks for always being there. Amen.   □

Words of encouragement span centuries

July 19, 2003

Failure and disappointment are not welcome in our lives, yet they visit every last one of us. Countless people throughout the centuries have testified: It's not so much what happens to us that makes the difference; it's what we do with what happens to us that leads either to triumph or defeat.

The moment we are born, life becomes a challenge. We either embrace life or struggle against it. These two extremes make up the substance of growth or the lack of it. If we resist nourishment in the form of things we don't particularly care for, we don't grow. If we balk at change, preferring only comfort and familiarity, we regress. If we rejoice in new possibilities, we seize opportunities for fulfillment and another growth spurt is charted. Growth doesn't just happen, it's a result of receiving, digesting, learning and exploring.

If life has taught me one thing, it's this: What I am, what I have and what I don't have, given as unto the Lord, comprise the best effort I can put forth in accepting life's challenges. In God, possibilities that don't exist are conceived. Successes that are impossible become bridges to future impossible successes. Ideas are only worth pursuing as they pertain to God's plan for life.

Now, that being said, I must also say this: I don't always put into practice what I've just said. How about you? Do you always embrace struggles, change, opportunities, challenges? I know, it's hard to admit, but we're a lazy lot! We would just love to have everything made easier. We would give up some of life's luxuries in a heartbeat if we could only go back to a less complicated era, the one we "oldies" refer to as the good old days.

The good old days are long gone. Too often the farther we travel away from them, the better they look. Some of them weren't so good while we were living them. Others were pristine and would definitely be worth regenerating if we could. We can't, so we go on from where we are, day by day.

Where we are. Just where are we?

Most of us are in a state of wearing out. Over-commitments, overwork, overloads of every imaginable nature are pressing down and around, threatening at any moment to become more than we think we can bear. Encouraging words help for a brief while; music soothes in some instances; exercise or a shopping break offers diversion. Ultimately, however, stress and pressure return and register full weight on the scales of life.

I was thinking about all of this the other day when Jim, my husband, handed me a print-out of something our friend Dave Niemira sent us via e-mail. It's a portion of the writings of St. Teresa of Avila (1515-1582). These words, having survived well-over-400 years, were not penned out of a life of ease or passive spirituality. They come to us through the miracle of affliction, time-tested endurance and timeless application.

According to a Web site on the Internet, St. Teresa, at age 14 or 15, faced the loss of her mother, later suffering serious physical ailment herself "with what seems to have been a malignant type of malaria." Teresa fought depression, endured tribulations pertaining to slander and was ridiculed as being a victim of delusion because of her visions and other manifestations of the evidence of the Holy Spirit in her inner life.

Yet, in time, recounting experience after experience of being drawn ever-closer to the Lord, St. Teresa realized victories through her struggles. Victories which span the centuries to give us these words of hope, encouragement and depth of trust:

> Let nothing disturb you,
> Let nothing frighten you,
> All things are passing.
> God never changes.
> Patient endurance attains all things.
> One who possesses God is wanting in nothing.
>
> — *St. Teresa of Avila*

When we invite the Lord to work in us, there's no telling what we, too, will one day leave behind in word or deed for someone else to ponder way down the line. One thing is certain: Future generations will need encouragement, then, every bit as much as we do today.   □

It's time for redemption, not doom

March 9, 2002

There are times in life when we all feel "doomed." For me, I often feel doomed to be forever behind. If my calculations are correct, to date, I'm roughly 125 years behind my estimated sigh of relief that I've finally accomplished what I set out to do. The older I get, the louder my lament.

One of the things I never seem to complete is correspondence. The list of people I want to keep in touch with keeps growing and, about the time I think I've got a new system that will work, I realize I don't and it doesn't.

Regardless of whether the cards and notes piled up on my desk, or at my end of the kitchen table, are from faithful readers of the " 'Joy ... in the Morning' " column or from family and friends far away, I no sooner set out to write responses than my intentions are interrupted, sometimes for weeks at a time, yes, even longer. The interruptions are not the usual run-of-the-mill stuff. And I know I'm not the only one saying that these days. People all around are saying the same thing: "Where is our world headed! Nothing is simple any more! I can't accomplish anything I set out to do! It seems like the world is turned upside down!"

One day last week I finally had a chance to scrape a few layers off the proverbial tip of the iceberg. The shavings probably wouldn't even fill one solitary footprint along the cold, heartless passage of time, but at least I have the peace of mind I made an effort.

For nearly one whole day, I wrote and wrote and wrote. Thank-you notes. Letters. Cards. I wrapped and mailed a belated birthday package to a dear cousin, Patty Jack, a couple of hundred miles away. At the end of the day I sighed. Not a sigh of relief that I was done (because I wasn't), but a sigh of awareness that perhaps I wasn't really "behind" in the first place. Perhaps this was the day the Lord had intended all along for me to do what I had done.

In my sighing, God's Word from Ecclesiastes 3:1 came to mind: "To everything there is a season, a time for every purpose under heaven" (NKJV).

For a few minutes, even stretching into a couple of hours, I felt peace. I felt caught-up. I felt less pressure than I've felt in a long time.

So what did I learn? I learned that either in the brief times of relief, or in a return of a "doomed' feeling, I can, in all honesty, confess to myself and God: *I do the very best I can. I pray for guidance, and even when there are delays and detours, Lord, I must believe this is exactly where You are guiding me. If and when You lead me toward accomplishment, then I trust this is the "season" for it. Whether my progress is slow, fast or standing still, if You are in it, then I'm right where I'm supposed to be. Thank You, Lord, for redeeming my sense of defeat.*

The next time *you* feel "doomed" remember it doesn't have to be a permanent state.   ☐

A fireplace of priceless stones
October 8, 1988

In the late 1970s and early 80s, we had a wood stove in our house around which the whole family gathered for warmth and a homespun atmosphere.

Sadly, I developed an allergy to wood smoke and our pioneer-like atmosphere had to go. Out went the closest I ever came to being the frontier woman of my dreams. Even so, there's a coziness about the memory of a wood fire that brings a spark of regret to mind every time I remember that we had to give it up.

Also hidden away in my memories of things that used to be, I recall a time involving friends of ours who once had a beautiful fireplace in their home that was very special to them. It was special not only because of the warmth it gave off, but also because they themselves had built it with stones they had collected at specific times and places in their lives.

Because each stone in the masonry work of that fireplace had significant memory value to our friends, it wasn't easy for them when they had to sell the home and move elsewhere. Their sadness at leaving their fireplace was summed up by a question that the wife asked, more of herself than of me, in a conversation prior to their moving: "Who else will know or care about each stone in that fireplace the way we do?"

Following that conversation, I wished that I could have had the right words to say to ease my friend's hurt. Later that same day, I began reading my Bible in 2 Corinthians, chapter 5, when I had some definite reactions to verse 1 which says: "...we will have wonderful new bodies in heaven, homes that will be ours forevermore, made for us by God Himself, and not by human hands" (TLB).

My friends' fireplace came to mind along with their reluctance to give it up because *they* had built it. But then I thought, "Could it not be that God will have a fireplace for them in their heavenly home, one day—a fireplace that *He* built special, just for them?"

I envisioned my friends saying to each other upon their future heavenly arrival, "Honey, look at this fireplace! The stones are so-o-o beautiful. Why...it's hard to believe...but this fireplace is even more lovely than the one we had to give up years ago."

And I could imagine God standing back enjoying their comments of appreciation and praise. In my spirit, I saw Him step up to the couple, place a hand on each of their shoulders, and say, "I'm so glad you like it, My children, because not only did I build it just for you, I built it with the most precious stones I could find.

"You see, children, I built this fireplace out of all the stumbling blocks in your life on earth, because, every time you stumbled over life's difficulties, you drew closer to Me."

Later, when I called my friend to share this with her, she laughed appreciatively and said, "Well, if that's so, it's going to take a lot of firewood (up there), because it will certainly be a big fireplace."

Lord, comfort us with the nearness of Your Presence every time we have to confront obstacles in our lives. Remind us that You can turn them into priceless treasures. Amen.

□

CHAPTER SIX

Faith

Patience is sure sign of strength
March 17, 2001

"Have patience, be persistent, keep the faith." This drop-quote in R. Franklin Cook's editorial on page 1 of the March issue of *Holiness Today* magazine drew me in. That's what it means to be hooked by a highlighted quote, a headline or opening remarks.

In this instance, Cook's hook (rhyming purely coincidental) was a godsend. I was blessed by being reeled in. I really needed to hear the rest of what the editor-in-chief of the monthly publication of Nazarene Publishing House, Kansas City, Missouri, wrote.

"The work of God does take time — time few of us are willing to give it," Cook exhorts. "Patience is not inactivity. It is not lethargy. It is persistent trust."

Nothing is harder to do than be patient, and trust, when we would much rather take the bull by the horns and make things happen — quickly, as in NOW! But if we are to *have patience, be persistent, keep the faith,* we must trust. Trust, as in waiting on the Lord. Waiting on the Lord is not a display of weakness. It's a promise, a guarantee of upgraded strength to come.

"They that wait upon the Lord shall renew their strength; they shall mount up with wings as eagles; they shall run, and not be weary; and they shall walk, and not faint" (Isaiah 40:31, KJV).

In my opinion, this passage of Scripture from Isaiah can not be overstated. It can not be quoted too often. It's like breathing air and drinking water — we never outgrow our need of it. There is no getting away from Isaiah 40:31's living, breathing, essential quality of eternal sustenance. But then, there is no surprise in this, because this is what all Scripture is: Alive.

Scripture is Alive! God's Word lives and breathes! Oh, what joy and power for living comes from feeding on God's living nutrients!

"The Word of God is living and powerful," we read in Hebrews 4:12 (NKJV).

Interestingly, this quote from Hebrews was featured Monday in the March 12 reading from *Our Daily Bread* devotional booklet put out by Radio Bible Class Ministries of Grand Rapids, Michigan. Short, but to the point, the meditation concludes with punch: "God's Word will always have an impact."

It's so simple to employ but so easy to overlook God's very own voice in His Word. We know the power that's there. But we forget. We neglect to reach for it as a weapon against depression. As a tool to defeat discouragement. As wings to take us soaring above our circumstances.

Ah, but thanks be to God The Father for reminders of His power placed here and there throughout our lives. Like spotting flowers along the pathways of our journeying, we either stop to appreciate them or we miss out. The choice is ours. But the choice is more obvious when we get hooked on something as life-changing as God's Word.

Actually, being hooked — daily — must be what Jesus meant when He taught us to pray as recorded in Matthew 6:9-13: "Our Father which art in heaven, Hallowed be Thy Name. Thy kingdom come. Thy will be done in earth, as it is in heaven.

Give us this day our daily bread. And forgive us our debts, as we forgive our debtors. And lead us not into temptation, but deliver us from evil: For Thine is the kingdom, and the power, and the glory, for ever. Amen" (KJV).

Have patience, be persistent, keep the faith. You can do it. I can do it. As long as we remember where our daily sustenance and spiritual strength originate.   □

Watering seeds of hope and faith

August 11, 2001

In the spring I bought a colorfully painted and artfully lettered wooden garden sign that reads: "Water the seeds, not the weeds." The sign never made it to the garden but instead is propped up against the wall inside the foyer of our home. But that's OK because the message of the sign is every bit as meaningful inside as it would be outside.

A home, like a garden, is a place to grow and a place to see results of sowing seeds. Watering seeds in a garden, however, is easier, by far, than nurturing seeds in the home. There is no comparison between watering seeds such as love, joy, patience and kindness or simply tipping a sprinkling can full of water over a green plant. One takes a few minutes, the other a lifetime.

In the case of tending seeds in our homes, there's the matter of words versus actions. All too often many of us say one thing and do another. For instance, we might sow a handful of seeds by expressing early in the morning that we hope today will go smoothly for everyone in the family. But the next thing you know, the very one who spoke the words of hope is caught up in a mood of despair because the bathroom sink is clogged.

Right away, when an event such as this hypothetical scenario occurs, it's wise to identify the clogged sink as an ugly weed and yank it out by pouring an unclogging remedy down the drain. Calling a frustration by its name and dealing with it is often the most productive way to keep watering seeds of hope and faith without losing sight of results and rewards.

Sounds easy enough, but life is never that easy, is it? Weeds of despair sprout up overnight, sometimes instantly, while seeds of hope and joyful anticipation seem to remain dormant underneath layers of confusion, delays, limitations and reversals. *Reversals.*

Financial reversals experienced in 1837 by the father of Anna Bartlett Warner, the woman who wrote the words to "Jesus Loves Me," could have been the undoing of the Warner family. Instead, as a direct result of Henry Warner's economic setbacks, his two daughters Anna and Susan began writing to help supplement the family's meager income. The rewards of these two women going about watering seeds of faith instead of succumbing to weeds of doubt and discouragement now span three centuries.

But look again at the year, 1837, of the Warner family's financial reversals. It wasn't until 1860 that Anna wrote "Jesus Loves Me" as a poem to be included in a novel her sister was working on. Twenty-three years passed between the time of the need and the sprouting of that particular seed. It was later still, 1861, when noted musician and hymn writer William Bradbury discovered the poem and composed the music for "Jesus Loves Me."

There's no telling how long seeds in our own lives will require watering and prayerful attention. Anna Bartlett Warner was 40 years old when she wrote "Jesus Loves Me." She lived 55 more years, dying on January 22, 1915 at 95 years of age. Gazing at a picture of Anna Warner my husband ran off for me from an Internet resource, I can almost imagine her saying

something along the lines of: *There's no hurrying a good thing.*
Take your time, trust the Lord and always hold onto hope and
faith while working to get rid of doubts and fears.

In other words, water the seeds of positive possibilities a
little bit every day. Don't spend any more time than is necessary worrying about the weeds, unless, of course, it's to do a
little weed pulling.   □

Victory requires a face of flint

November 10, 2001

More than once I've "lost" my favorite Bible verse and
more than once I've been blessed to find it again. Each time
this happens I discover anew the power of God's Word to reach
out and grab hold of one's heart, mind, soul and spirit in a
flash.

It happened again Tuesday morning: I "uncovered" my verse.
It was right where I left it — tacked to the wall beside my
filing cabinet. Only problem was, I hadn't seen that part of the
wall for a good, long while because of boxes and research papers piled high in front of the sign.

The sign is nothing more than a four-by-six index card held
up with a red thumbtack stuck into our barn-board wall. But
it's the message on the sign that never fails to cut to the heart
of the matter — whatever "the matter" is any time I feast on
this Scripture from Isaiah 50:7: "Because the Lord God helps
me, I will not be dismayed; therefore, I have set my face like
flint to do His will, and I know that I will triumph" (TLB).

This is a verse I quote often. It's a verse I hope to remember
always. No life is devoid of circumstances that threaten to dis-

may. I've not met anyone who has managed to escape a face-off with the threat. But, oh, praise God, the face-to-face encounters with dismaying circumstances need not defeat us. The reason we can make this claim is because we need not stand alone in the face of dismay.

Moreover, when dismay boldly and abruptly plants its feet in our pathway, we have every right to expect that we won't be disheartened or tempted to abandon our progress. We can, as the Scripture announces, set our face like flint and know that we will triumph. The qualifier comes in setting our face to do *God's will*. Then we can know we *will triumph*. Obviously, the key is locking our sights on God's will, not our own.

Is it easy to set one's jaw with a determined focus and cut through obstacles that often defy description? Of course not. If it were easy, I and others wouldn't waste our time writing, preaching, teaching about the challenge. If it were easy, you and I wouldn't bother reading, listening or responding to suggestions about dealing with dismaying situations.

Instead, we take heed because life is hard. Precious few moments come and go in anyone's life that could be labeled uneventful and non-threatening. You need to set your face like flint. So do I. Most of the time when we're called on to do this we don't feel comfortable. We aren't prepared. We don't look our best. We'd rather not be seen taking a stand.

Whenever we find ourselves about to make an excuse to turn the other way, it's a safe bet we're trying to avoid the boulder that's impeding our progress down a contrived easy road. If we're going to win the victory over life, it's time to sharpen our resolve to search for God's will in whatever lay before us and, with His help, expect to claim the prize. Sounds like a plan, does it not?

Oh, Lord, establish our plans according to Your will. Engrave our gaze directly on You. Fill us with confidence that

nothing will veer us away from the course You have ordained.
Remind us, again and again, that we need not be dismayed
and that, in the end, with Your help and in Your will, we will
triumph. In Jesus' Name. Amen.   □

'Let us lift up our heart with our hands'

April 26, 2003

Let us lift up our heart with our hands unto God in the heavens (Lamentations 3:41, KJV).

Do you ever cry out, "Oh, Lord, my heavy heart weighs me down!" If we're willing to be honest, most of us will say I do. It's not a fun place to be, weighed down with weariness, worry and woe, but it *is* a place frequented by the masses.

Oddly, though, when you or I are there, we don't see the masses. We only see our own plight and fear our own demise. Not necessarily a physical demise, although that is sometimes a possibility, but rather a spiritual, emotional, financial or other imminent death.

When we are in such a place, we're certain there is no way we're going to survive "this one, this time." We just know we're in danger of being crushed. But we can't give up. We can't let life defeat us. The weight of our circumstances need not impede our eventual success and victory, even in the face of impossible odds.

If only our hearts could rise above the dread of reality long enough to lift our spirits and give us a breath of unpolluted hope and revived faith. It may seem simplistic, but there *is* a way to do this. It's called being childlike. I call it being like Lily. Lily is my granddaughter.

Lily Grace Strauch was born Chinese and spent the first year of her life in an orphanage in China. In December 2001 she became the daughter of our daughter April and her husband Allen. Lily's mommy and daddy could not love her more. And neither could her four grandparents. Although Lily is not quite two-and-a-half, it's as though she has belonged to our family since forever.

As a member of our family, Lily teaches us as much, if not more, then we all teach her. She doesn't know it, but she has taught us God's way is not only the best way, it's the only way. She has also shown us that faith and trust are best expressed with abandon. When I came upon the verse the other day in Lamentations 3:41, "Let us lift up our heart with our hands unto God in the heavens" (KJV), I saw this scripture come alive by picturing Lily reaching up to her "Bompaw."

Of course, *Bompaw* is Grandpa. And when Lily runs toward him with her straight-black hair flying in the breeze of her rushing, her arms are raised in anticipation of her Bompaw's embrace, better known as a hug and a squeeze.

But you know, it's not really Lily's arms that are raised in confidence with sheer abandon. When her arms are up and extended as she makes a beeline for Grandpa, it's actually her heart that is lifted up. It's her heart that is saying, "Bompaw, Bompaw!" And it's her heart that knows Bompaw will scoop her off her feet and hold her tight, where nothing else matters to either of them for a good, long while.

If you and I could be like Lily at least once a day, we could breathe easier. I just know it. If we would only *lift up our heart with our hands unto God in the heavens* we could walk, even run, with less weight on our shoulders. The weight literally falls off when we raise our arms up to praise the Lord and embrace His love and devotion to us.

If you don't believe me, try it, right now. Look up to the ceiling. Throw your head back and raise both arms up to the sky, hands open, ready to receive all the Lord is waiting to give. The Lord gives release and relief. It's His offering to us as we present the offering of ourselves to Him.

Dear Lord, Who but You could bring Your Word down to earth in the shape and form of a childlike expression of faith? Of course, You have done this in the shape and form of Your Son—The God Who became a Baby to become a Man to stretch forth His arms on the cross so that we might be offered salvation through the sacrifice of Our Savior. If this isn't Love, nothing is. Because of what Jesus Christ did in lifting up His heart with His hands unto You, You have shown us, clearly, what we should do in response to Your love and grace extended to us. In Jesus' Name. Amen.   □

Nightingale sings mostly in the dark
May 31, 2003

I call to remembrance my song in the night (Psalm 77:6, KJV).

With so much darkness from distress and heaviness of spirit prevalent in our world today, who among us feels like singing? Huddled in the dark, where worries and fears press uncomfortably close, we cower; we tremble. Singing here seems out of place; even ridiculous, if not impossible. We don't feel like singing when we can't see what is lurking in the shadows. There might be danger and that's no cause for song. Darkness is something to dread, and who hears music in his soul when surrounded by dread and darkness?

Nevertheless, there are characteristics of dark nights of fear that do, indeed, induce song. When the darkness is deep and dense with uncertainty, cries of travail in the night produce a God-ward plea. A plea that resonates with a gripping, desperate hope that the night will end and the dawn will birth victory.

Not many of us can sing like the nightingale. I know I can't. But did you know that the nightingale sings mostly in the dark? Its rich, complex melodies are heard when the sun is hidden and the night is thick with blackness. Fables portray the nightingale performing its best song with its breast pressed against a thorn all night long. Due to the nightingale's intense fear of snakes, the pain from the thorn keeps the night-time caroler awake and alert.

Fable or truth regarding the nightingale makes no difference because, either way, these things are certain when applied to your life and mine: You and I are often asked to sing when we'd rather just hide from the vast unknown. You and I must believe in the Light of God's presence even before He pierces our fears and drives away the gloom of doubt and anguish.

Even in the dark; especially in the dark; our song of faith in God's almighty power pulsates from our heart when, in an attitude of worship, we give voice to our reliance on Him despite the depth of our despair. Our confidence in the Lord's able-ness to overcome darkness with His Light might be only a distant note; but no matter how faintly we hear it, if we will tune our melody of pain and sorrow with His Might, we have the makings of a song. Yes, a song in the night.

The Bible speaks of a "song in the night" and encourages our "remembrance" of it (Psalm 77:6, KJV). However, in order for us to *remember* it, it must first occur. But how? The entire chapter of Psalm 77 addresses "the how" along with anguish, troubles, complaints. The chapter is full of questions:

How do we sing when we are crying out to God, feeling forgotten? How do we declare the Lord's greatness when He appears to be withholding from us His tender mercies? How do we rest; we can't sleep; the troubles are so deep we can't even speak?

The answers, of course, are also in Psalm 77: We "remember the works of the Lord" (v.11) from the past. We meditate on all He has already done. We talk of His deeds. We declare His strength and "remember the years of the right hand of the Most High" (v. 10).

Herein lies our song: Our anguish and His glory go hand in hand. There is harmony between our bearing the pain and His right to be glorified; not necessarily *for* the pain, but in the midst of it. Deep, dark trials like "great waters (v. 19)" are no hindrance to God. They merely represent another place for His Light to shine.

This *is* our song. Our song in the night. Remembering it is our melody. We are more like the nightingale than we might think.   □

Should we expect faith to strike like lightning?
June 27, 1992

There's nothing like a middle-of-the night summer thunderstorm to wake a person from a sound sleep. The effect is similar to the way a profound statement alerts us to a truth we hope we'll never forget, especially if it's something we can pass on to another person at just the right moment.

That's kind of how I felt recently when I happened upon the words of the late, world-famous preacher, evangelist Dwight L. Moody:

"I prayed for faith and thought that some day faith would come down and strike me like lightning. But faith did not seem to come. One day I read in the tenth chapter of Romans, 'Faith cometh by hearing, and hearing by the Word of God.' I had [up to this time] closed my Bible and prayed for faith. I now opened my Bible and began to study, and faith has been growing ever since."

Only a few days after I had read Moody's words in the *Topical Encyclopedia of Living Quotations* (1982, Bethany House Publishers) under the topic of "faith," a woman from New York State expressed a personal concern to a small group in which I was present.

The woman shared how she has been waiting until she has enough faith to approach the elders in her church and ask them to pray for her that she might be healed of a chronic condition causing her frequent, medically unexplainable bouts of pain.

"I don't think their prayers will do me any good unless I have enough faith to believe," the woman sighed.

All of us around her seemed to disagree with her assessment: She didn't have to have tons of faith before she could be prayed for. We tried to encourage her to rely on the faith of others if her own faith was weak right now.

Then I remembered the words of Moody, with two exceptions: At that moment I couldn't recall the exact words or even who had said them. What I did remember was a concept, and so it was the concept I passed on right then and there.

What I said to this woman as several of us were sitting or standing around the kitchen table was something like this:

"You don't have to wait until you can muster up all the faith in the world. That might never happen. But what you can do, is believe what the Bible says somewhere in the Book of James, I think: 'If any of you lacks faith, let him ask God for more faith, and it will be given.' "

Imagine my dismay when, a few days later, I discovered that in my attempting to quote Moody I had actually misquoted a Bible verse.

The verse I had botched was James 1:5: "If any of you lacks wisdom, he should ask God, who gives generously to all without finding fault, and it will be given to him" (NIV).

In trying to encourage the distressed woman, I had inadvertently transposed "wisdom" into "faith." My error wasn't intentional and the woman did seem relieved when she said, "OK, I'll try. I'll try to believe that God can help me, even if I don't have all the faith I think I need."

It seemed to me like the woman was given wisdom at that moment. Wisdom which sounds a whole lot like added faith. Perhaps that resulted from the Lord's intercepting my words and allowing the woman to focus on the concept of trusting Him to supply her with what she needs.

Lord, forgive us if we, in our human imperfections, sometimes make mistakes that only You and Your power can transform into just the right thing at just the right time. In Jesus' Name. Amen. □

CHAPTER SEVEN

Focus

Talents, choices can lead to obsessions

July 23, 1994

Do you ever feel like you're trying to live in two worlds, each fiercely important to you? I do. In one, Jesus is "driving the bus"; and in the other, He's a little harder to find. In the first scenario, when the secondary character is yours truly, I profess a commitment to living my life for the purpose of loving, honoring, praising and serving my Lord and Savior Jesus Christ. Not only do I write and talk about living for Him, but I really and truly live for Him.

Perhaps you, too, believe Jesus should be first in your life, first in your heart, first in your thoughts, first in your dedication. He deserves anything you or I can possibly do to glorify Him and His Name. We've been taught to strive to consume Scriptures concerning Jesus' supreme worthiness, such as this verse, Revelation 5:12: "Worthy is the Lamb who was slain, to receive power and wealth and wisdom and might and honor and glory and blessing!" (RSV).

Speaking personally, I love and am devoted to my husband and to our family; I care deeply for our friends, neighbors and church family; yet ever since I was old enough to give my heart and my life to Jesus, I've tried to put the Lord first. I never want that to change. But there's always this other world that I get myself into. It's the place in my mind, in my choices and activities, where Jesus gets shoved back the aisle of the crowded bus. He is no longer driving. I am. Do you know what I mean?

Take my latest domestic project, for instance: sewing. Please, feel free to draw a parallel in your own life. As for me, I'm in the process of sewing curtains, a bedspread and a blouse. I've got plans to make dresses, pillows and tablecloths. The ideas tumble out of my head faster than I can collect yards...and yards...and, believe me, more yards of bargain-priced fabric. Last week alone, I not only bought yards and yards of fabric remnants, but I also bought fabric on bolts; one bolt contained five yards, one had 88 and the other, 90.

The best part of these recent purchases is that all this new, high-quality fabric cost me only a little more than $30 (total!) at a yard sale. The worst part is I now want to sew and sew and sew. I see visions of redressing all the windows in the house and creating a new wardrobe of comfortable, attractive outfits for myself. After all, I enjoy investing time, effort and energy doing something I love to do — and I love to plan, design and feast my eyes on the finished product.

"So, what's wrong with that?" I hear myself asking myself. Well, what's wrong is that I get carried away. I don't like to eat or sleep until everything I see in my head is at long last completed. It's hard to exercise restraint when it comes to wholesome, creative but challenging projects.

This part of my personality forces me to continually readjust my focus. I *want* Jesus Christ to be the uppermost priority in my life. But honestly, if I was not committed to keeping my sights on Jesus and on His will and plan for my life, I could easily go on and on obsessing on plenty of worthwhile activities and choices, none of which are violent, or criminal or even sinful or harmful, in any way. But the bottom line has to do with temptation: Again and again, I'm tempted to put talents and personal interests in the front seat — the seat belonging to the One who gave me these very talents and interests in the first place. Do you relate to what I'm saying? Surely some of you see yourself in this picture.

Even when you and I rationalize that God wants us to use *all* He has given us, that's not the ultimate point, is it? I believe He wants us to use our time, our energies and our talents *wisely*. Moderation and balance help us maintain perspective without compromising convictions and priorities.

We may never totally "get it" in this lifetime, but letting the Lord know we'd like to keep working at it is one way we can bring Him glory, honor and praise.   □

New perspective dawns with a blue-sky day
July 16, 1994

If I heard it once, I heard it dozens of times early this week when my husband's brother Bill, our sister-in-law Kate and their family visited us for a few days: "Aunt Dotty...Aunt Dotty...Aunt Dotty!"

The insistent "Aunt Dottys" sprang from Emily and Billy, our three- and six-year-old niece and nephew, who were neither still nor quiet until their little eyes blinked shut almost at the same instant their little bodies climbed up onto the hide-a-bed in the living room each night.

But my favorite "Aunt Dotty" episode can't be fully appreciated without a bit of background information. The background info is brief and familiar to anyone living in northeastern Pennsylvania this summer: hot, humid and hazy weather conditions — day in and day out. As a matter of fact, it's been so hot, so humid, so hazy, for so long, if you're like me, you nearly have forgotten the sky up there is actually blue. Enter Billy with one more "Aunt Dotty" and color-appreciation senses are joyously awakened.

It happened like this...

Tuesday dawned, finding me with a horrible headache. I had no choice but to tune out the "Aunt Dottys" as best I could while Billy and Emily did try to keep their voices soft and their exclamations to a minimum. But when Billy burst in the front door from having been out on the porch after breakfast, he forgot about my request for quietness and breathlessly exclaimed, "Aunt Dotty! You have to come outside! It's a beau-u-u-tiful day! Oh, it's so beautiful out there! Look! Look!"

How right he was! There wasn't a cloud in the sky! The sky was blue! It was like seeing the sky and the color blue for the first time.

Now, it was my turn: "Oh, Billy! Oh, Billy! It *is* beautiful!"

For a few moments my headache was forgotten, and I'm sure as time goes by, my memory of the blue-sky day will, by far, outlive any recollection of the pain in my head. But as wonderful as the miracle of God's blue skies is, there is something more wonderful, more miraculous when we take the time to think about it; when we pause to let God lift the haze from our routine, often troubled, lives.

The wonder, the amazement, the thrill of a lifetime comes each and every time we look at Jesus instead of obsessing over our unsolved problems. Instead of fretting about our confusions. Instead of wallowing in our disappointments and losses. Every time we look up to Him, and really "see" Him we begin to perceive our sins, our shortcomings, our worries, our pains in a new light. The light is the Light of His love and forgiveness.

Seeing Jesus, His love, His forgiveness and the breathless realization of His presence are like seeing Him for the first time. And yet, whether it *is* the first time or the zillioneth time, we recognize the Light immediately and vow, "I'll never forget this moment.!"

Of course, we do. Forget, that is. The haze, the clouds, the weight of the burdens, they all return. But He is there; He is here. If we keep looking, we will know, we will see.

Dear Lord, keep us on the right path. When our eyes stray, bring our focus back in line with You and the Light of Your will. When we finally see, again and again, help us to know there is no other way than the way You have prepared for us. And, oh, yes, even when we can't see the way, fill us with the assurance we need to persist. In other words, keep us faithful, keep us trusting, keep us. Whether skies are black, gray or gloriously bright, keep us, keep us, in You r sight. In Jesus' Name. Amen. □

Staying on track with the Lord's help
January 8, 1994

Clothespins disappear at our house faster than socks get lost in the wash. Even so, the explanation of the vanishing clothespins is much less mysterious than the sock-eating-washer-and-dryer syndrome introduced years ago by humor columnist Erma Bombeck.

The clothespins vanishing from our laundry room do so only because they are snatched up for other uses besides fastening clothes on a line. For example: I use clothespins to clip notes to my purse as reminders for the next time I go shopping; my husband and I both use clothespins on bags of cookies, pretzels, potato chips, cereal, crackers and other foods to help seal in freshness.

Dozens of clothespins defy gravity by drifting upstairs into my writing room. There they hold together various papers, notes, ideas and projects in secure little groupings for future reference. Clothespins are much better than paper clips for organizing some types of paper work because, No. 1: clothespins hold more; and, No. 2: the clothespins stick out and are easier to grab.

Although I could go on and on about other duties assigned to clothespins at our house (such as book and magazine markers and coupon organizers), this column is not about clothespins. Rather, this column is about holding a life on course. Whether we're speaking of your life or my life, it's a task so significant as to warrant keeping reminders of God's purposes in every room, in every imaginable nook and cranny of our habitation.

Personally, alone, I can't keep my thoughts on track, can't keep my heart and mind focused without help. I need visual crutches. If I may, I'll call these crutches "spiritual clothespins" — handy little gadgets to help organize my spiritual life and keep my prone-to-wonder mind feeding on fresh insights everywhere I go.

These crutches, these gadgets, these spiritual clothespins are none other than devotional books and booklets scattered, while at the same time strategically placed, around my house: in the bathrooms, on the dining room table, in reading corners, within reach of my favorite television-watching chair and at my computer desk. Through the years some of you readers have told me you do likewise.

Unwittingly we can place so much stock in the devotional arena, we have to be careful not to let any of the readings replace God's Word in the Bible. That's why it's wise to keep a Bible within reach of all the devotional materials. In my case, I try to let the devotional writers' thoughts inspire me to pick up God's Word, inspire me to look for spiritual parallels in my own life and, above all, inspire me to turn my face God-ward.

Nothing — no devotional material, no inspirational literature and no writer or familiar personality — should ever replace the Lord. He is the One Who puts "the profound" and "the fresh" in His Word. That's why His Word is the Living Word.

"The Lord's promise is sure. He speaks no careless word; all He says is purest truth, like silver seven times refined" (Psalm 12:6, TLB).

When we're dealing with holding things together, especially our very lives, gimmicks such as *spiritual clothespins* might figuratively or literally be found marking the highways and byways in our hearts and homes. Even so, we must never let anything replace the Lord, Jesus Christ, the Holy Spirit, the Bible. Anything that takes our eyes off *this focus* is not going to hold our life together, or keep us on track, for very long.

□

How much is our time worth to us?

December 31, 1988

Do you and I spend our time as carefully as we do our money? If every second was worth a dollar, the value of each day would be $86,400. No one I know has that kind of money to spend however he or she chooses on a daily basis. Instead, every person alive is given 86,400 seconds to spend each day.

When we awaken each morning, suppose we valued this gift of time as much as we might if the figure of 86,400 was preceded by a dollar sign. Would we rush out and spend all that time impulsively? Or would we, at the beginning of each day, thoughtfully and prayerfully make plans for how best to use that day's "account"?

Look at it another way: When each day draws to a close, like right before we put out the lights, do we rejoice over how we spent the day? Or are we glad it's almost over and want to forget it as quickly as possible?

Whether we reflect on each today with joy or regret might be a good indicator of how we ought to view the opportunity to start a new day tomorrow. Perhaps we might bid farewell to the day just ending and prepare to greet the approaching one by asking ourselves some goal-setting questions:

• What bad habit do I have that I could set out to get rid of first thing tomorrow morning? What healthier habit could I replace it with?

• How many people did I pray for today? How many more can I add to a list for tomorrow?

• Is there anyone I hurt or offended during the last 24 hours? What can I do tomorrow to set things aright and how can I try to be more thoughtful in the future?

• What more can I do than I've ever done before about my own spiritual growth? How can I expand my outreach to people who don't know Jesus Christ?

• What can I do to improve my relationship with my spouse? My son? My daughter? My friends? My boss? My neighbors?

• Am I willing to change if it will show someone close to me how much I love him or her?

• Am I willing to ask God what He wants me to do about

the mistakes I've made today? If God actually answered that question, am I willing to follow His instructions?

• Is there anything I've always wanted to do, but didn't, that the Lord and I together could begin doing tomorrow?

At the close of each day, you and I have little choice but to accept that it's likely too late to improve upon today. But it's not too soon to resolve to make tomorrow a better day. A day to know God, ourselves and those we love more intimately than ever.

It's also probably safe to assume that spending $86,400 per day is beyond the reach of most of us. So why not give ourselves over into the hands of the One who can best advise us how to spend that many seconds each day, every day.

Dear Lord, I would rather have You in charge of each day of my life than anyone else I know, including myself. Please help me as I draw the curtain on today to turn more of myself and my life over to You than I did in the hours just past. Thank You in advance for hearing my heart. Amen.

□

Distractions spoil recipe for faith
November 20, 1993

Years ago I wrote about my infamous pumpkinless pumpkin pies. The secret recipe is easy to repeat: Simply forget to add any and all pumpkin, and you've got it down pat. But some things in life are a lot more complicated than my tongue-in-cheek recipe for pumpkin pies.

For example, keeping our spiritual eyes focused on Jesus—no matter what storm is raging in our lives—is easier said than done. And I, for one, have tried to say it more often than I've been able to accomplish it. When I have succeeded in keeping my focus, it has not been without effort.

Just like the other day. My intent was to forget about everything piling up around me, sit down in my rocking chair and read the Bible, hoping to focus on the Lord through His Word. But instead of getting and keeping the focus, I looked up at the clock on the wall every few seconds. I was irritated that time was passing so quickly and my goals for the day were not being met. One of those goals was a desire to focus on Jesus before proceeding with the rest of my day.

Determined, I continued trying. With the rhythm of the rocker, my eyes read a verse or two and then darted toward the clock. Back and forth, my eyes read and darted, read and darted. Even chiding myself aloud didn't help: "No way am I going to 'see' Jesus if I can't keep my eyes where they belong!"

At last, there was only one thing left to do. I got up from the rocker and taped a full sheet of paper over the face of the clock. Then I sat down again, Bible in hand. Each time my eyes darted upward, I found it a relief not to see the hands of time moving.

Finally, after I glanced up at that blank sheet of paper several more times, my mind and spirit began to relax as I read from the book of Jonah in the Old Testament. The tension suddenly drained away when, in chapter 1, verse 15, I read: "...and the storm stopped!" (TLB).

What I gained from reading the rest of Jonah (about his ordeal with the sea after being thrown overboard and swallowed by a "great fish") was rather a long list of positive, encouraging insights, from a personal perspective. But not one of them is as relevant to my fixation on the passing of time as is the peace that can come from focusing on Jesus when the storms of life are raging on all sides.

Once again I learned what I've known for years, but often

forget: Sometimes I have to physically get distractions out of the way before I can see my Lord.

The distractions are ingredients well left out of any recipe for time spent with Jesus.

Dear Lord, with the passing of time ever before us, we find our lives either full of activity or full of loneliness. Either way we can be distracted. Either situation can get in the way of our "seeing" You. Show us how to boldly remove distractions from our lives, and help us to reach out to others who may need help with their distractions. In Jesus' Name. Amen. □

The march of time

July 14, 2001

They...searched the Scriptures daily to find out whether these things were so (Acts 17:11, NKJV).

As the clock on our living-room wall struck midnight earlier this week, I was struck anew with the realization of how time marches steadily onward. It refuses to stand still and wait for me to catch up. The same is true for you, too. Neither you nor I can outrun time.

No matter how fast-paced or slow our day has been, one stroke of the clock and today is over. No turning back, ever. One moment is all that stands between yesterday and tomorrow. We can never relive one second of the day just ended. Oh, we can, and do, mull it over in our minds and perhaps wish we would have said or done things differently, but we can never actually live it again. Each day begins and ends the same way. In one split-second today becomes yesterday and tomorrow becomes now. It all happens at the stroke of midnight.

It's not always fun to be up that late. You end up feeling like you're borrowing from life without any way to pay it back. There are times, however, when staying up until midnight and beyond is the only way to hear yourself think. Better yet, it is sometimes the only way to "hear" God "speak."

"In the stillness of my soul," sings contemporary Christian artist Carman in his song "Bless God," "I reflect to see how [God's] love and power have grown and move inside of me."

The stillness of the soul is worth seeking, early or late. Midnight represents both extremes of time. But whether you or I wait until the last minute of today or avail ourselves of the beginning of tomorrow, we need to be still, reflect and search daily.

Personally, I like to be still more than once a day. I like to be still and quiet before I ever open my eyes in the morning, when my mind is barely awake. It's an ideal time to silently praise the Lord and pray for many of the people and situations on my mental prayer list. It helps to settle my anxieties concerning the day ahead.

At meal times, either before or after the usual prayer of thanksgiving, I like to pause before that first bite and whisper an additional, "Praise You, thank You, bless You, Lord." It helps to quiet my spirit and calm my digestive system.

Throughout the day I like to turn my attentions God-ward so that I can keep my focus and my priorities lined-up with His will as I perceive it. Of course, the way to arrive at any kind of perception as to what the Lord's will might be for one-self, you and I have to search for His will.

God's will is found in His heart. His heart is found in the Scriptures. God's heart is in His Word. And His Word is where we must go daily to search and to find answers to life's uncertainties and demands.

Whether at the stroke of midnight or before, sooner or later the only way to face the present and deal appropriately with the past and the future is to look to the Lord. Look to His Word. Look to His Son. Look to His Way. There we find out what to believe and what to do. In my opinion, it's the only way to begin or end each day.   ☐

'Spiritual crutch' can help us retain focus

January 27, 2001

At last count I have in my possession 28 different devotional books. With the diverse number of things I have to think about and deal with, I'm thankful that there is a volume of meditational readings almost everywhere I turn in our house. Why? Because in today's world it's downright hard, if not impossible, to keep focused without help.

Keeping focused in the midst of life. That's where I am, or at least where I know I need to be. Perhaps the rest of you are there, too. When I refer to keeping focused I feel the need to offer a bit more definition. It's not enough to just keep focused on any old thing, but rather we've got to keep focused on the Lord.

All of us — not only ministers, Bible teachers, youth leaders, Christian parents and others "called" to fill Christian roles — all need to be focused on the Person we are following. The Person we are serving. The Person of Jesus Christ who is what we are supposed to be living for.

Living for Christ, although this is our proclaimed goal, is not something we do automatically. We certainly don't do it in a vacuum. We live for Christ when we make such a commitment a way of life. We do it as part of our life. Not a separate part, but as a total part of who we are and all we do.

That's why having inspirational resources at one's fingertips, always along with the Bible, is such a boon to helping a person keep the focus. It's a lot like taking vitamins and nutritional supplements in conjunction with eating healthy foods. The combination is what helps a body stay strong and promotes growth.

When it comes to adding vitamins and other supplements to our diet, we know that their nutrient contents are usually most effectively absorbed and used throughout our body in combination with food. There are exceptions. A few need to be taken on an empty stomach, but most vitamins bind themselves with food to be transported throughout our system.

So, too, are the Bible and biblical principles best absorbed and used for growth and development in conjunction with our daily lives, our thoughts and our routines. I know of no better way to keep the absorption merging with life than to keep focused.

OK, so how do 28 devotional books do the job — for me, that is? Well, for one thing, when I experience those days when my thoughts are all in a jumble because life has a way of pulling in all directions, I know I need to get on track. But I also know I need help in finding where to start.

Usually I start by reading one of the Psalms from the Bible or I look up a devotional reading for that day. A good devotional book is one with an appropriate Bible verse or passage accompanying each meditation. It's this suggested Bible verse that often gets me off and running. I look it up in my Bible and read what comes before and after it. Many times this is where my focus comes from for the day, the moment or for a particular need.

Of course, the Bible verse or the devotional reading only jumps to the "ah-ha" status when I can identify how it specifically applies to right where I am right then. That's when I feel fed, nourished and focused.

That's when either I bow my head and whisper, "Thank You, Lord," or lift my hands and shout, "Praise God!" That's when I know that valuable spiritual nutrients are going to be coursing through my veins and energizing my life, at least for the next little block of time. That's also why I need more of the same scattered throughout my physical environment. When I run low on nutrients and my focus starts to get fuzzy, I grab another, and then another, helper.

Call it a devotional addiction, a spiritual crutch or whatever. It works. But it only works because it's a way to get me, and keep me, in touch with the Lord.

If you, too, use a similar method, in addition to regular Bible reading, you know what I mean. If, by chance, you haven't tried a variation of this, you might want to consider it. Making a conscious effort to turn to Bible-based nutrients placed in key locations throughout your day-to-day routine, and then prayerfully applying these nutrients to your life, is one effort that will not go to waste. It's backed by a lifetime guarantee.

□

Quiet times and peaceful places
December 7, 1985

Our whole house was cluttered. There was an unfinished project here, a stack of newspapers there. Mail on the kitchen counter, bills on the dining room table, shoes on the living room floor. Mending in the clothes basket, clean clothes to be folded in another basket and dirty clothes piled in a third. College brochures and homework papers decorated the stairway.

Everywhere I turned in our home there was something waiting for someone's attention. All of these things would eventually get taken care of by various members of the family at various times, but for the time being, the clutter remained.

Much worse than all the domestic clutter, however, were the piles of mental clutter that I was struggling to plow through. My mind was overwhelmed with thoughts of all the upcoming plans and events written on the calendar. Oh, how I wished I could stop thinking about all the places we were going to be going, all the appointments we had to keep, all the deadlines we had to meet.

One corner of my mind said, "Do this now in preparation for that," while another corner piped in with, "No, no! You have to do *that* before you do *this*."

At the same time that my mind was racing from one thing to another, I got an idea for an article, an idea that had to be jotted down right then. But while I was doing that, another part of my mind said, "You ought to be doing something else instead of this, like planning the menu for the weekend guests that are coming next week. And you know you ought to be typing the letters that need to go out in today's mail."

My overactive mind was driving me up a wall. "If only I had time to get away from all this," I thought.

With that, I knew what I had to do, where I had to go. I headed for the landing at the top of our stairs — one of my favorite spots in the house.

There on the wall hang four of the most peace-inducing objects I know: a painting done in restful shades of blue by a friend of ours, a wooden cross, a praying hands plaque and a framed copy of "The Serenity Prayer." You've all heard the prayer, I'm sure:

"God grant me the Serenity to accept the things I cannot change...

Courage to change the things I can...
and Wisdom to know the difference."

I began to see that, although I couldn't change the forth-coming scheduled events, I needed the *Serenity* to change my mental attitude toward each of them. I could try by beginning to think of each one as something I *wanted* to do, not something I *had* to do. I could make an effort to stop my mind from running way ahead of me by saying to myself, "One thing, one step, one day at a time."

But what about *Courage to change the things I can*? Well, I can try to keep next month's calendar page a little less filled than the current one. I can pray for the *Courage* to say "No" when I don't want to say "Yes."

And while I'm at it, I can ask for *Wisdom* to know when to come back to the top of the stairs to rearrange my cluttered mind.

Dear Lord, remind me, on other days such as this one, to search for quiet times and peaceful places. And help me to find them when I need them. Amen.   □

Look over your shoulder

April 6, 1985

It was the third time in less than three months that I was down with strep throat. I was sick of being sick.

To make matters worse, there was an urgent task in front of me. It looked like my husband, our daughters and I were going to have to move within a couple of weeks. I was too weak to pack. I prayed for strength, but I felt none. I tried to convince myself that the Lord was with me, but I didn't *feel* His presence. Like many other times in my life, I simply couldn't *see* Him in my situation.

Retreating to the Bible for comfort I began reading John, chapter 20.

In this passage of Scripture, it was early on what we call Easter morning. Mary Magdalene had come to the tomb where the Lord's body had been placed after He had died on the cross. Mary found that the tomb was empty. Jesus was gone and she didn't know where they had put His body. She ran to tell the others. The others checked it out and verified that Mary was correct: Jesus was not there! No one could find Him.

After the others went on home, Mary returned to the tomb and stood outside crying. As she continued to weep, she looked inside. Two angels, sitting at the head and foot of the place where Jesus had been, spoke to her.

"Why are you crying?" the angels asked her.

"Because they have taken away my Lord," she replied, "and I don't know where they have put Him" (v. 13, TLB).

I knew how Mary must have felt — alone, helpless, confused — the way I was feeling. How was I going to be strong enough to do all that had to be done if the Lord wasn't with me? Hoping for an answer I continued reading...

Just then Mary glanced over her shoulder. Someone was behind her. She didn't recognize Him until He spoke her name.

"Mary!" He said.

She turned around. He was there! Jesus was standing there!

It was then I realized why I couldn't see the Lord in what *I* had to do. I, like Mary, had been looking in the wrong direction. I had been looking into the emptiness of doubt and impossibility. When I stopped my worrying and turned around, I found that Jesus was right behind me. I knew He would take care of my need.

He did!

The next day the move was postponed. I had time to fully recuperate.

Since then I have wondered how often the Lord stands behind us ready to say, "Child, look over your shoulder. Turn around. I've been here all along." ☐

CHAPTER EIGHT

Forgiveness

What do you 'listen' to during the weekly sermon?

January 25, 1992

Last Sunday morning during the worship service at church, sitting next to my husband in a pew, I designed, cut out and sewed a bedspread with matching pillow covers. I also made new curtains for our living room and a framed fabric picture for the bathroom.

No one, but God, could see me doing all of this, because I wasn't doing any of it with my hands. It was all taking place in my mind as I sat there going through the motions of "listening" to the sermon.

With my eyes focused on the minister as he read from the Book of Colossians in the Bible, I was instead "seeing" some of the many bolts of fabric I had touched and handled the day before in the craft and fabric section of the newly opened Wal-Mart store in Lewisburg.

After running errands in various places in Bloomsburg on Saturday, my husband and I had decided to head for Lewisburg to check out the new store while looking for a few household items. Mainly, though, Jim and I simply wanted a day away from all the things occupying our minds at home.

We purchased items on our little list, but the ideas I carried out of there in my head were impossible to confine in the space of time between our visit to the store and Sunday's sermon. Thus the spilling over into the sermon time, and even into the nap I didn't get Sunday afternoon because my mind went on a "creating binge."

But, anyhow, back to the sermon.

As the Rev. Howard West read from Colossians (while I sewed my imaginary creations), I was jolted free from visions of fabric bolts by hearing these words:

"Let heaven fill your thoughts; don't spend your time worrying about things down here. You should have as little desire for this world as a dead person does...don't worship the good things of life, for that is idolatry" (Colossians 3:2-6, TLB).

Quickly and silently, I asked the Lord to forgive my wandering mind:

Lord, I'm sorry for not paying attention to what I'm here for. I'm sorry for putting ideas and projects ahead of You. It's just that I haven't done much sewing for a long, long time, and seeing all that beautiful fabric has started me thinking about... o-o-oh, I wish I would have gotten a couple of yards of the green material with the tiny tulip print...I could have used it to make one of the shelves in the bathroom into a little vanity... Oh, Lord, I'm really sorry, but I just can't help myself this morning.

Before I knew it, the service was over, and I felt bad for not being more attentive. I knew I hadn't committed any horrible crime, and I didn't feel tons of guilt, but I privately lamented having allowed myself to be so distracted.

But it happens. It happens to all of us. Big things, little things. Things come between us and our Lord. Things that can cause us to lose sleep, lose blessings. Things that cause us to miss what the Lord would like for us to hear and to see.

Many times, however, if not most of the time, He gives us other chances. If we don't pay attention to this week's sermon like we know we should, we can try to do better next week. Just like, if we argue with a mate, we can apologize and go on growing in our love for each other. Or if we dent a fender because we forget to look into our rear-view mirror, we can get it repaired and be more careful next time we back out of the garage.

Obviously, some mistakes are not as easy to fix as a dented fender. And some marriages need more repair work than simple apologies. Sometimes we even put off tuning into the Lord's will for our lives, for so long, that we no longer care about Him. If we find ourselves in any of these extreme situations, we may be in need of major help and major forgiveness.

In such cases, I am not trying to minimize the significance of extreme times and extreme needs. Instead, I'm only sharing an incident that I hope makes this point:

Let's not incapacitate ourselves by getting hung up on things that are common to all of us. Let's accept ourselves as human in some areas by forgiving ourselves and accepting the Lord's forgiveness. Then move on.

Whether moving on to next Sunday or to the next time we stumble and fall short of perfection, we can make the most of what the Lord gives us in terms of time, talents and His correction and direction.

As Rev. West read from Colossians 4:5, we can "Make the most of [our] chances to tell others the Good News [of Jesus Christ]" (TLB, brackets added).

No, I didn't actually "hear" him read the above verse on Sunday, but I did hear him say he was reading the whole Book of Colossians, so I looked up what I missed later this past week.

Thank You, Lord, for the times You give us second chances, often third and fourth and upwards to seventy-times-seven chances. Help us to make the most of all You give us, and help us to use as much of it as possible for You and Your glory. In Jesus' Name. Amen.   □

Oven cleaning illustrates God's intense love

May 19, 1990

A friend of mine at *Press Enterprise*, Cathy McQuown, did something recently I seldom do — she cleaned her oven. Cathy admitted her oven is self-cleaning, but she had to push the right buttons to set the whole process in motion. That means—in her opinion and mine—she cleaned her oven!

But Cathy said she got more out of the experience than a sparkling oven. She tells it like this:

"When I set the oven to begin the self-cleaning process, the oven door automatically locked and could not be opened until the extremely high temperatures of the process completely burned off the burnt-on dirt and grease. This reminded me of how the Lord removes sin from our lives. Asking Him for forgiveness sets the whole process in motion.

"Concerning our sins, our hands are tied. We're helpless to forgive ourselves. We have no control over what's going on inside us when the Lord is purifying us, just like we have no control over what's going on inside our self-cleaning ovens.

"The heat in the oven is intense, just as His love is for us! And when either one of these purifying processes is completed, there is nothing left but ashes.

"With the ashes in the oven, we have but to brush them out, throw them away and that's the end of it. However, the ashes in our lives are a little harder to get rid of. But it can be done. Those ashes are the memories of our sins. Once we're forgiven, the sins themselves are gone, but we tend to hang on to the guilt feelings.

"Although the guilt itself is removed, we may still feel embarrassed or ashamed because of our sins. We'll continue to have the ashes lying around in our ovens and in our lives, unless we consciously remove them. Sure, it's harder to 'sweep out' unsightly memories than it is to brush out ashes from an oven. But that sweeping out, the letting go and moving on is part of the process."

As Cathy and I talked about this, we mentioned how the Lord says in Psalm 103:12 that our sins are removed as far away from us as the east is from the west; and in Isaiah 1:18, how they are washed as white as snow.

"Those ashes in my oven were white," Cathy continued, "all the blackness of the burnt-on oven spills was removed, totally gone. It really struck me that that must be like the blackness the Lord removes from our lives when we're cleansed of our sins. With the blackness gone, the white ashes can be scattered and blown away by the wind," Cathy concluded.

Makes a person want to do some deep cleaning, doesn't it? The kind that brings peace of mind, forgiveness of sins and a guilt-free future.

Lord, we can scrub and clean our houses, our windows and even our ovens. But only You can clean our hearts. Help us to be receptive to Your cleansing process. Then help us to accept and believe how truly clean You have made us. All we have to do is ask. So we're asking You today: Help us be as clean as we can be, from the inside out. In Jesus' Name. Amen.

□

CHAPTER NINE

Fulfillment

Our life is meant to fulfill God's purpose

October 27, 2001

One by one each leaf leaves its tree in autumn and floats to the ground. The leaf then dries out, curls up and becomes brittle. Life as a healthy green leaf is a thing of the past. And yet that dry, misshapen, brittle leaf is still a leaf, even if it blows away, even if it gets stepped on or raked into a pile. A leaf is still a leaf.

A leaf doesn't have a mind or a will. It has an appointed purpose and a lifespan. Part of that lifespan is to fall, decompose and fertilize future growth of other leaves. If a leaf could have a passion it surely would be to fulfill its purpose.

What about us, you and me? What and where is our passion?

One of my own passions is to get organized. I've spent a lot of time, years to be exact, trying to get organized for the future. Here I am, in the future, and still not organized. And yet I am still trying.

Through the years I've wanted to get organized for a variety of reasons. For one thing, I like organization. I like to know where everything is and I like to have everything in its place. It hasn't yet quite come together, but I can still dream of it, can't I?

Another reason for craving to be organized is synonymous with being prepared to take action when action is needed. Whether the action is baking a loaf of bread or welcoming visitors into our home, if I'm organized, things go more smoothly. However, life has taught me that things can go smoothly even when organization has flown the coop.

Although trying to get organized is a worthwhile goal, it doesn't constitute our ultimate purpose for being alive. It isn't what we were created for. It isn't what life is all about.

Life is about fulfillment. Fulfillment is about being used of God for His purpose. For His plan. For His desire. For His design. You and I are "organized" when who we are, where we are, what we have and what we don't have are all "lined up" with our being available to God.

I can't speak for anyone else, neither can you. However, each of us has a responsibility to seek out a way to find God's purpose for our lives. This doesn't mean we will ever be 100 percent sure of our exact purpose. Our purpose today might be fulfilled one way and tomorrow another. The key is trusting God for accomplishing His purpose, His way, in us and through us, each season, each year, each day of our lives.

Dear Lord, the closest we can come to knowing our purpose is to know that we were created to glorify You. The way we do this, the timing of it, the fulfilling of it and the culmination of it are aspects of our existence we place in Your hands. Take us, use us, draw out of us all that can be pulled together to fulfill our purpose in You. In Jesus' Name. Amen.

□

Saying something matters doesn't 'cut it' if we ignore it

February 22, 1992

I used to think everyone else had his or her life in perfect order except me.

If I read a good book or a good article I'd think, Wow! The person who wrote that certainly has it made. She couldn't have written anything that outstanding unless everything in her life and in her house is neat and clean.

Or I'd think, that writer either has nothing to do but write all day or he has everything else done very early every morning so the rest of his day is free and clear for writing.

How foolish I was! Thanks to a wise God, I saw the error of my thinking. Little hints I'm sure He planted here and there opened my eyes.

One day, maybe eight or nine years ago, I read from a magazine for writers something I recall almost every time I have to step over a pile of this or that that gets in my way. The writer was trying to encourage others with a bent for writing, and he showed me that if my bent for the craft is strong enough, something else will have to go undone. In speaking of himself, he wrote something like this:

"If you want to know where I live, just look for the house on my street with the unmowed lawn and the flower beds full of weeds."

Another time, my friend Barbara Clark said she knew there is a Bible verse somewhere that speaks of not waiting for perfect conditions before we act. Her paraphrase of the concept was along these lines:

"If we wait for perfect conditions, we'll never get anything done."

Even as she was speaking to me, God was speaking to both

of us, because this woman, a busy wife and mother of a busy, creative household, eventually enrolled as a non-traditional student at Bloomsburg University, where she not only completed a bachelor's degree but also a master's. And on top of a full house and a full schedule, she was battling rheumatoid arthritis.

Still another time, one of God's seeds sprouted and blossomed in the form of a star I had previously penciled in the margin of my Bible above 2 Timothy 4:1-2:

"And so I solemnly urge you…to preach the Word of God urgently at all times, whenever you get the chance, in season and out, when it is convenient and when it is not" (TLB).

I especially couldn't ignore the words "urgently" and "when it is convenient and when it is not".

And so it went, the Lord helped me overcome a mind-set of having to get everything done before going out to play or taking a vacation or going to bed. He showed me how to write when the sink is full of dirty dishes and the hamper is full of dirty clothes. He gently, but clearly, taught me how to pick up paper and pen and write what's on my mind or in my heart "when it is convenient or when it is not."

You'd think after all these years, I wouldn't need reminded. But I do, and so I was this week by words, once again, from God's Word, this time as quoted by freelance Christian writer Marlene Bagnull in her book of Bible studies for writers, *Write His Answer* (1990, Joy Publishing):

Marlene writes that she senses the Lord gently saying to her, "But what I ask you to do, and what I will enable you to do, is to [and then Marlene quotes Scripture] 'put aside your own pleasures and shoulder your cross, and follow me closely. If you insist on saving your life, you will lose it. Only those who throw away their lives for my sake and for the sake of the Good News will ever know what it means to really live' "(Mark 8:34-35, TLB).

Even when the advice to "put aside our own pleasures" comes from the Lord Himself, it's not easy to readily comply.

Many times (and this week was one of those times), I'd rather have my housework all done, my hair looking its best and supper in the oven before I write even one word. But sometimes I wonder, "When will I stop insisting on having everything the way I want it?" Often the answer comes quickly when I boldly seize the moment and write the first word.

Perhaps you, too, are someone who talks about being a writer for the Lord. Perhaps it's a lifelong dream, but you're waiting for a time when you'll feel inspired, or when the the kids are grown, or when your husband gets around to building you a writing desk. Perhaps you are the husband and your wife laughed at the desk you built for yourself, so you have vowed never to even bring it into the house, let alone sit at it and attempt to write.

Whatever the excuse, the stumbling block or the lack of resolve, it can be overcome with prayer, persistence and paper and pen. To a list of "p" words, add one more: "procrastination." Write it down, cross it out, then go on to write how you are going to defeat it. Today.

By the way, today's suggestions also work for anything else the Lord might be asking You to do that you are putting off until the perfect day. Guess what? Today is that day!   □

CHAPTER TEN

Hope

God is strength of all the ages

October 20, 2001

One of my all-time favorite Bible narratives centers on the parting of the Red Sea. Any time I read Exodus 14:13, I experience a stirring within my soul. When Moses, faced with no other option than to lead his people into the sea, declares to the Israelites who are being pursued by Pharaoh's army, "Fear ye not, stand still, and see the salvation of the Lord" (KJV), I, too, feel as though I'm standing on the verge of disaster with nothing but a shredded strand of hope to cling to. Suddenly, coursing through my veins, in the midst of almost certain destruction, is a realization that even in a mere remnant of hope there is the strength of the ages.

This strength is none other than God Himself of Whom there is no such thing as a little bit of God. God is God, full-blown. His strength is not limited by any measurement. Hope in Him is all-encompassing. A shred of hope is the same as Hope. A remnant of Hope is not a remnant at all. It is the whole ball of wax. Hope is Hope. God is God. And in Him I am secure.

I thought about all of this Monday evening right before dusk when I walked around our yard, back and forth on our lane.

The beauty of autumn is virtually indescribable. The palette of vibrant color is an indicator that God's hand is near. Yet God's hand can not be near without God Himself being here.

What God has done with His artistic touch is not merely a representation of a piece of God's presence. God's presence is God's presence. When He is here He is all here. When you and I witness anything God has done, we witness God. He is not separated into measurable components or manifestations. He is whole. Who He is and what He does are whole — and Holy.

Something stirs within whenever one realizes, or senses, God's strength, His power, His very Being is at hand. It's a stirring that sets off a chain reaction of hope, belief, renewed determination, focus and life. If ever there was a need for such a stirring, the time is now.

Now is when our nation, our world, our neighborhoods, our families, our own selves are ripe for a harvest of embracing Our Holy God, wholly, without a shred of doubt that He is in control. Can we do it? Can we believe that no harm will come to us if we but *Fear ye not, stand still, and see the salvation of the Lord*?

It's a lot to ask of ourselves. It's a lot to expect. It almost sounds like a giving up to "stand still." How can we possibly overcome if we do nothing?

As I see it, Moses and the Israelites did both on the edge of the Red Sea. They stood still at the same instant they moved forward. Within the same moment there was no where to turn and then there was. The Red Sea parted by the Breath of God. And as the people stood still they stepped into the path provided by God's hand.

How does this apply to where we are now? As a nation pulling together since September 11, 2001, we are standing firm, strong and confident as we take steps to secure our position as a world leader. As communities, families and individuals we are expressing a desire to keep our lives as normal as possible while we prepare for the unknown.

At the same time we must be wise and take action, we must also be watchful and still. God's hand will lead us if we keep our eyes, our hearts, our destinies centered on Him.

Fear ye not, stand still, and see the salvation of the Lord.

□

Fragrance of roses strongest in the dark

June 7, 2003

There's nothing worse than having no hope. Without hope life is meaningless. A lack of hope is like parched earth where no water ever fills the cracks. But such a state, although real, need not be permanent. Not for you. Not for me. Even when appearances decry hope, there is hope when we turn to the Lord. I know this to be true. I've been there.

Time after time, after time, after time, there have been, and will continue to be, times when the only place to turn for peace and hope in the midst of emptiness is literally at the feet of Jesus. If you can relate, you don't need to know my particular circumstances because you can fill in your own.

Whether our circumstances, yours or mine, pertain to health, family, finances, church, relationships, careers or anything imaginable, there is no better resource for dispensing what is most needed than going directly to God Himself. God the Father; God the Son; God the Holy Spirit. The Three-In-One God has Hope to spare.

No one of us can speak for the other, but it's been my experience that when hope seems to have vanished, I can't recreate it. It simply won't regenerate itself. Always, always, always, when hope has been reborn within me, it has come from the Lord. It has come from His Word as in reading it; praying over it; meditating on it. Hope has come from the Lord's presence as in seeking Him on my knees; crying out to Him with a broken heart; a wounded spirit; a bucket of tears.

Hope is not a mist; it is not a dream. Hope is a Light in the dark. Not just any light though. It must be the Light of Christ. Otherwise, it's counterfeit. Counterfeit hope is not hope at all, it's deception.

When I'm in need of hope, I don't want to be deceived. Neither do you. When you or I are seeking the kind of hope the Lord gives, we can be sure it's real. We might not be able to photograph it or plant a fence around it, but we can "see" it; we can "feel" it; we can "taste" it.

Real hope is as evident as the difference between night and day. Even so, I can't give it to you and you can't give it to me. But you and I *can* encourage each other that it does exist. We can steer each other where to look for it. We can remind each other the search for it is worth the effort. Most importantly, we can lift each other up in prayer until hope is restored.

Finding hope doesn't mean we'll get everything we want. It doesn't mean our problems will be solved or that troubles will disappear. The Presence of Hope in our lives is realizing the nearness of Jesus Christ. Quite honestly, we usually experience Him, not in the sunshine, but in the shadows. We usually find Him in the dark. That's when His Light is the brightest.

Consider the way rose petals are collected for maximum fragrance in making perfumes and rose oil, known as attar of roses. This essential oil obtained from the rose is the most valuable of the volatile oils. Three-and-a half tons of rose petals go into the processing of 2.2 pounds of attar of roses which is equal to the price of gold, according to a Web site on the Internet.

Although the extreme value placed on attar of roses is note-worthy, there is another component of this picture that per-tains directly to the concept of our most often finding Christ in the dark: Unless roses are harvested in the darkest hours of the night, they will not retain all their fragrance. It's been recorded that scientific tests reveal that "fully 40 percent of the fragrance of roses disappeared in the light of day." (From *Streams in the Desert* by Mrs. Charles E. Cowman, 1928, 1965, Cowman Publications.)

Whether we're searching for Hope, the Hope of Christ, or harvesting roses for maximum fragrance, what we find might be equal to or greater than the value of gold, with one excep-tion: When "the find" is Christ, we have found the only Price-less Resource. A Resource unsurpassed. Christ is Hope in its Maximum Strength. Remembering this in the darkest of cir-cumstances is most assuredly the best way to harvest Hope.

□

Three words give hope on road to despair

October 1, 1994

When I was a girl growing up in western Pennsylvania, my parents took me to the annual Butler Farm Show nearly every year. And every year without exception, I drank a Dixie Cup full of free buttermilk at one of the exhibits.

Funny thing is, I didn't like buttermilk. (Still don't.) But it was free! So not only did I drink it, but sometimes I went back for seconds on the few occasions when we stayed at the farm show all day.

What is it about free things that makes them so appealing? Of course, this question answers itself, but many other concerns in life aren't so readily resolved.

For instance, what do we do when, without warning, we're hit with a situation that seems hopeless? Perhaps all of our life we've professed a belief in Jesus Christ as the answer to all doubt. The answer to all fear. The answer to all of life's impossibilities. And yet, in the midst of a here-and-now whirlpool of uncertainty, swirling doubts and fears threaten to pull us under.

Giving up seems an unthinkable option, and yet, there it is, right before our eyes, a free and clear consideration for the taking: Give up! This thing is never going to work! Not even Jesus can solve this problem!

Whoa! We've got to stop right there! Right this minute! We can't take another step in the wrong direction!

When we've been raised on the belief that Jesus Christ is the answer, we've been raised on The Answer. We've been raised on The Right Way. We've been raised on The One whose touch can work miracles. The One whose voice calls out and is recognized the instant we truly listen.

A week ago Wednesday I was driving home to Benton from Bloomsburg. My mind was preoccupied with overwhelming doubts about a concern I'm not free to share publicly. But, daily, for months on end, I've had to give it to the Lord. It's too heavy, too hopeless, too impossible for me to handle. And that day, I was never more in need of a bold reminder—a reminder of Who the Lord is and what He can do.

And there it was. The reminder. Three words I've known all my life. Three words I've believed. Words I've spoken. Words I've written. Now someone else had put them right where I needed them. Right where I couldn't miss them.

The words?

"Christ gives hope."

Plain black letters on a white marquee-type sign and message board by the side of the road in front of the Benton Assembly of God Church, along Route 487, near Stillwater:

Christ gives hope.

It was free. It was what I needed. It was what I've always believed. What I've always told others. And I thank God for the person(s) responsible for putting that reminder right in front of me. It's the kind of thing someone like me can't keep to herself. Why? Because there's always the chance, someone like you (if you're like me) might just need the same reminder, today.

Christ gives hope.   □

CHAPTER ELEVEN

Memories

⌒⌒

Summer prompts legacy of memories

June 23, 2001

*[God's] mercy extends to those who fear Him, from genera-
tion to generation (Luke 1:50, NIV, brackets added).*

Memories of departed loved ones and summer go hand
in hand. Perhaps it's sitting on the porch swing telling stories
or using Granddad Heckler's garden hoe that starts the memories flowing. Whatever it is that prompts us to "remember
when," there's no denying life's legacy of memories. As I write
about some of the memories my ancestors left to me, I hope
you, too, might be encouraged to search your own memory
bank for precious deposits. What you and I choose to remember and, in turn, share with our living loved ones will one day
become part of the legacy we leave to them.

Now, for a couple of personal cherished memories.

Bees buzzing on a sweltering day, along with the pungent
smells coming from the edge of the forest as I mosey along on
a "thinking" walk the other day, take me back to the huckle-
berry bushes and ant-hill days of childhood. Across the road
and deep in the woods from where I grew up, my mother and I

went berry picking almost every summer with Grandma Heffelfinger, Pup, Aunt Rebecca and Uncle Cal Fair.

Pup was actually my grandfather (Guy Heffelfinger), but because he was barely five-feet-tall, he was nicknamed "Pup" long before any of us grandkids were born. Aunt Rebecca was Grandma's sister and Uncle Cal was Rebecca's second husband. Her first husband Basil had died years earlier. I never knew him, but I did know that my dad was named after him. Aunt Rebecca, who had no children of her own, had been granted permission by my grandma to name my dad when he was born. Anytime Aunt Rebecca spoke the name "Basil," either in reference to her first husband or to my dad, her otherwise sad eyes sparkled.

And so it was with Uncle Cal. He had been married twice before he married Rebecca. Mona was his first wife who died of cancer in her thirties. Mona was Cal's first and only love. Although he married Mona's sister Flora and she, too, died in her thirties of cancer, he never let go of Mona. His eyes, also, betrayed him, even when he and Aunt Rebecca told knee-slapping stories about their own courtship.

But anyhow, back to the berry bushes, picking, sweating and watching out for snakes.

Once our swinging (oops!) pails and blue-speckled-enamel canners were filled to overflowing with berries, stink bugs, leaves and small twigs, we trudged back home with either Pup or Cal pointing toward the ant hills as though these two-feet-high pyramids of sand were sophisticated landmarks. "The black-top is right over that way. Follow me!" one of the men would call over his shoulder. No need though. We all knew the way. But some gestures are simply part and parcel of life.

Then there are the memories of mosquito bites and green thumbs from being in the vegetable garden too long, especially picking tomatoes. Even without the inevitable insect bites, tomato patches always made me itch. I would turn green from the tips of my fingers to my armpits from reaching into and under tomato bushes for the biggest, juiciest, ripe beauties. If and when I whined about being itchy, Dad would usually say I could quit picking if I wanted to and Mum would try to coax me to "just pick a few more and then we'll go in."

The memories of tomatoes — buckets, bushel baskets and boxes full of them — go way beyond scratching and turning green, however. Home-grown tomatoes, along with corn on the cob and fresh strawberries, were the reason for living in the country. As a matter of fact, I didn't know there was any other place to live unless it was one of three small towns where we shopped and visited other relatives.

Most often, nowadays, when I recall a long-ago memory, I attach it to a thankfulness to God for His hand on my life. I know that in the place of cherished memories, I could choose to highlight a peppering of bad ones. Negatives and positives alike, in your life and mine, help to form our opinions, our personalities and our priorities. This is true for each and every one of us. It's by God's mercies that we survive — from generation to generation — regardless of pleasant or, in spite of, unpleasant experiences.

That's why it's the positives I recommend we all spend the most time remembering. It's a choice each of us can make as we trust, by God's mercies, and as we reverence Him, that He will impact future generations, quite possibly through you and me...and the "remember when" stories we share.

☐

Revival memories need resurrection

June 30, 2001

Let everything that has breath praise the Lord (Psalm 150:6, NKJV).

Continuing a theme of "remember when" from the preceding memory, I'd like to turn from everyday-type memories such as berry picking and bug slapping to the ones seasoned with lively congregational hymn singing and gospel trios and quartets. Sound familiar? Oh, yes, many of us remember the good old-fashioned revival services at open-air campground tabernacles.

It was there everyone sang his or her praises to the Lord as loudly as possible. Rain or shine, summer heat or evening breezes, in storms or in drought, we were there with our families and church friends. We were there to hear Bible-thumping preachers and globe-trotting missionaries tell us their stories of faith. We were there to shed tears and shout "Amen!" We were there to be taught. We were there to grow. We were there to be revived!

Today, we don't talk about revival as much as we did then. But for any of us who experienced being "saved" at a revival service, we need to revive the memory. We need to keep the very word "revival" alive for future generations. That's why I'm writing here about my personal testimony. I hope, you, too, might share yours with somebody, soon, very soon. All of us who call ourselves Christian must keep the message of Jesus Christ's saving Grace and Power in the forefront of who we are and what we do. We must refer often to Bible passages such as Luke 1:50: "[God's] mercy extends to those who fear Him from generation to generation" (NIV, brackets added).

When I was seven years old I attended a series of youth revival meetings in Kittanning, a western Pennsylvania town in Armstrong County. When the invitation was made for anyone who wanted to be saved by accepting Jesus Christ as Savior and Lord, I went forward to the altar, got down on my knees and prayed with the adult leaders who spoke privately with each of us who took this step.

I was not forced. I was not brainwashed. I was not bribed. I was *saved*. Because I came to know Jesus at such a young age, I was saved from a life filled with regrets. I am so very thankful that I "met" Jesus early. I knew He loved me and I openly and willingly loved Him. He has been my Friend all my life. He has been my Guide. My Master. My Teacher. My God.

Even so, I'm not sharing this to brag or to talk about me. I'm sharing my testimony because I'm burdened for young lives that aren't being exposed to faith in Christ. They aren't hearing or responding to altar calls because there aren't any. Instead of knowing about revival services, our children and youth know how to "surf the 'net" and end up in "web" after "web" that may or may not be wise habitats for vulnerable minds and untrained curiosities. Our young people see and hear too much, too young, about too many destructive ideas, concepts and issues. They hear and see on TV, on the streets and in their homes too much about sex, violence and corrupted lifestyles.

Oh, I know, some might say I'm out of line or narrow-minded. But that's OK, if the end result is that one person, one parent, one grandparent echoes a concern that I know many of us share for some good old-fashioned biblical wisdom to be revived in our land. Revival starts with remembering what can and does happen when lives are rescued, transformed and set on the right path.

There is no time like the present to recall, restate and revive the concept of revival.   □

Memories swirl in old tea cup

July 27, 2003

Memories of simpler times abound when one cleans and clears out the spare bedroom. I relearned this recently when I tackled the cleaning and clearing of said room.

One of the stray items I came upon and promptly relegated to a future yard-sale or give-away box is an old coffee or tea cup minus its saucer. The monetary value of the cup ranges somewhere between a nickel and a quarter, at the most. The sentimental value of the cup is much higher. Therefore, as you might suspect, the cup was immediately retrieved by yours truly from its "box."

I just can't do it. I can't get rid of the cup. That cream-colored cup with its green Pennsylvania Dutch floral pattern is all that remains of a set of dishes Jim and I acquired in 1966 when, for our first anniversary, we purchased a brand new 12-by-60-foot mobile home. The mobile home dealership included the set of dishes as a courtesy gift because we selected a deluxe model home where we lived for the next five years.

We lived in that mobile home when I graduated from college. It's where we lived when both of our newborn daughters were brought home from the hospital. It's where we lived when we were a young family with our whole lives and the rest of our dreams stretched out before us with unlimited potential and promise. It's where we lived when we outgrew the 12-by-60-foot space and moved on to "bigger" things.

We moved into a bigger space with bigger responsibilities. From there we moved again, and then once again, each time into bigger domains and bigger responsibilities. Often, as we all know, bigger and bigger gets heavier and heavier. But then one day, like I said, one comes upon a cup that one can't part with because it represents the kind of security that accompanies memories of simpler days gone-by.

And yet, even this is not entirely true. The simpler days that our own family encountered in that mobile home included pain, grief and suffering.

There is where I returned home from the hospital after major emergency surgery and the loss of an unborn child. It's where we picked up the phone in the middle of a cold February night and learned of my father's untimely passing. It's where I fell and broke a bone in my foot. It's where some dreams expired and others were put on hold indefinitely.

Simpler times are a matter of perspective. Usually they are only simpler in retrospect, much like the way the proportion of objects behind us diminishes in size in our rear-view mirror as we proceed toward other destinations.

When we are living in the present, as each of us is required to do on a daily basis, we generally see the enormity of our problems and difficulties. We wonder how we will ever get through the obstacle course set before us. We question our own abilities and face countless uncertainties.

But, then, as today passes and some of its burdens are lightened, today eventually becomes a memory to be either hurtfully forgotten or lovingly cherished for its simplicity.

Of such are the days of "the cup." The cup I found is not only a comforting symbol of the earlier days of our family's life, it's also a remnant of reality. Reality being, as I see it from where I am today, that no life, no past, no present or no future is so simple as to be perfect.

Even so, reflecting on life, along with its past, its present and its future, is worth an expenditure of time and effort. Often such reflection is where we see things we might otherwise have discarded as insignificant. Reflection, especially God-guided reflection, serves to remind us, not of a cup half-full or a cup half-empty, but of a cup overflowing with His love and provisions.

That's why I can't get rid of the cup. Because every step of the way, from the early days until now, God's love, His guidance and His providential sustaining power have been ever-present. And I don't ever want to forget that. So I hang on to every reminder that crosses my path. With a lone cup in hand, I recite:

"The Lord is my shepherd; I shall not want. ... Thou anointest my head with oil; my cup runneth over. Surely goodness and mercy shall follow me all the days of my life; and I will dwell in the house of the Lord for ever" (Psalm 23: 1, 5-6, KJV).

□

Memory Lane is a godly journey
April 6, 2002

To me there's nothing quite like a long, leisurely walk in the forest on a blue-sky, gentle-breezes spring day. Indulging myself thusly late one recent morning, I pleasured in one whole hour just poking around a forest trail with my walking stick.

The tranquility of the valley where I strolled was punctuated from time to time with the welcomed melodies instinctively pouring forth from the just-arriving-from-the-south feathered friends of spring, but that was about it, except for the crunch of dry leaves underfoot.

In that one hour I felt closer to the breath of God than I have in months. It was more than refreshing; it was a revival. I wish I could have stayed there, but of course no one can do that. Life calls all of us back into the real world. It's that way for you, and it's that way for me.

But, oh, how important are the times we separate ourselves from life's demands and poke around on paths that meander away from the stresses and pressures of the day, all the while leading us into "God's world" of peace and serenity of thought.

It's a place where a glance upward toward the blue sky is a prayer. A place where a whispered sigh is a song of praise. A place where doubt and fear are forbidden to enter. A place where confidence in the Lord reigns supreme.

Such a place is where we all need to travel on a regular basis. But circumstances don't allow it. Most of us are "lucky" to get away at all, let alone do so with routine frequency.

This is one reason I repeatedly thank the Lord for the gift of memory. When I can't stroll on a real lane or poke around in a real forest, I rely heavily on memories of such experiences of the past.

Often, and I do mean often, I fall asleep at night or wake up in the morning to the "sights and sounds" of earlier times. Times like when I "find God" in a quiet place; when I "hear Him" in a cloud shaped like a shepherd. Times when I "know" every-thing — absolutely everything — that goes wrong in my life will be all right. It will be all right because God is with me. He is with me because I have found salvation through Him in my heart, in my mind, in my spirit, in my memory.

Finding God comes from seeking Him. That's Scriptural. "Seek, and ye shall find; knock, and it shall be opened unto you" (Luke 11:9, KJV).

As life advances, I don't like to miss out on any of the joy. And yet, no one can take it all in. We are all bound to miss a lot. That's just the way it is. But what we do manage to capture — more accurately, what captures us — often lasts a lifetime in our memories.

Dear Lord, not all memories are worth carrying around, but please help me to be fed long-term by the ones that are. The ones that begin and end with You are like a spring day that never draws to a close. When You remind me of such times, may I always give You the praise for making it hap-pen. In Jesus' Name. Amen. □

CHAPTER TWELVE

Praise

Applause is due 'His Majesty'
March 14, 1992

For the Lord is great beyond description, ...Let the heavens be glad, the earth rejoice; let the vastness of the roaring seas demonstrate His glory (Psalm 96:4 and 11, TLB).

It may sound ridiculous, but one afternoon a couple of weeks ago, I was jealous of a small flock of sea gulls fluttering at the edge of a cornfield outside Benton.

Knowing the sea gulls were undoubtedly en route to the sea was the source of my envy, for I would prefer, on almost any day, going to see the sea rather than doing many of the things in front of me.

The waves, the rhythm, the sounds, the smells of the sea are attractive to many of us. And, if you're like me, each time you experience the sea, it's like meeting an old friend for the first time.

Seeing that flock of gulls reminded me of the day in June 1990 when my husband and I spent a whole afternoon sitting on a boulder along the coast of Maine in Acadia National Park near Bar Harbor.

Well, actually, *I* sat there all afternoon. Jim came and went periodically, but I didn't budge except to find a more comfortable spot on the boulder each time the spot I was on became a little too hard.

But the hardness of the rock is the last thing I remember when I think of that day. What I remember first is the sheer joy I felt every time the waves crashed and exploded on a particular rock below.

The display of power, the roar of wave meeting resistance and the resulting fireworks-like spray were so awesome that, more than once that afternoon, I cheered and applauded aloud in praise of God's magnificent, creative genius.

Does that make me odd? Eccentric? Better or worse than anyone else? I don't think so, but that's up to you to decide.

All I know is, when I see a flock of sea gulls migrating to the sea, I envy them because of where they're headed. But that shouldn't stop me from praising and applauding the Lord for all the things of the earth that demonstrate His glory.

Praise Him for the growing fields, for they display His greatness. Let the trees of the forest rustle with praise. For the Lord is coming to judge the earth; He will judge the nations fairly and with truth! (Psalm 96:12-13, TLB).   □

CHAPTER THIRTEEN

Prayer

Squirming at truth leads way to peace
September 10, 1994

Picture this: You're on your knees. You're praying. No, you're pleading:

Please, Lord, answer this longing. Lift this burden. Solve this problem. Do this thing in such a way that Your Name will be glorified.

Your posture is both biblical and traditional. Likewise your praying; even your pleading. Your breaking heart is crying out to the Right Person. You may even be saying all the right words. But when you get to the part beseeching God, telling Him He *must* do something so that His Name will be glorified, what you really mean is:

Lord, please, answer this prayer so I can have peace of mind and get on with my life.

The other day, at the side of our bed, I was in the above picture. While begging God to take the sting out of my hurt, I was trying to fool Him, and myself, by expressing that all I wanted was for Him to receive the honor, the praise and the glory when the answer comes.

Was I wrong to pray what I prayed? Wrong to feel what I felt? Wrong in saying what I desperately wanted to believe? I hope not. Eventually, though, I saw the truth.

The truth? Yes, I squirmed at it, but I had to admit that, to me, the bigger burden was my own aching heart. The actual problem I was trying to persuade the Lord to solve was secondary. Shortly thereafter an amazing thing happened. I'm convinced it was because I was finally honest with God, and myself.

Peace of mind began descending into my morning. I wasn't as worried. I wasn't as tired. I was smiling and looking at the chores I had already accomplished, not at all the things yet to be done. Instead of seeing only yesterday's and today's burdens, I was remembering times past when the Lord answered other prayers.

Other prayers. How many others have there been? Who can count? Some, at the time of their urgency, were just as agonizing as the one I was dealing with in the present. Then I knew. I really knew that, when the answer comes, when the situation is finally in check, God will be glorified by the outcome.

Trust. Trust in the Lord. That's where it's at. I am trusting Him to take care of the problem. Trusting Him to do it His way, in His time. He really did take the sting out of my hurt. At least for the moment, for the hour.

If things drag on as things often do in this life, I'll be back in the same posture as I was earlier, day after day, perhaps morning, noon and night. But if God can be trusted, as I know and am reminded anew that He can, His Name will be glorified over and over, again and again.

Is this the end of my pursuing peace while awaiting the resolution of my concern? No, it's only the beginning. But square one isn't the end of the world, after all.   □

What do we expect when we pray?

July 28, 1990

Do you ever write down your prayers?

On separate occasions several years ago I kept a daily prayer journal for a month at a time, writing out my prayers to the Lord each day and, later, recording how and when the answers came. I called it an experiment because I wasn't sure how it would turn out. It was something I wanted to test.

It turned out the prayers were answered. Some with a cut-and-dried "Yes" or "No." Others with the hope of "Maybe" or "Later," but unmistakably "Not now." No, I didn't hear an audible voice giving me any of these responses, but they did come through clearly.

For instance, my then-elementary-age daughter balked one morning about going to school because she expected to have a bad experience with a particular teacher. Together we prayed. We asked for the day to go well and that the Lord would work things out between her and the teacher. When Lori came home skipping and laughing at 3:10 that afternoon, I knew I could record a big "Yes" in my journal.

But there was more.

God also showed me a touch of humor in the way He answered that prayer. It turned out that Lori had a terrific day because, as she put it, "My day was great! We had a substitute."

And that was that. When the regular teacher for the class returned, Lori dealt with the situation in a positive way.

Since the days of my experiment in prayer, I have often made the suggestion to others that they try it, too. So once again I suggest it, for anyone who would like to give it a try, even if you, too, have done this before. During the next month (or other preferred block of time), write down at least one prayer each day along with how and when it is answered.

Where do you start? What kind of prayers should you spell out?

Why not begin at the best possible place. Start with whatever is important to you. Whatever matters enough to keep you awake at night.

Your prayer might be for a loved one with cancer. For a family member on the verge of a breakdown. For energy for yourself just to make it through another long day.

You might pray for someone to help you with the dishes. For God to grant you a good night's sleep.

You might ask for career direction or wisdom about which car to buy.

Nothing is too big or too small to pray about, because God can reach high and low with His answers.

The size of the pray-*ers* doesn't matter either. Even children or grandchildren can do this experiment with you. All you need is a notebook, tablet or several sheets of paper and a prayer a day. Finding time each day to write out the prayers might be the hardest part of the project, so why not begin by praying:

Dear Lord, my life is pretty full already and what I don't need is one more thing to do. But if You would like me to attempt this project of writing out my prayers for the next month or so, please help me find the time. Better yet, show me how to make the time to do it. Thank You, Lord. Amen.

□

Since God knows everything, why bother to pray?

October 23, 1993

Sometimes you or I can say a whole lot in a few words. Or we can talk all day and say nothing. I'm afraid the latter is what I did the other day, going on and on about something that was bothering me. I'm sure I made no sense at all. Fortunately I was "talking" to God. Since He knows everything, He knew what I was trying to say. Do you ever wonder, *since God does know everything, why bother to pray?*

My girls used to ask me that question a lot, especially when their spiritual lives were young and tender. You know the age, when it's still possible to help mold and shape a life. The scary part about it is, when your kids are that age, you, the parent, are faced with answering questions that perhaps hold eternal significance, and you aren't sure you're giving the right answers. So you pray a lot. That's exactly what I did.

When the girls were in school, I walked two and three miles almost every day, praying for wisdom. Praying for strength. Praying for patience. Praying for whatever would help me be a good mother. Sometimes I envied other women I knew who said they prayed better while they cleaned the house. Not me. I often had to get out of the house to do what I thought was the best praying. Sometimes walking a few miles wasn't enough. At times I had to get in the car and drive around until I was all prayed out.

Quite often being all *prayed out* simply meant I talked through whatever it was, out loud to God, until I was all *talked out.*

Occasionally, on such a day, one of the girls would come in from school and ask me a question that I could actually answer in a few straightforward words. It didn't happen all the time and, when it did, it didn't make me some kind of a super mom. But once in a while it felt good to have the answer.

"Mom, how do you know exactly what to say?" one of the girls might marvel as I found my neck being squeezed and a kiss planted on my cheek.

"Oh, praying helps, Honey. I did a lot of that today. But I sure didn't get much of anything else done," I might add under my breath.

"Oh, Mom, who cares? Someday we'll be all grown up and you'll have all the time in the world to do other things," was a common reply to my lament.

That time is now here. But guess what? I'm still not doing many of the other things. I'm still praying for wisdom. Praying for strength. Praying for patience. Praying for whatever it takes for me and those I love to hear our Heavenly Father.

Dear Lord, I suppose life will always be just hard enough to keep me talking to You until I'm all talked out. But once I'm all talked out, please help me to listen carefully. I don't want to miss anything You might have to say. In Jesus' Name. Amen.   □

Pulling weeds, praying: Both bring us to our knees

August 6, 1994

Whatever do you suppose God was thinking when He created weeds? For those of you who might be sighing, "Please, don't talk to us about weeds!" I can only say, "Sorry, weeds it is."

Slating weeds for what they are — a notorious nuisance — I'll try not to run this topic too far into the ground. Even so, being on our knees, as in the weed-pulling posture, is often the best way to learn certain lessons or truths. Perhaps this is because it's also the posture of prayer.

Early one recent morning as I knelt on a vinyl cushion beside my flower beds, I felt as though God had me where He wanted me. But simply being in a prayerful position did not ease the heaviness in my heart for all the people I know and love who are hurting. Yanking out weed after weed did nothing more to soothe my troubled spirit than to keep my hands busy while my mind raced for answers to so many problems, so many heartaches.

Eventually, seeing humor in God's design of the kneeling position (humbling at best) for the battle of humans versus weeds and humans versus life, I tried to smile and reach for yet another fistful of weeds. At the same time, I searched my heart, wondering for whom or what I should pray first, and then next, and next.

As I fought off tears thinking of people I'm helpless to comfort, the praying helped allay some fears. Soon I became absorbed in other observations about numerous parallels between weeds and life. I noted the various sizes of weeds and the degrees of their tenacity. Long before my disposable plastic gloves were thoroughly stained green, I reflected on how some weeds, like certain problems and worries, are harder than others to uproot. Yet, left to grow wild, many problems, like many weeds, take over the spaces meant for beauty and enjoyment.

More and more parallels on the weed front piled up in my head nearly as fast as the mountain of weeds beside me. I frowned at how easy it was to pull out a flower by mistake when I got too anxious and randomly grabbed a tangle of weeds. The sacrificed flower reminded me that I was sure to miss the color, fragrance and texture of the blossoms if I became obsessed with focusing on only the nasty, greedy, choking weeds.

Seeing only weeds in a bed of flowers is not unlike seeing only the negative side of a spouse's or friend's personality; not unlike dwelling only on the down side of raising children; not unlike constantly tearing apart a job or a boss we don't particularly care for. Right there I sensed a good, all-purpose prayer any of us might pray while in a figurative or literal weed-pulling posture:

Lord, help me not to miss out on the beautiful aspects of a relationship or a task simply because I think I'm the only one who is working at it. If I have eyes only for flaws, for weaknesses, for critical comments, give me new eyes to see another dimension of life, another dimension of love, another dimension of friendship or responsibility. In other words, help me not to overlook the flowers because all I see are weeds.

It was then I came upon the stubborn, root-goes-all-the-way-to-China weed. The weed embedded in the crack between the sidewalk sections. The weed that almost monopolized all my efforts and energies, threatening the certainty of unchecked proliferation of the rest of the weeds. This weed-of-all-weeds reminded me of the temptation to nag, nag, nag on the same stupid things — things none of us may ever be able to change, or things that may require a lifetime of gradual persistence — while letting other manageable problems destroy house and home.

"So how should I handle this breed of weed?" I sighed. Before long the tugging was wearing me down, but the wearing-down process brought to my mind how many of us struggle with deeply-rooted problems.

Eventually, I had to let up on the enormous weed and reach for ones young and tender, ones easy to pluck out of the earth. At sensible intervals, I returned to the stubborn weed, again and again, until at long last the weed cluster in the sidewalk moved ever so slightly. Encouraged, but continuing to pace the effort, sometime later, after many more attempts, my hopeful expectations were at last realized: "The" weed came up, lock, stock and entire root.

The thing I didn't expect to learn is now a given: There's a lot more to pulling weeds and learning about life than I'll ever master. The good part of the realization, for me, is the acknowledgment that God *always* knows what He is doing. Therefore, if He had good reasons for "inventing" weeds, He has even better ones for creating solutions to uprooting problems we all face. We simply have to trust Him, time after time — on our knees.   □

Hymn shows no day is ordinary
June 9, 2001

It is commonly assumed that one day is not much different than another. The sun rises; the sun sets; life's routines roll on. Every now and then, however, something grabs our attention and convinces us that extraordinary events do, indeed, occur on ordinary days. One example of this is illustrated by circumstances surrounding the writing of "I Need Thee Every Hour," a well-known prayer-hymn that has touched countless lives for more than 125 years.

On a sunny June morning in 1872, Annie Sherwood Hawks, a 37-year-old Brooklyn, New York, wife and mother of three children, was simply carrying out her duties around the house when divine inspiration entered the picture and hymn history was made. Resource books record Annie's writings of her personal account of that day:

"As a young wife and mother...I was busy with my regular household tasks.... Suddenly, I became filled with a sense of nearness to the Master, and I began to wonder how anyone could ever live without Him, either in joy or pain. Then, the words were ushered into my mind and these thoughts took full possession of me — 'I need Thee every hour...' ."

Eager to write down the words as they began flowing into her mind, Annie sat down at her desk near an open window and wrote what she considered to be a poetic prayer. While the ink was yet drying she penned a series of brief couplets:

I need Thee every hour, Most gracious Lord; No tender voice like Thine, Can peace afford.

I need Thee every hour, Stay Thou near by; Temptations lose their power, When Thou art nigh.

I need Thee every hour, In joy or pain; Come quickly and abide, Or life is vain.

I need Thee every hour, Most Holy One; O make me Thine indeed, Thou blessed Son!

Although Annie felt she had been surrounded with the presence of Christ at the time of writing these lines, she later hesitated to show them to her pastor, Dr. Robert Lowry, at Hanson Place Baptist Church. Annie rationalized that her words were surely too simple to be significant. But then she remembered that Dr. Lowry had always encouraged her poetry writing and he had insisted that she show him everything she wrote. On the following Sunday morning after the church service, Annie gave Dr. Lowry a copy of her lyrics.

Dr. Lowry, a prominent gospel hymn writer and composer of such favorites as "Shall We Gather At the River" and "Marching to Zion," was deeply moved by Annie's four stanzas. Going to his Brooklyn parsonage and sitting down at the modest organ in his living room, he quickly composed the music for "I Need Thee Every Hour."

Even as Dr. Lowry considered the piece, indeed, to be fine, he was sure it needed a chorus to render it complete. He had long prior to this been convinced that a chorus should accompany every hymn. He felt the repetitious singing of a chorus assured congregational involvement, especially from the children. Thus the familiar refrain was born from Dr. Lowry's own pen:

I need Thee, O I need Thee, Every hour I need Thee! O bless me now, my Savior, I come to Thee!

That's how it came to be that circumstances on an ordinary June morning in an average household soon embraced the world. First the song was sung at the National Baptist Sunday School Association Convention in Cincinnati, Ohio, in November of that year. Then, only a year after Annie Hawk and Dr. Lowry created "I Need Thee Every Hour," it was included in a new songbook, *The Royal Diadem,* compiled by Lowry and William Doane.

In time the song was popularized by Ira Sankey and Dwight L. Moody in the Moody-Sankey evangelistic campaigns. Swept across America and reaching all the way to Great Britain, "I Need Thee Every Hour" began touching and comforting God's people everywhere. It started a wave that ever flows deep in the heart of Christendom.

Stories such as this serve to remind us that no day is too ordinary in the eyes of the Lord to be used of Him. We never know when, at any given moment, inspiration might be extended through Him into the uttermost corners of time and eternity. We continually need Him and we praise Him every hour!

(References consulted and quoted: *Living Stories of Famous Hymns,* by Ernest K. Emurian, 1955, Baker Book House Company; *101 More Hymn Stories,* by Kenneth W. Osbeck, 1985, Kregel Publications; *Hymns of Faith and Inspiration,* by Pamela J. Kennedy, 1990, Ideals Publishing Corporation.) □

Alphabet prayers weed distractions

May 26, 2001

Planting a garden. Oh, how I pine for it all winter. Come spring, I just can't wait to get started. Perhaps that's why I found myself "making a garden" recently when I should have been sound asleep.

On a couple of nights last week I awoke too early: 2:30 a.m. the first night and 3:30, the second. Wide-awake after only three or four hours of sleep, I began digging, planting and mulching, in my head of course.

The tomatoes will go here and the lettuce needs a "roof" because you're supposed to grow it in the shade. My burpless cucumbers went crazy last year vining up on cut tree branches I stuck in the ground, but this year I'd like to try a pole-like teepee. And the flowers, oh, the flowers! I can't wait to get my hands dirty!

After an hour of placing wave petunias in pots and honeycomb marigolds in the ground, I shifted my attention to the placement of the new perennials I had purchased.

Should the golden yarrow go in the center of the first flower bed or on the edge of the one by the well? How would a triangle of daisies work as long as it appears they grew that way without human design?

On and on went my mind. I focused on the most minute details, planning, rearranging, selecting the right spot, hopefully, for each plant, all the while wishing it wasn't the middle of the night. I would have much preferred going outside to actually do what I was mentally visualizing.

Each of the two nights I lost three and four hours of sleep because, once my mind starts, it won't stop. (Oh, yes, you're nodding, you and I are like peas in a pod.)

The first night, after the first two hours, I tried to think about other things because gardening by moonlight was wearing me out. I tried to pray but distractions prevailed. I continually returned to gardening.

The second night, when the tossing and turning started all over again, another idea began to take root. It stemmed from knowing in my heart something needed weeded out. It just wasn't right that I could be obsessed with details of gardening if I didn't give equal time to the Lord, focusing on who He is and praising Him for countless details to which He eternally attends.

A wide-awake conscious decision became clear: *If sleep is going to escape me, again, I am going to dedicate this time to God. I'm going to tell Him why I love Him, why I follow Him, why I serve Him and why knowing Him makes life worth living.*

Starting with the letter "A," I thought-prayed, "Lord, You are worthy of worldwide *adoration* because of who You *are*. Your Name is a *blessing* to utter because You are *beautiful*, You are *bright* like the morning star and You *bring* hope to a dark, lonely world. Praise You for *caring* enough to *create* the world and then offer us *Christ* as our Savior. You are *divinely diligent* and *deserving* of all honor as You *direct* our lives."

What I found myself doing was a variation of alphabet praying. Instead of praying for people by name from "A" to "Z" or petitioning God for personal needs and concerns starting with each letter of the alphabet, this was a special time of detailing one sleepless soul's appreciation of God for who He is.

If you're wondering at what point I fell asleep, I didn't. I made it all the way to "Z," thanking God for His *zealous* desire that none of us should perish but that all would come to know Christ (2 Peter 3:9).

In the morning I knew I was suffering from two short nights, back-to-back. But although I was tired the second morning, I felt more refreshed from having detailed God's attributes and His character than I did the first night I "worked" in the garden.

For any of you who might find yourself in a similar pickle, I recommend the type of prayer I've outlined here as one way to squash your frustrations over sleeplessness. It certainly is a good way to fertilize one's spiritual garden.

Happy prayer planting!   ☐

'Fishy' story nets a parallel on prayer

June 28, 2003

If the story I'm about to tell you sounds a little fishy, that's because it is. Oh, it's true all right, so it's not fishy in the sense of being contrived, but my latest cooking episode, of which you are about to hear, really did have a fishy taste. And trust me, there's no fish in the "recipe."

The experience, however, is a reminder that preparation and the proper "tools" can make a huge difference in the outcome of whatever any of us tries to accomplish. In the end you will see, hopefully, that a day beginning with adequate preparation affords even greater benefit than the avoidance of a fishy aftertaste.

OK, so much for the buildup. Tuesday morning dawned with my craving something I've never actually eaten before, although I've thought of making it for a number of years. Somewhere years ago a tidbit of trivia about Elvis Presley stuck in my brain. I heard or read that one of his favorite foods was a grilled peanut butter and jelly sandwich. Or was it a grilled peanut butter and *banana* sandwich? Regardless of the accuracy of the second ingredient, I decided to try my own version: cashew butter, a banana, cinnamon, honey and nine-grain bread.

My grilled breakfast sandwich would have tasted quite good, I'm sure, had it not been for this fact: A few days earlier I fried catfish in the same skillet. You said it! Yuck! Even though I washed the skillet with detergent and hot water, either I didn't do it thoroughly or our non-stick skillet is now permanently catfish-flavored.

Not being one to waste food, I managed to eat three-fourths of the grilled sandwich, washing it down with a cup of cinnamon-orange tea. But I felt kinda' sick the rest of the morning.

Perhaps that's what I get for remembering something about Elvis before turning my focus God-ward at the beginning of my day.

This is where proper tools and preparation escort the theme for a parallel on prayer. It's not a complicated notion at all. It's about as basic as you can get: If you or I neglect or rush our time alone with the Lord and His Word, we can try as we might to cover up our negligence, but, in the end, there will be fishy consequences.

In other words, if our day stinks, perhaps we are to blame. We just weren't careful enough; or faithful enough; or diligent enough. All right, I'll let the rest of you off the hook. Maybe I shouldn't be saying "we" here. Maybe it's just me. Maybe I'm standing alone as one who doesn't always begin my day with a Bible in my hand and a prayer in my heart. I doubt it, but hypothetically let's say I'm the only one. The real issue is: What am I going to do about it?

As you can guess from my fishy sandwich incident, I'm about to expand on the parallel: I must cherish my time with my Lord to the extent that I guard and protect the preparation of my audience with Him. Shortcuts and haste are not options. Deliberate, thoughtful approach is a must. Instead of thinking, "I wonder how quickly I can 'meet with God' and tell Him what's on my mind," I need to realize I have a unique opportunity available to me. An opportunity that not only can transform my day, but also will transform my life.

Just the mere thought of being in the presence of The King (not Elvis, but The Lord) should bring me to my knees even before He actually "enters." Being on my knees, if not literally, at least in my spirit, is more than a symbolic invitation for the Lord to come in. It's a sign of worship. Respect. Humble expectation. It says, "I'm devoted to You, Lord, and although I'm not worthy of time with You, I'm deeply grateful You see my neediness. I truly honor this chance to tell You how much I appreciate whatever time You will give me."

Before I go on, I am compelled to tell you that not all of the ideas here are strictly mine. Yes, the fishy sandwich episode is original. But the concept of viewing prayer as being "an audience with God" and the subsequent transforming power behind such an "approach" to prayer time are highlights from a book written nearly 80 years ago by a native of Hoboken, New Jersey, Reuben Archer Torrey, known as R.A. Torrey in the theological literary world. The book Torrey authored, *The Power of Prayer* (subtitled *And The Prayer of Power,* 1924, Fleming H. Revell Company; reprinted 1960, Zondervan Publishing House), came into my possession 39 years ago on my nineteenth birthday as a gift. And what a gift the volume has been since I rediscovered it recently on my dusty bookshelves!

Not only am I struck with the underlinings I drew back when I was a freshman in college, but also I'm revived by renewed understandings as clear as the dawn of the clean slate of a fresh day. A day fresh with promise. A day brimming with opportunities to come before The King of Kings asking Him, in a paraphrase of the words of Torrey: not how much time must I devote to prayer, but rather "how much time will [You] the King [actually] give me?" (Brackets added).

Thank God, I know the answer is however much time I need. Also, I thank God for His using an unsavory kitchen episode along with Torrey's words to re-teach me something I should not ever take for granted: Time with the Lord in prayer is "one of the most highly esteemed privileges of life." Acknowledgment of this is essential when it comes to proper preparation for each day.   □

CHAPTER FOURTEEN

Strength

New way of life might be better
September 29, 2001

If ever there was a time to desire a getting back to normal in our nation, it's now. But it's not going to happen. In the aftermath of September 11, 2001, the evolution of a redefined normal is still in progress. Terrorists not only killed thousands of innocent people and reduced to ashes significant symbols of American pride and confidence, but they also robbed us, perhaps forever, of our former way of life.

The only good that can come from the evil that has befallen us is the hope that our "next" way of life will be an improvement over the last. If we all care more deeply for our fellow man than we did before, we will see the fulfillment of God's promise in Romans 8:28: "And we know that all things work together for good to them that love God, to them who are the called according to His purpose" (KJV).

If we turn our hearts toward the Lord with renewed commitment and dedication, we will reap the rewards in eternal terms. If we ask the Lord to equip us for the long haul of service in His Name, we will find strength and resolve we didn't know we had. If we spend more time learning the ways of God than we do demanding our own ways, we will witness a transformation both within and without.

If we commit to a sacrifice of our time and spend it in fervent prayer, we will begin to understand what is meant by the Scripture in James 5:16: "The effectual fervent prayer of a righteous man availeth much" (KJV).

In the Bible, Joshua 6, we read of God's instructions to Joshua about bringing down the walls of Jericho with strict attention to a faithful observance of God's plan. It worked, just as God said it would. Imagine what might happen in our own lives, today, if we truly sought after the Lord's will and His plan for NOW.

There's nothing that says you or I can't be a modern-day Joshua. God knows, there are plenty of walls that need brought down as we face our future. Walls of selfishness within marriages and families. Walls of bitterness built from years of regret and guilt. Walls of immeasurable height and depth that separate us from the best God has to offer those who love and follow Him.

All it takes is doing something that any of us can do. Any of us can ask God to be Lord of our life. We can accept Christ's free gift of salvation and grace and become "new creatures" in Him. We can serve Him instead of the almighty self. We can drive around our neighborhoods and communities — yes, literally, drive around — and stop at key spots and vistas and pray for the Lord's Holy Spirit to descend on the hills, plains and valleys we call our homeland.

We can beseech "Our Father who art in Heaven" (Matthew 6:9, NASB), to stir into flame the dying embers of a once strong faith that carried our nation into past victories. We can accept that the tasks before us will not be easy, but that they *will be* worth the effort. Future generations deserve our best shot at our rising above some of the pits we have dug for ourselves in our former mode of complacency, apathy and lack of awareness that "unto whomsoever much is given, of him shall be much required" (Luke 12:48, KJV).

The time has come to move into a new era of dedication to

the cause of Christ.

Lord, help us all to swiftly forget our laments of having been stripped of what we once called normal. Help us, then, to courageously reformulate our concept of what normal should be. Show us how to succeed at following Your lead. Amen.   □

All of us need God's strength
February 23, 2002

Life often extracts more from us than we think we can give. No one is exempt from this dreadful, draining squeeze. The key to survival is how we handle the pressure of being pressed on every side, both from without and within.

Nearly 10 years ago I shared in one of my columns that I was going through a time of unrelenting demands. A faithful, caring reader responded by sending me a note of encouragement and a promise to pray for me. In her note she also enclosed a little card stating: "I can do all things through [Christ] who strengthens me" (Philippians 4:13, NASB, brackets added).

The Bible verse is one I had memorized as a child in first or second grade. Over the years I have been sustained by reciting it many, many times while growing up, reaching even far into adulthood. But that day when the little business-card-size reminder fell out of the envelope onto my lap, I couldn't have needed it more.

For four or five years that card was displayed on the window above our kitchen sink and it always seemed to catch my eye when I felt depleted of all strength. Then we moved. One day the Bible-verse card resurfaced and has been attached to the bathroom mirror ever since.

The message of God's power, being what is needed to provide the strength for life, is never more meaningful than at any given moment when you or I need it most. And most often that moment is day by day, hour by hour, minute by minute.

Life without a source of strength is merely an existence on the verge of death. Without God's strength, His breath, His power, His presence, we are nothing and we have nothing to give.

Billy Graham writes in his daily devotional book, *Unto the Hills*, that "God's idea of strength and man's idea of strength are opposite one another" (Copyright 1996, Word Publishing).

From 2 Corinthians 12:9 we learn that God's strength is perfected in our weakness. If we aren't first weak, then we can't experience God's perfect strength.

You and I don't set out each day to be weak or inadequate — we just are. It's our nature. It's also a blessing. If we weren't so weak, in and of ourselves, we could never fully appreciate the real Source of our strength for living.

When life extracts more from us than we think we can give, that's as it should be. I'm not saying it's pleasant or that it's a breeze to humble ourselves in God's presence asking for His strength and power to descend upon us. What I am saying is that we can't change a basic fact of life: We need the Lord!

The sooner any of us acknowledges our need of God's strength, the stronger we will be—for now. The need, however, will return, again and again. Praise God, His supply of strength is unlimited!   □

Garden provides renewal for the soul

May 29, 1999

If I had to describe in one word why I love gardening with all the sweat and dirt that accompanies such a habit, I would have to say: renewal. Renewal as in revived physical and spiritual strength.

When I'm out there pulling weeds, chopping at the long root systems in a effort to "get it all," I feel like a kid again. I remember, as though it were only yesterday, digging holes and planting tomato plants and onion sets with my dad even before I could read and write.

Just remembering brings renewal. I remember everything from hoeing and raking with kid-size garden tools to eventually learning how to run Dad's Gravely garden tractor when I got older. I've never outgrown my love for seeing seeds become sprouts and sprouts turning into big, leafy salads at our supper table.

I feel renewed when I pick the rocks out of the soil and toss them, clunk, one at a time into a pile "over there." I feel renewed when I mix topsoil with compost in the wheelbarrow and then dump it in just the right spot. I feel renewed when I move from one location in the yard to another in an effort to stay in the shade.

I feel renewed when I plop a straw hat on my head and walk around the corner of the house carrying the four-pronged weeding, spading hoe that used to be my Granddad Heckler's. I feel renewed when I go back inside much later, take off the hat and glance in the mirror to see a crop of flattened "hat hair" on my head.

Yes, gardening is about renewal as much as it is about growth. Growth evolves out of the process of being renewed, and gardening is one of the best ways to see the fruits of our efforts in this process.

But there's more. There's another stage of renewal that takes place in a garden. It's a freeing from other cares and worries. It's an opportunity to pray without interruptions and distractions. It's a place to feel close to God. A place to see His hand at work.

A place to be encouraged that God's hand is also at work everywhere else in the world. A place to kneel and to expect answers. A place to bury the impossible and wait to see what new life God breathes into it.

The garden is a spiritual classroom, a prayer closet and a sanctuary all in one.

Dear Lord, there is more to gardening that producing the biggest roses or the juiciest tomatoes. There is finding You there. You are the Source of any garden's renewal or growing capabilities. You are why gardening is worth the work, the sweat and the wait. Thank You. In Jesus' Name. Amen.

□

CHAPTER FIFTEEN

Timing

Big Ben delivers timely message

February 24, 2001

There are times when a thing happens without explanation. It just happens. Later, reflecting on the event, it's all very clear. It might be days later. Even years. On the other hand, sometimes only mere seconds pass before we are struck with knowing we've just witnessed a significant moment.

One of these moments happened to me a week ago, Saturday, February 17. It was late. Around midnight. My husband and I were still working in our home offices. One of the drawbacks of working "at home" is that you don't just work at home. In essence, you live "at work." But back to "the moment."

It happened as I was removing the contents of a storage cabinet so the cabinet could be used elsewhere. As I reached for the next item on the shelf, my hand wrapped around an antique clock. To be exact, it is the Big Ben wind-up clock my parents always had setting on their bedroom dresser when I was growing up. Realizing instantly what I was holding, I cupped the clock in both hands and hugged it to my heart.

Carrying the clock down the hall to show Jim my find, I took a deep breath. That clock hadn't been wound for 30 years. It stopped ticking about the same time my dad died. Dad was the one who wound it when it ran down every couple of days. He was the one who set and wound the alarm every night. The last time Dad held that clock in his big calloused hands was the night of February 15, 1971. The next morning at the breakfast table Dad suffered a stoke that landed him in the Armstrong County Memorial Hospital. He never again wound Big Ben.

Although Dad was partially paralyzed from that stoke, his doctor thought he would live. Less than 42 hours later, around midnight on February 17, the doctor changed his mind. Dad suffered another stoke and it didn't look good. We were awakened by a phone call and then came a second call a little while later. Sometime between midnight and 3 a.m., Dad died from the effects of a third stroke.

Thirty years since Dad's heart stopped. Thirty years since my mother stored Big Ben. Thirty years, and now I find the clock on the anniversary of Dad's good-bye to our family.

At first I thought the finding of the clock at this time was purely a subtle irony. Coincidence. Strange. Odd but true. Within moments I knew the event was significant. I didn't know how to explain what I knew, what I felt, I just knew it affected me deeply.

This isn't the first time in my life I've written about Dad's untimely death at 55 years of age. It isn't the first time something reminded me of him and I was affected by it. It is the first time, however, that I wound Big Ben. It is the first time Dad's clock is now ticking away within a few feet of my desk. It's one of those times when you know, you just know, that life sets forth two uniquely opposite and yet equal actions. Life in the form of death stands still and, although time is no more for the individual who passes away, life and time continue to move on.

The fact that our family's Big Ben was silent all these years does not alter reality: time has advanced. But, oh, what comfort and what peace I have just knowing that, although my dad's voice has been silenced, his being lives on eternally. Months before he died, Dad gave his heart to Jesus Christ. He claimed Jesus as his Savior and was forgiven of his sins. Dad's "ticking" stopped but his soul moved on. Just as yours and mine will whenever our life here on earth is ended.

Finding Big Ben was, indeed, personally significant. But not as significant as God's eternal plan for each of us. It is not His will "that any should perish, but that all should come to repentance" (2 Peter 3:9, KJV). This is why "God so loved the world, that He gave His only begotten Son" (John 3:16, KJV). Any of us who makes the decision to believe on Him will be saved. If you haven't yet done this in your own life, perhaps now is the time to repent and believe before your heart, too, stops ticking. Believe it or not, one day it will.

□

Telling God, 'Take Your time'

January 4, 2003

"Time and tide wait for no man," states an old English proverb. No matter how hard we might try, we can't grab ahold of time and slow it down. And yet, I fear, it's not time we'd like to put the skids on. It's life.

Life, no matter how fast-paced, can not keep in sync with the ticking of the clock. The clock ticks at the same speed, day in and day out, while life races on. And we, you and I, strive to keep up.

When is the last time you or I told anyone, or anyone told us, "Take your time"?

Taking our time is virtually an extinct concept. It's been replaced by: Hurry up. Get to it. Do it yesterday. Don't think, just do.

Whatever happened to the idea of taking enough time to do something right, and actually enjoy doing it? Which generation, perhaps the one just now being weaned from diapers, will be the last to ever have known anyone old enough to remember the good old days, when time served man, not the other way around?

Ironically, as much as we demand speed of action, thought and decision, we still have sense enough to wish things could be different. Also ironically, as much as we wish we could be given the luxury of taking our good old time to accomplish our jobs or tasks these days, we seldom, if ever, offer the Lord this courtesy. We don't say to Him, "Lord, take Your time."

What might happen if we did? What might our lives be like if we expressed to God that we trust His judgment regarding His timing of the things we pray about? His timing surrounding the agonies we endure? The burdens we struggle with? The problems we think we can't deal with another minute, let alone another day? Beyond that, what if God actually does *take His time* and doesn't appear to respond to our need until we label it "too late"?

Far too often we, men and women alike, rush ahead of time, especially ahead of God. There's no telling what a difference we might see in our lives if we begin loosening the reins on God. Yes, it's great we hang on to Him, but it's not so great that we try to steer Him, control Him and spur Him faster and faster. That's not a display of confidence, it's arrogance. We're trying to tell Him we trust Him at the same time we're yelling hurry up.

Assuming God might like to hear you and I say, "Take Your time, Lord. You know what You're doing. And that's all that matters to me," then let's do just that. Will you pray with me:

Dear Heavenly Father, I trust You. I trust Your timing. I trust Your tenderness. I trust Your eternal sense of how and when things will be done. You, and You alone, know what's right about speed versus the fullness of time. Help me to give You what is Yours anyway: the power, the wisdom, the strength and the responsibility to bring about everything in Your time, Your way. In the Name of Jesus. Amen. □

CHAPTER SIXTEEN

Tributes

Mother 'bequeaths' a shining example
May 10, 2003

W hen my mother died in February she was bent and worn-out. Through the years, osteoporosis compressed her spine; arthritis twisted her knuckles and invaded her knees; Alzheimer's disease robbed her of mental and physical pleasures. Other age-related deterioration was evident. Nonetheless, something else was evident, too.

At 88 years of age, Dorothy Heffelfinger's light, her Christian witness, was still shining. My mother never lost her quiet, calm ability to touch lives. She was a lot like one of her "prized" possessions — an out-of-shape candle, melted and bent down by the heat of affliction, but still capable of giving off light.

The story of mother's misshapen red candle seems a fitting tribute to her memory.

Seven years ago this summer, our family was in the process of packing up my mother's things in preparation for her moving in with my husband Jim and me. On one of the days when our daughter April was helping me fill boxes at Gram's house, April suddenly exclaimed, "Well, Gram, here's one thing we can definitely throw out! What in the world is it anyway?"

Spying the bent-low-to-the-ground red candle April was holding in her hand, my mother was quick to respond. "Oh, Honey, we mustn't get rid of *that!*"

"Gram!" April lovingly quizzed her again. "Why not?"

"Well, Honey," Mum began explaining, "it's like this. I've had that candle for a long time. When I was away visiting my sisters one summer it got pretty hot in my trailer. When I came home the candle was drooped all the way down in that S-shape. Since then, every time I look at it, it makes me laugh. And when you've lived alone as long as I have, you need all the laughter you can get."

With a shake of the head, a rolling of the eyes, April and I hugged each other and Gram, too. The candle and the story would be preserved. April knows that someday she and her sister Lori will probably find the candle amongst *my* treasures. And once more the issue will arise as to "what in the world should we do with this candle *this* time!"

In the meantime, the candle illustrates a profound truth. A truth I shared with all those who gathered in March at my mother's memorial service. The candle is still a candle with a wick. If we were to light that wick, it would give off a bright light. Just like my mother in her final years, bent and out-of-shape, she, too, was still a gentle, kind, human being. She, too, had a purpose. A great part of her purpose was to brighten the lives of others. And she did.

We miss her very much. There are days when I forget, momentarily, she's gone. I catch myself thinking I'll just run out to the nursing home to see her. The last time I went out there a few weeks ago to visit with some of the staff, they reassured me that, in *their* memory of her, my mother's light, her witness, still warms their hearts. That pretty much sums up a life well-lived. The shape Mother was in didn't alter who she really was.

When my time comes, to be worn and bent, I hope I have it in me to shine like you, Mum. You left me a lot to live up to.

□

Mother-in-law is a blessing, not a target for disrespect

February 20, 1999

This weekend my mother-in-law Mona V. Moore turns 80. Not only do I thank her for giving birth to the man I married, but I also have her to thank for Jim's asking me to go on our first date 36 years ago.

As a sophomore at Slippery Rock State College (now University), Jim had gone home disgruntled because he still hadn't found "Miss Right." His mother suggested he consider dating Dotty Heffelfinger, a "good Christian girl who lives just over the hill," she said. "She is someone we've all known for a long time."

So he did — ask me out, that is. The rest is history. But this piece is not about us. Instead it's a tribute to Mona and to all other deserving mothers-in-law.

I've never liked, and seldom laugh at, disrespectful mother-in-law jokes. Perhaps I would feel differently if I had a bad mother-in-law, but since I have a good one, I don't find such humor funny.

A year or so ago, I told Mona what a good mother-in-law she has always been. "Well, I thank you, Dotty," she said, "but no one had a better mother-in-law than I did."

She then told the story of how, years ago, her own mother-in-law Pearl let Mona have the brand new refrigerator Pearl had bought for herself. It all came about when Mona and Dick were moving into a second-story apartment. Their old (very old) refrigerator wouldn't fit up the stairs, so Pearl took their old fridge and let them use her brand new one. By the time Pearl got the "new" refrigerator back a few years later, it was no longer new, of course, but Mona's praise and appreciation of her mother-in-law lives on to this day.

Another story Mona told recently was how she got her name. Her own mother Beatrice Booher was pregnant with Mona at the same time that Beatrice's sister-in-law Mona Fair was dying from cancer. Mona Fair made a request.

"Beatrice," she had said, "if the baby you are carrying turns out to be a girl, will you please name her after me?"

Mona Fair died around Christmas in 1918, only two months before Beatrice gave birth. Although the two Monas never "laid eyes on each other," the two of them certainly have a bond.

Speaking of bonds, when I entered the Moore family, Mona said from day one, "I'll treat you like a daughter, Dotty, not an in-law." And she did. So much so, that one time she shared a secret, asking me to "never tell a soul." I haven't...and I won't.

Mona is a farm girl who has always been a classy lady, in my eyes. She can look fantastic dressed up in a suit and heels or in a sweat shirt and blue jeans. With always-neat hair, necklace and earrings, she peels potatoes, watches TV or runs the sweeper looking as though she could be ready to go shopping or visiting a friend on short notice.

Naturally, I know she is going to read this and she is probably going to wonder if I'll say *anything* negative about her. Well, it's like this: if I did, I wouldn't write it here. I would tell her face to face. That's because that's the way she would do it, and I know that's the way she would want it done to her.

When I first got to know Mona I learned right off that she was a hard worker and usually expected the same of everyone else. (That's not a negative, by the way. It's a fact.) So I was really touched by something she did when I was a young mother with our second daughter only a few days old.

Mona had come to stay with us to help out, and when the eighth day came after I had delivered Lori, Mona said that evening, "Now tomorrow, Dotty, I don't want you doing anything. Nothing at all."

I'm sure I gave her a funny look, but she went on, "I was always told a new mother shouldn't lift a finger on the ninth day. So that's the way it will be. You will do nothing but rest."

So I did. She took care of everything else.

Weather permitting, our family is coming together from Buffalo, Syracuse and western Pennsylvania for a celebration today and tomorrow. We'll be helping Mona celebrate 80 years of life, 80 years of memories, 80 years of joys and 80 years of sorrows.

Mona's hasn't been an easy life. She's lost a husband, a mother and father and two brothers along with scores of other close friends and family, but Mona prays and leans on God for strength, always.

She was married to Richard Moore on her birthday in 1942. She will undoubtedly be the first to say, "I wish Dick could be here now, but somehow I'm sure he is."

Mona isn't afraid to say what she thinks, so you always know where you stand with her. Right here and now, I want her to know that I and the rest of her family are all proud to stand up and say, "We appreciate you, Mum, Mona and Grandma. You always let us know how much you appreciate whatever any of us does for you. Now it's our turn to tell you likewise. We love you. Happy Birthday!"   □

Our neighbor was quite a 'treasure'

June 8, 1991

Nothing in life requires more strength and courage than facing the death of a loved one.

People everywhere go through it every day.

Often it's someone we know.

Such was the case this week with the death of Ruth (Treasure) Dildine of Third Street, Benton.

Ruth was my next-door neighbor.

Many people knew Ruth as a former home economics teacher in the Benton Area School District. Many knew her as a victorious lady who faced and recovered from heart-bypass surgery twice with remarkable courage and an obvious love of life.

Ruth's love of life also brought with it two separate battles with cancer, the latter ending in a different kind of victory than we had all hoped.

That final victory was the strength and courage seen in Ruth's husband and family at her funeral on Thursday in the Benton United Presbyterian Church.

Many people will long remember Ruth as a woman who loved flowers and trees and who knew how to plant and grow almost anything with great success.

Her husband Jim knew her as a dedicated, faithful wife. Her children and grandchildren knew her as a loyal, committed mother and grandmother. Friends knew her as a warm, gracious hostess.

As a neighbor, my family and I, along with other neighbors, knew her as an easy-to-talk-to, generous woman who shared beauty and quiet enthusiasm with everyone around her.

The seven-or-eight-year-old locust tree in our front yard was once a seedling Ruth herself had planted and cared for until it was ready to go from flower pot to permanent spot in the ground. It was kind of an extra—Ruth had intended it for her own yard—but when she saw she didn't need it, she immediately offered it to someone who did.

But back to the strength and courage of Ruth's family at her funeral:

- The strength and courage that was displayed in son Jim who spoke of his mother as the best in the world and read the poem, "Thank You, Mom," in her honor.
- The strength and courage of daughter Janet who chose just the right hymn about peace, "Be Still, My Soul," for the officiating pastor, the Rev. O. Allen Lumpkin, to sing.

- The strength and courage of daughter Linda who also read a poem and spoke of her mother's sense of humor by reflecting on things her mother said and did "right up to the day she died."

- The strength and courage of husband Jim who nodded support and approval for each of his grown children as they all participated in the funeral service.

- The strength and courage of sister-in-law and neighbor Eleanor Klementik who flawlessly played the organ accompaniment for the hymns sung at the funeral.

Flowers will bloom around the Dildine house and yard this summer, and for many summers to come, because Ruth had the foresight to plant perennials as generously as she planted strength and courage in the lives of those she loved.

There is no doubt in anyone's mind who knew and loved Ruth Marie Dildine that she knew how to nurture strength and courage. I wonder if it's because, in 1919, she was born on July 4 — July 4, the day we celebrate the birth of a country known for its strength and courage.

It's more likely Ruth's strength and courage came from "the Father of our Lord Jesus Christ, the source of every mercy, and the one who so wonderfully comforts and strengthens us in our hardships and trials. ...So that when others are troubled, needing our sympathy and encouragement, we can pass on to them this same help and comfort God has given us" (2 Corinthians 1: 3-4, TLB) .

If we dare to imagine the Lord having a garden full of strength and courage in and around His "home," I think we can also dare to imagine that every now and then His blossoms burst forth through some of the lives He plants on earth.

Ruth Dildine, you were one of these blossoms.   □

One woman inspires many

October 19, 1991

I press on toward the goal for the prize of the upward call of God in Christ Jesus (Philippians 3:14, NASB).

When the rest of us — assuming you're like me — get tired from doing some of the things God asks of us, we might be encouraged to press on, if we think of Mary Aten of Fifth Street in Nescopeck.

Back around 1926, at 14 or 15 years of age, Mary, who turned 80 in May, began doing something that many adults find ways out of instead of saying "yes" to: She began teaching Sunday school at St. Mark's Evangelical Lutheran Church on Third Street in Nescopeck. Recently, Mary was honored for 65 consecutive years of service there.

At an age when young girls today are concerned with such things as hair styles, make-up, "when can I date" and "I can't wait until I can drive," Mary volunteered to teach children, one-and-a-half to 10 years of age, in what later became the primary department of the church.

She volunteered because, as Mary said in a telephone interview this week, "They needed someone...and I liked children." Thus begun, the obvious, natural match continued.

Mary, modestly, admits never having gotten tired of teaching Sunday school. For her, "the children" always made it worthwhile. For her, even the ones who were hard to handle in the beginning, "the children" were her reward. "Once you got to know them, everything was OK," she said.

The world has seen a lot of changes in 65 years, but Mary feels the attitudes of each generation of young students have remained predictable: "If they come [to Sunday school], they're interested."

For Mary, the joy of being with the children is why she was

a teacher and/or superintendent of the primary department until about a month ago. Now, she plays the piano for Sunday school and substitutes where she's needed.

Where she's needed.

Perhaps that's why there is a plaque at St. Mark's hanging in the primary department in Mary's honor. Perhaps that's why the congregation threw an appreciation dinner for Mary on Sunday, October 6. Perhaps that's why Mary was surprised when a couple of her favorite, former pastors showed up at the dinner.

Perhaps being needed is what keeps Mary going, and going and going.

Dear Lord, You must need all of us right where You have us — that's why we're still here. Thank You for confirming that through the Mary Atens of the world. When we get tired, revive us. When we get discouraged, refresh us. When we forget, remind us. In Jesus' Name. Amen.

(Mary Aten lived until January 15, 2001 when she died at 89 years of age. St. Mark's Evangelical Lutheran Church was officially renamed Faith United Evangelical Lutheran Church as of Novermber 2003. The name reflects a consolidation of St. Mark's in Nescopeck and Mt. Zion Lutheran Church of Briggsville.) □

CHAPTER SEVENTEEN

Trust

Sleepover is service lesson
March 10, 2001

When it comes to telling stories about our granddaughter Dallas, no one has to twist my arm twice. So here it is, the latest Dallas episode in my life as Grandma.

The recent blizzard forecast early this week brought Dallas to our home for a two-night, two-day sleepover. She loved it and so did Grandpa and I. Dallas knew when she arrived that she would be here a "long time" and she kept track of it by reminding me, "I haven't been here long enough yet. There is still a very long day and a very long week to go."

To Dallas' almost four-year-old mind, two days and two nights was a long week. I even overheard her on the phone telling her mommy, "I'm staying here for two nights and two weeks." Dallas wasn't the least bit bothered by the exact length of her stay as long it qualified as a "long time."

Smiling at her innocent enthusiasm about being here for however long "long" turned out to be, I thought how pleased God must be, if and when we place a similar confidence in loving Him, trusting Him and serving Him for the long haul without fidgeting or complaining about the duration. But how seldom, I imagine, He sees such unconditional devotion.

Naturally, I can only speak for myself, but, from what I hear others say, it appears that many of us struggle with this. We want the Lord to tell us or show us: "How long will this hard time in my life go on?" "How much more am I going to have to take?" "How long will I have to wait for things to get better?"

If only we were more childlike. If only we looked up to the Lord with loving eyes, trusting hearts and willing spirits expressing to Him: "I don't know how long all of this will last, but I'm so glad I'm with You and You're with me!" "There might be no end in sight for all that I have to endure, but praise You, Lord, praise You, not for the burden, but for Your strength that sustains me." "Hopefully things won't get worse before they get better, but regardless, Lord, keep me safe and hold me steady."

Too often, I fear, too many of us go around acting as though we are doing the Lord a favor by trying to follow Him. In so doing, we let Him know rather boldly how displeased we are that He isn't making our life and our circumstances easier. Too often we display an arrogant attitude that boasts, "Pat me on the back, Lord, and then give me an easy road!"

Life is inherently uncertain and difficult. Moment by moment can be as troublesome as trudging uphill in 14 inches of snow. "No one ever said life is supposed to be easy," we all quote the wise words of some anonymous "Duh." So why, then, do we demand the easy road, the light load, the clear sailing?

The only answer that makes any sense is: We are human. We can't see what God sees. We don't know what He knows. And we don't always like that. We would prefer being little gods and having more control. Until, that is, we got in over our heads, which we are bound to do sooner than later, and then we would surely blame Him for our shortcomings.

God must shake His head continually at our naivety. We are so blind and so foolish. When are we going to learn that storms, steep pathways, heavy burdens and dark skies are often the passageways into the warmth and security of God's loving arms.

It shouldn't take a blizzard to wake us up, but sometimes it does. Other times it takes only a child to lead us. This, too, is an unexplainable act of God.   □

Strength comes by trusting God
July 21, 2001

In quietness and in trust shall be your strength (Isaiah 30:15, RSV).

How many of us wish we could recline in the cool shadows of ease instead of facing the blazing trials of reality? Probably most, if not all, of us long for less stress and more relaxation. But it's not going to be. Not in this life. Not for the majority of us.

Most of us have no choice but to accept that the only real peace we'll ever have is the peace that defies explanation. It's the peace that passes understanding (see Philippians 4:7). The peace that comes from our being so weak that we rely on the One who is strong (2 Corinthians 12:10).

When your strength and my strength come from trusting in the Lord's strength and power, we are strong indeed. These words are written not because they sound good but because they have been lived. Lived by yours truly and by countless others who have experienced faith and strength growing out of impossible circumstances. It's not necessary for me to share here and now all the details of my firsthand knowledge of God's strength and power, but if you are human, and I know you are, you can fill in your own details of your own struggles and triumphs. You and I alike can give credit to the Lord for getting us through rough times.

Sometimes the roughest of times turns out to be the pivotal point of our facing the future with confidence as we walk away from the defeats of our past. Often this is possible only when, in the stillness of relinquishing our all to the Lord, we take the first step of trust by refusing to identify with our former fears. In so doing, we can shed shackles that were meant to ruin us.

For instance, take the story of Alma and Leo Barkman. Alma tells of her and her husband's experience in *Daily Guideposts, 1996* (Copyright 1995, Guideposts). The two of them, Alma and Leo, were attempting to harvest the vegetables from their garden before the cucumbers, tomatoes and herbs might rot due to excessive amounts of rainfall.

Alma writes that the garden had turned "into a quagmire" making it nearly impossible for her and Leo to walk through the rows of vegetables. Even with rubber boots on, their feet "sank into the squishy clay" and the suction created by each step, I imagine, was like trudging through wet cement.

Exasperation and exhaustion set in quickly. At last Leo voiced a solution. He suggested they go barefoot.

"Having more fun than a couple of kids," Alma says it worked. "No longer bogged down by those heavy big boots, it was much easier to pick the vegetables."

Not only was the job easier but also it was the first time in nearly 50 years that Alma had walked barefoot in cool, wet mud. The experience was liberating, refreshing and downright memorable.

Isn't that the effect we seek in our walk of faith? We want to exhibit confidence and trust in the Lord that He will supply our needs and give us strength, and yet we allow ourselves to get mired in the details of impossibility. We are either weighed down or held back because circumstances impede our progress. And then, it happens. The Lord imparts an idea or encourages us to do the unexpected, and the answer appears. It's obvious. And to think the solution was there all along! Lo and behold, in the quiet and confidence of a moment of clarity or a moment of unexplainable peace, we are free to be strong. We are free to succeed!

It's not that all struggles for all times have suddenly ceased and disappeared, but rather, episode by episode, we will see the results of trusting in the Lord. Indeed, He shall be our strength.   □

Learning how to walk without fear
May 5, 2001

I am the Lord, your God, who takes hold of your right hand and says to you, Do not fear; I will help you (Isaiah 41:13, NIV).

W henever I see our young granddaughter reach up and take hold of her grandpa's hand, sometimes I drag my feet just so I can lag behind and observe the two of them from a casual distance. Although I can't see their faces, I know the look each of them has.

Grandpa's is one of pride and honor that this child trusts him completely, not only to lead her but also to proceed at a pace that is comfortable for her. His face reflects an awareness of his position, and you know without a doubt, he is blessed beyond measure by Dallas' unwavering trust and devotion. Her well-being and enjoyment of the journey ahead are uppermost in his heart and mind.

Dallas' look is one of pure pleasure just to be where she is. She doesn't pull away and run ahead; she walks confidently right by Grandpa's side, her stride telling the world, "I may not know exactly where I'm going, but I know my grandpa. And where he goes, I know I'll have fun. I'll be safe because he is strong. I'll see wonderful things because Grandpa is wise. I'll have a new adventure to tell others about because that's what Grandpa and I do, we have adventures. Yep, me and Grandpa and Grandma are having an adventure!"

About that time she throws her head back and calls over her shoulder, "Grandma, come on! We're going on a adventure! You better catch up and take my other hand!"

The scene and the insights that go with it are a lot like imagining being a follower of Christ. First you observe from a distance and are enraptured by what you see until, all of a sudden, you take the necessary steps to catch up. You no longer want only to imagine, you want to actually be there with Him, to feel your hand in His and know that you have nothing to fear.

You know from having memorized such Scriptures as the Twenty-third Psalm that the Lord is your shepherd. It's head knowledge, even heart knowledge, but you also desire moments *with* Him that can't be explained by your head or your heart. You want Him to walk beside you, hold your hand and fill you with His peace. You want Him to tell you, "Do not fear!"

There's nothing like having nothing to fear. But who of us has that kind of knowledge and peace all of the time? We have moments. You do. I do. Sometimes these moments are so fleeting they're virtually non-calculable. Other times we recognize the peace of Christ hovering over us like a slow-moving cloud of angels.

Most of the time, however, we walk and work in our own strength and power. We forget about putting our hand in the Lord's hand until we get into troublesome, downright frightening circumstances or we face a life-and-death crisis.

"Where are You, Lord, where are you!" we cry, searching everywhere for a sign that He's near. We look to the sky, we look behind us, we peer around corners, we dig into the Bible, we fall to our knees, we request prayers and we agonize about what's going to become of us.

Then it happens. A word comes to us. A song. A sight. A Presence. A Hand. The Hand of Jesus stretches forth and we reach up.

We don't know exactly where He will lead us, but we know *Him*. We know we can trust Him. We know we'll be safe. We know He will help us and that there is nothing to fear. We are His child and He will never let go.

The walk with Him begins, again and again. The walk continues. It's a walk that needs never to end. You and I can daily pray:

You are Lord, God, and right here and now I give You my hand. I give You my life. I give You my all. In the depths of my soul I see You and me going on a lifelong adventure. Even into eternity. In Jesus' Name. Amen.   □

Bluebird encounter parallels God's mercy
May 24, 2003

A bluebird is a sight to behold. Who wouldn't love to see one perched on the kitchen windowsill every morning? But finding one trapped inside a home heating system, now that's a horror story. Luckily for the one telling this story and the bluebird who stars in it, the horror part of this very tale was erased when the gentle, yet strong hand of a rescuer returned the "bird of happiness" to his natural habitat.

To begin with, I'll back up to the discovery phase of this tale. As I was walking past our stone hearth one recent afternoon en route to the laundry room, I heard a fluttering sound and simultaneously realized the sound was coming from something live trapped inside our Franco Belge oil heater. (The heater had been off for weeks due to the warm weather.)

At first sight of the flailing, flapping creature I thought it was a bat. Imagine my disbelief when a closer look through the glass door of the stove revealed an orange chest and bright blue body with feathery wings aflutter.

"Oh, my! Oh, my!" was all I could get out before I ran up the stairs yelling for my husband Jim to get down here. "Jim, Jim, quick, there's a bluebird trapped inside our stove! He must have tumbled down the chimney!"

The bluebird was in as much or more of a panic than we were. "Not a dear little bluebird!" we muttered as we raced around looking for some solution, some way out of this predicament for this innocent creature. We knew he would never make it out of there alive going back the way he came. Not with all the right-angled turns and drops in our stovepipe! We also knew we didn't want to yank open the door on the stove and have this bird, no matter how cute he was, sailing all through our house.

At last we devised a plan. Jim pulled on thick leather work gloves and I shook open a large plastic bag. As we eased the glass door on the stove open just far enough for Jim to get his fingers inside from the bottom of the door, I covered the top and side opening of the door with the bag. One way or another, we hoped we could get that bluebird out of his prison and back to freedom. We did it!

We were absolutely thrilled when Jim was able to wrap his one hand around the bird's body and wings. Out through the patio door we went together and together we momentarily fussed over the bluebird and admired his sapphire-like beauty.

He seemed fine and proved it when Jim opened his hand and gently released the bird skyward.

Mr. Bluebird didn't fly far, but he did settle on a tree branch not far from where we stood. For a few minutes he watched us while we watched him. Jim even had enough time to grab the digital camera and snap a few shots before the bird flew to the next tree. Jim sent me back inside for the telephoto lens. All in all, Jim took 20 pictures of this lovely creature before it flew away for good. Out of all those photos only two were keepers, outstanding is more like it. But as good as the two photos are, that's not where the significance of this story lies.

The thing that strikes closest to home for Jim and me, perhaps for you, too, is how our bluebird encounter reflects what happens when we, as creatures of a loving Heavenly Father, are trapped in circumstances of life beyond our control. Like our bluebird friend who was helpless and hopelessly at our mercy, we, too, time after time, can be rescued only by a merciful hand. The Hand of God.

This doesn't mean we won't face fear. It doesn't mean there are no risks involved. It doesn't mean we won't have our doubts about the short-term outcome. But it does mean the Lord has our best interests at heart. Even when the stakes are high, especially when they are, He can be trusted with His strength. With His gentleness. With His compassion. With His grace and mercy.

God the Father created us all. And He knows the best way, the best path, the perfect plan not only for our rescue and redemption, but also for our future. Our future flights, if we draw a parallel. Flights which are assuredly upward and onward as we acknowledge Him as the guardian and overseer of our very soul. □

Putting a lid on 'the burden box'

September 21, 2002

Cast thy burden upon the Lord, and He shall sustain thee: He shall never suffer the righteous to be moved (Psalm 55:22, KJV).

You don't come across very many people these days who aren't carrying a heavy load. Whether the burden is for self or someone near and dear, virtually everyone has a weight on his or her shoulders that seemingly can't be lifted.

In the fight to survive life and its worries, there are no pat answers and no money-back guarantees. There are, however, Scriptures that offer hope; biblical promises to lean on. One of my motivations for writing is to provide glimmers of hope and encouragement to those among us who are in need. Here you find Scriptures, personal stories, spiritual parallels that are intended to help us all, yours truly included, to "keep the faith."

But, I'll tell you, and I can just hear you telling me, keeping the faith is not as easy as it sounds. It might look neat and to the point in black and white print, but there are times in all of our lives when it's the hardest thing we've ever done. It's during these desperately trying times that keeping the faith, although difficult, is the only — and I do mean only — option.

A few days ago, my husband Jim and I were discussing a burden which is both directly and indirectly related to our ministry — Jim's as a Christian counselor and mine as a writer. The burden is many layers thick and several tiers high. No one can lift it. We can do nothing but wait, work and pray while the Lord implements *His* plan.

It's no exaggeration to say that some days we must dump our burden, more precisely burdens, into a big hulk of a figurative box and say, "Here, Lord, they're Yours! Keep them! Fix them! At least hold them for a while!"

In a recent long-distance phone conversation, I was sharing

the burdens-in-a-box concept with my mother-in-law. I told her that we have been trying to throw our burdens concerning many matters into that box. But, I confessed, no sooner do we unload *this* burden and *that* burden into "God's box" than another burden, and then another and another, enters the picture.

As I was describing the box of burdens all I could see in my mind's eye was a huge boxful of things we are attempting to give to the Lord. Problem is I can still "see" what's in the box, I implied to Mona.

"Well, Dotty," Mona said, "then I guess you and Jim will have to put a lid on the box and walk away from it for a while."

Wow! Instantly I knew she had hit the mark. "Put a lid on it!" It's a phrase we've all used in a slightly different context, especially when we want someone to quiet down or back off. But in the case of a boxful of burdens, putting a lid on it is a definitive act of faith. It gives a burdened heart breathing room, space to take a deep breath. Inhale hope. Exhale fear. Inhale a sense of release. Exhale the need to know NOW! the outcome of the burdens.

Dear Heavenly Father, there is no better way to keep the faith than to exercise confidence in You. Give us the strength to give You our all. All of ourselves. All of our energies. All of our talents. All of our weaknesses. Especially all of our burdens. Then, as we try to put a lid on our grave worries and concerns, forgive us in advance for all the times we know we are going to pry open that lid and begin the whole process anew. Even if it amounts to a hundred times a day — that we must give it all to You — by Your strength and by Your might we can keep going. In the Name of Jesus. Amen. □

Doubting merely shadows our fears

July 13, 2002

Eighteen years ago in June I entered a prestigious writing contest that I was positive I would win. Fifteen winners were to be chosen from roughly 7,000 entrants, so I calculated the odds and continued to feel confident throughout the entire summer of 1984. I knew the outcome of the contest would change the life of anyone who emerged as a winner.

As it turned out, the contest *did* change my life, but not because I won. My life was changed because I lost. When I received notification that I was "a loser," I gave up writing — forever. However, in the midst of what I deemed was my final rejection, unbeknownst to me a seed was germinating. Months later, that seed sprouted and grew into what became the " 'Joy ... in the Morning' " column.

Defeat gave way to a completely unexpected course of events. If I would have won the contest I entered in 1984, I might have written, from time to time, a few articles for a Christian publication. Instead, a secular door opened where I've written close to 900 weekly columns. In terms of sheer numbers, there is no comparison. In terms of discipline and faithfulness to a deadline, there is no comparison. In terms of loyalty from a faithful readership, there is no comparison. In terms of what I planned and how God led, there is no comparison.

There are obvious reasons for sharing here about a defeat and a victory in my life. Who among us hasn't lived both? Who among us hasn't had his or her life changed by a reversal of plans? Admittedly, this a condensed version of how " 'Joy ... in the Morning' " came about. Even so, you know as well as I do, when you're living the unexpected, when the waiting seems endless, there is no condensing or minimizing the pain. When pain subsides, however, as it usually does, from disappointment and defeat, new outlooks surface and new direction appears. In the meantime, when hurt, confusion, rejection and often devastation prevail, there is little consolation.

The only consolation, at times, and I do mean *only*, is knowing we belong to the Lord and He belongs to us. Knowing Him and knowing He has a plan can change your life and mine. Trusting Him and trusting His plan changes your life and mine, even more.

If ever we doubt, and we do because we're human, our doubting can only be one-dimensional. The reason there is no depth to our doubting is because doubting is merely a shadow of our fears. And fear is not a living, breathing reality with vision, substance, motivation and action. Fear is a feeling. And although our feelings are explainable, they are not God.

God is power. God is victory. God is wisdom, might, Creator, Savior, Lord, Redeemer, friend. God is everything good. He is strength. He is conqueror. He is the answer to the desire of every heart. He is our comforter for every rejection. He is our sustainer for every defeat. And He is our reason, yours and mine, for calling ourselves, not losers, but winners — even when circumstances declare otherwise. □

CHAPTER EIGHTEEN

Gleanings from the far end of the table

February 17, 2001

If one more piece of mail gets added to the pile at my end of the table, I'll have to sit on the floor when it's time to eat, I sighed to myself the other day. *Where does it all come from!* I shrieked inside my head.

Casual conversations confirm that none of us is alone in bemoaning an overwhelming abundance of stuff that walks right into our lives through both solicited and unsolicited mail and printed material. The only consolation we have is that when any of us complains, we know others are doing the same.

Information, information, information. How rich we would be if only information — and knowledge — held the key to the door marked wisdom. But, alas, information and knowledge are not synonymous with wisdom.

It's like Billy Graham said a number of years ago: "Knowledge is horizontal. Wisdom is vertical — it comes down from above."

Oh, how thankful you and I ought to be that God does not send us His wisdom in the form of junk mail!

Of course not all mail is "junk" and not all "paper work" that piles up in our homes and offices is annoying "stuff." A lot of it is necessary, even vital, to running today's households and successful businesses. But the whole scenario of dealing with it certainly involves wisdom and the wise use of time, space and talents.

Wisdom. It's been said that we are wise either because we have found God and want to serve Him; or because we are actively seeking Him because we have not yet found Him. Nothing else we are, or are doing, quite measures up to being wise.

"He who provides for this life, but takes no care for eternity, is wise for a moment, but a fool forever," said John Tillotson (1630-1694), pastor and Dean of Canterbury, as quoted in a volume called *12,000 Religious Quotations* compiled and edited by Frank S. Mead (1989, Baker Book House Company).

Many things come under the heading of providing for this life: We have to eat. We have to shop and plan for what we are going to eat. We have to live in houses. Houses have to be cared for. We have to stay healthy. Stay clean. Get rest. Exercise. Be informed. Be wise. And in being wise, we must also beware.

"For the wisdom of this world is foolishness to God," the Lord tells us through the writings of the Apostle Paul in the Bible (1 Corinthians 3:19, TLB). Our wisdom, like Billy Graham says, must come from above.

"If any of you lacks wisdom, let him ask of God, who gives to all liberally and without reproach, and it will be given to him," we read in James 1:5 (NKJV).

You and I can be wise and still live in this world. We might have to sift through a variety of distractions along with undeniable necessities, but with the Lord's help, with His answering our pleas for wisdom, we can do it.

Fortunately, this is what I managed to glean from my recent encounter with a pile of stuff at one end of the table. Out of desperation to run away from it, the Lord steered me to Him-

self and to His Word. There, finding wisdom, I feel empow-
ered to tackle today. May my testimonial to this fact also encourage you, if by any chance, you, too, can't quite find a spot
at your own table.

God bless.   □

Springtime is a call for wisdom

March 24, 2001

Spring is here! And with it comes an unmistakable temptation: Anything goes! That's why it's so easy to go a little
crazy this time of the year. It's also precisely why we have to
be careful we don't hurt ourselves.

After the long winter we are tempted to do all the things we
couldn't do when it was cold and blustery. Things that are harm-
less when done in moderation but devastating when overdone.
You know what I mean. Things like wearing ourselves out by
not knowing when to quit. Things like going overboard with
cleaning, painting, gardening, ripping and tearing. But did you
know there is a Bible Scripture for this, too? Consider:

"See then that ye walk circumspectly, not as fools, but as
wise, redeeming the time, because the days are evil. Wherefore be ye not unwise, but understanding what the will of the
Lord is" (Ephesians 5:15-17, KJV).

OK, I know. This Scripture is not referring specifically to
spring and flamboyant spring projects. But when you think
about it, it could be. It could be warning us to be as wise in the
spring as we are supposed to be at any other time. Even so,
perhaps spring is when temptations are greatest.

Why spring? Well, as I see it, it's an awakening time. A time to be free to be ourselves. To do what we want. Go where we want. Think and say what we want. A time to let go of restraints. A time to be expressive and explore. A time to be careful we don't hurt ourselves or anyone else.

That's why Ephesians 5:15-17 *does* pertain as much to spring as to any other season. We *always* need to be wise about how we spend our time. We need to be mindful of making the most of the days given to us. Opportunities to live and grow closer to the Lord are precious. The freedom to love the Lord and serve Him with obedience is redemptive.

To redeem this time is to reserve it for the Lord's will. For the Lord's work. For the Lord's calling. It isn't to be squandered. It is, instead, an opportunity to expand our witness. To give birth to new insights. To explore new areas of service as followers of God.

Although it might be easier to go crazy with the arrival of spring and ignore common sense about discipline and proper planning regarding the use of our time and energies, it behooves us to be wise.

This is not to say that gardening, spring cleaning and fixing up the premises are bad. Of course they aren't. But if that's all we do. If that's all we think about. If that's all we live for, we are neither walking circumspectly nor are we redeeming the time. We're simply doing "our" thing for "our" reasons. We all do it to some extent. I know I do. However, the Scripture stands: *Be ye not unwise, but understanding what the will of the Lord is.*

It seems quite safe to imagine that the Lord, too, looks forward to spring. He, better than anyone, knows how impulsive spring renders us, His children. This makes Him the best place for us to turn for guidance and direction regarding our choices of what to do, now, next and so on down our list.

Once again, as in times and years past when you and I admittedly have been tempted to virtually explode with springtime ideas, perhaps we might pause to glance God-ward and whisper:

Lord, please oversee my endeavors. Help me work and produce results, both indoors and outdoors. Especially take the lead in keeping me focused on the spiritual commitments of time spent with You. Time spent in reading and studying Your Word. Time spent in prayer and witnessing about You and Your will. Time spent in redeeming the time for You and Your priorities. In the Name of Jesus. Amen.   ☐

Divine lessons need repeating
March 31, 2001

One day this week, I encountered a challenge. (Chances are as you read on, you'll soon echo, "Been there!") As daylight dawns, everywhere I turn there is work to do; and work not to do. The hardest part is differentiating between the two. I want to do it all. I know I can't. But that doesn't stop me from trying to figure out: How *can* I do it all!

The work I label "to do" is work that must be done now, today. The work "not to do" is work that must be done also. It needs done as soon as the must-do work is done.

All of it is overwhelming because all of it has been put-off too long. The bottom-line reason: I'm always behind where I think I should be in terms of accomplishing what I think I'm supposed to accomplish.

Yes, I'm somewhat of a procrastinator. But I am more of an over-estimator. If something needs done today that *can* wait until tomorrow, I'll wait. Then comes tomorrow and I figure I can do everything I could have done earlier along with everything that must be done today. So I push myself.

The harder I push myself, the more I add to my expectations. Like the morning in question when I tell myself, *If you can shake 14 throw rugs and stuff half of them in the washing machine in less than 30 minutes (which is what I did), you can certainly shake the second dozen or so. By the end of the day you can have them ALL washed and dried.*

The only problem is, since we all know you can't put clean rugs back down on dirty floors, I immediately assume I will find a way to vacuum and/or mop every floor in the house. The second problem is, I know from past experience that it takes more than a day to vacuum and mop our entire house. But little old me thinks I can do it in one day.

Suddenly, I remember: This is the very thing I cautioned against in the preceding column!

"Spring is here!" I wrote in "Springtime is a call for wisdom." Along with it comes a temptation "to go a little crazy" and "not know when to quit," I said. Talk about eating your own words. I even quoted an all-too-appropriate Scripture:

"See then that ye walk circumspectly, not as fools, but as wise, redeeming the time, because the days are evil. Wherefore be ye not unwise, but understanding what the will of the Lord is" (Ephesians 5:15-17, KJV).

The will of the Lord. What *is* His will regarding the tasks you and I choose to do and the tasks we choose not to do? When I wrote what I did earlier, I didn't expect that I would find myself back at square one this quickly. But none of us ever has it down pat. We must return continually to the Lord for wisdom and direction. Daily we must seek His will for the time allotted to us.

In my case, regarding the throw rugs, I decided to settle for stopping with the first batch. I knew I could wash them in one day and mop one floor, but no way was I going to try to do another dozen and wiz through the whole house. God was showing me moderation and common sense. He was showing me faithfulness to other tasks.

I looked around as I looked within. There were dishes to do. Mail to sort. Phone calls and appointments to make. Most importantly, there was a deadline to meet for "Divine lessons need repeating," the piece before you. If I had followed through on going plum crazy over rugs and floors, how could I walk circumspectly to my computer and write, again, about being wise and redeeming the time?

If there is a lesson in this for me, hopefully there is one here for you, too. Each of us can expect to relearn what we think we've already learned. We all need the Lord's help in differentiating between what we can do and what we can't. Therein is our need for wisdom and understanding of what the will of the Lord is for each of us, this day and every day.

Seeking His will is a never-ending prayer. *Amen.*   □

'God's Word is like a key'

October 19, 1985

One morning last month I was out looking for insects for my daughter's biology collection. (Family and friends were permitted to help with the assignment.)

After walking more than a mile without seeing any "bugs" that we didn't already have, I went back home to discover that I had accidentally locked myself out of the house. Trying all the doors and checking all the windows confirmed there was no way to get in.

It was 10:30 in the morning. Did this mean I was going to remain locked out until my husband came home at 5:15? Hopefully not. Maybe one of the girls had taken one of our spare keys to school with her. Returning from a walk to the high school, which is only a couple of blocks away, I had the key I needed to get back into our house.

As I went in and got on with my day, I thought how this day could have been ruined if neither April nor Lori would have had a key for me to use. If I would have been locked out all day, everything would have gone differently than I had originally planned. I would have been prevented from doing all the things I had wanted to do. I would have missed out on the satisfaction of accomplishing my goals for the day.

Sitting down to read the Bible, I reflected on how God's Word is like a key. When we prayerfully read it, it can open the door to power and wisdom. There is no limit to all the Lord might want to reveal to us through His Word.

However, if we neglect the Bible, we might find ourselves locked out of the knowledge of whatever it is that God wants us to do today. We might miss out on the peace and joy that come from receiving guidance and direction from God.

How can we prevent this from happening to us?

Well, just as we usually make sure we have our keys to get us into our homes, we are wise in being certain we have God's Word in our hearts. One way to do this is to read our Bibles before the day is too far spent. Doing so gives us access to one of the keys that opens the door for hearing what God has to say to us.

Jesus' promise of this truth echoes down through the ages: "Ask, and it shall be given to you; seek, and ye shall find; knock, and it shall be opened unto you" (Matthew 7:7, KJV).

☐

God knows about half-eaten bananas

October 24, 1992

If I had my choice, I'd rather waste time than food. That's why I hate it when someone leaves a half-eaten cookie or sandwich on the kitchen counter and the abandoned food has to be thrown out because no one will claim it.

This happened at our house on August 3 of this year. The reason I know the date is because I wrote it down. The reason I wrote it down was because God taught me a lesson through a half-eaten banana.

There were only four of us in the house and each one of the four declared, "I was not the one who ate half of the banana and left the other half to turn brown in the folded-back banana peel!"

Ordinarily, I would have trimmed off the brown parts and cut up the remainder of the banana in a bowl of cereal. But since two of the four of us were not feeling well, the only sensible thing to do was throw the banana in the wastebasket.

As I did, I imagined God asking me, "How do you suppose I feel when you waste *My Food* by not feeding on My Word each day?"

At first I tried to "convince" Him that I would never do that. That was about as bright as hoarding a box full of burnt-out light bulbs.

The Lord knows better, and so did I. I simply couldn't deny there are plenty of times when I waste opportunity after opportunity to fill myself with fresh wisdom and insights because I don't take time to savor His Word.

There are plenty of times when I only grab a bite of God's Word and "eat" it on the run. For instance, take today, the day I'm writing this. It is now 9:20 in the evening and I haven't yet picked up my Bible and read until I was full.

Oh, I glanced at a verse here and there, but I didn't really "taste" any of them. None of those bite-size glances were enough to stick to my spiritual ribs.

I guess God might say I was throwing out a half-eaten chance to be a stronger Christian, to be closer to understanding His will, to be nourished by something He labored to provide.

Oops...did I just say *something He labored to provide?* That includes time, doesn't it? And at the beginning of this column I said, "I'd rather waste time than food."

H-m-m, looks like I'm guilty of throwing out more than a bunch of half-eaten anything.

Lord, help me to discern what is a waste of time, talents, food or anything else You give me. And help me to make wise choices when it comes to balancing my work with worthwhile relaxation; balancing the use of my talents with spending the right amount of time with people who love me; balancing all kinds of nourishment You provide with the proper amounts of intake and sharing with others. In other words, help me not to waste opportunities to give, receive, partake, share, enjoy and be joyful. In Jesus' Name. Amen. ☐

CHAPTER NINETEEN

Witness

Time to consider your last words

September 15, 2001

Rarely do I write a column in advance of my weekly deadline. The one written and dated for today is an exception. Because of a heavy upcoming schedule, I wrote five advance columns last week. Naturally, there was no hint, then, of what would transpire this week in America. On Tuesday evening (September 11, 2001), countless numbers of people gathered around our country in churches to pray for our nation and the thousands of lives ripped apart by terrorism. I sat among more than 100 people at such a service in Town Hill United Methodist Church. After offering an opening prayer, the leaders of the service invited all in attendance to stand and sing "Stand Up, Stand Up for Jesus." Although I've sung this hymn all my life with conviction and commitment, this time I was chilled to the bone. You'll see why as you read the following column, written one week before terror struck our land.

No one likes to dwell on morbid thoughts. They can be harder to swallow than lumpy oatmeal. But sometimes it takes a stick-to-your-ribs experience to grab one's attention. That's why, for starters, I'll share a personal encounter with some parting words. Then you'll hear another story that more than meets the criteria for standing the test of time.

It was an innocent chance meeting my husband and I experienced a few weeks ago when we bumped into a longtime friend at the Lycoming Mall. After chatting for a while, the three of us went our separate ways. The last thing I spoke to our friend was, "Have a good day [and his name]."

Within minutes I swallowed hard. *What if*, the thought in my head was almost an audible voice, *the words you just said were the last words you ever spoke?*

It did more than make me think. It prompted me to realize, anew, none of us ever knows when we will draw our last breath. Will we die with hurting words or healing words on our lips? Will we die living for Christ or following the world? Consider the story of a dying preacher who at only 29 years of age spoke a final message that still resounds in church hymnals 143 years after the reverend's passing.

The preacher was Dudley Atkins Tyng. He and his father, the Rev. Stephen H. Tyng, shared the reputation of being "bold, fearless and uncompromising," states an account in *Living Stories of Famous Hymns* by Ernest K. Emurian (Copyright 1955, Baker Book House Company).

The younger Tyng, on Tuesday, March 30, 1858, preached a noonday lecture sponsored by the Philadelphia Y.M.C.A. at Jayne's Hall (then located at 621 Chestnut Street), according to *Living Stories*. Out of 5,000 men gathered for that meeting, more than 1,000 of them were converted to Christianity on that very day when they responded to Dudley Tyng's invitation to accept the Lord Jesus Christ as their Savior.

Tyng's message that day was reportedly cited as "one of the most successful of the times." The *Living Stories* account says "the entire city was being aroused; a religious awakening was gaining force." One day short of three weeks later, Tyng died. The cause of his death was the result of a farming accident on Tuesday, April 13, 1858. Tyng and his family lived on a farm outside Philadelphia, and on that fateful Tuesday, Dudley was watching some workers operate a corn thrasher in the barn. Raising his arm to pet one of the mules powering the machine, Dudley's sleeve got caught in the cogs, severely lacerating his right arm. Four days later his arm had to be amputated close to the shoulder and two days after that "the shock to his system proved fatal."

As Dudley lay dying on Monday, April 19, according to a newspaper story at the time, he took his elderly father's hand, beseeching him to "Stand up for Jesus, Father. Stand up for Jesus and tell my brethren of the ministry, wherever you meet them, to stand up for Jesus." These were his last words.

After hearing of the drama surrounding the death of Dudley Tyng, one of his friends, the Rev. George Duffield, Jr., then pastor of Temple Presbyterian Church in Philadelphia, composed a six-stanza poem inspired by Dudley's dying comment. The poem begins:

"Stand up, stand up for Jesus, Ye soldiers of the cross; Lift high His royal banner, It must not suffer loss. From victory unto victory, His army shall He lead, Till every foe is vanquished, And Christ is Lord indeed" (as quoted in *Living Stories*).

Later the editor of a hymnal paired the words of the poem with a tune created by George Webb, a tune originally composed to accompany a show song on a ship cruising somewhere in the mid-Atlantic.

Stand up, stand up for Jesus! A powerful witness to proclaim when considering one's last words, wouldn't you say?

☐

Simply stated Gospel:
'Jesus Loves Me'

August 4, 2001

An island, a summer home, two sisters and financial struggles each played a part in giving the world "Jesus Loves Me." The story is one more example of how the Lord, time and again throughout history, uses the ordinary to accomplish the miraculous.

Each month in the mail I receive *Songtime* newsletter published through the ministry of Dr. John DeBrine from Hyannis, Massachusetts. My favorite part of the newsletter is a regular feature called "A Hymnstory" by columnist and hymn researcher Bill Dagle. A mechanic by trade, Bill Dagle has been interested for many years in the background and origins of hymns. For the August newsletter he writes about what he calls "the hymn history of all hymn histories." It's the story of "Jesus loves me, this I know, for the Bible tells me so. Little ones to Him belong; they are weak, but He is strong."

The setting is the lower Hudson River Valley of New York State. There, on Constitution Island across from the U.S. Military Academy at West Point, Henry Warner, a successful New York City lawyer, and his family, including daughters Susan and Anna, vacationed each summer in the early to mid-1830s.

In 1837, however, Henry Warner faced financial reversals and had no choice but to "move the family to the island for year-round residency," writes Dagle. Henry's own brother, Thomas, who was chaplain at West Point, was the one who had encouraged Henry to buy the island in the first place as a summer home. Once it became the family's permanent residence, Susan and Anna, who were both highly educated began writing to help supplement the family's meager income. In time their books grew so popular that one of them gained a rank second only to *Uncle Tom's Cabin*.

Even so, the novels written by the Warner sisters did not imprint the world across the centuries with the same intensity as Anna Bartlett Warner's song "Jesus Loves Me." When Anna first penned the words, they were the words to a poem she created as part of a story in a novel written primarily by her sister. The story involves the fictional character of a little boy named Johnny Fox who is dying. A man by the name of Mr. Linden comes to console Johnny with a poem. You guessed it, the poem is "Jesus Loves Me."

Once the novel was published, the poem was discovered in the real world by musician and composer William Bradbury. In his hands "Jesus Loves Me" became a melody of hope, joy and love sung by all ages around the world in dozens of languages.

What this story does for me, and hopefully for you too, is remind us not to agonize quite so much over what the Lord is doing when He seemingly permits misfortune and troubles to come our way. Although it's unlikely you and I will ever produce anything that parallels "Jesus Loves Me," we *will*, nonetheless, produce whatever the Lord wants to create through us, if we but ask Him to use us in His way, in His time.

In the case of Anna and Susan Warner, they never married but continued writing after their widowed father's death and spent their Sunday afternoons teaching Bible classes and Sunday school for the young cadets at West Point. Bill Dagle's column in *Songtime* along with other information found through Internet resources, confirms this fact: The Warner sisters lived in an area pretty much secluded from the rest of the world, yet they served the world simply and faithfully.

Anna's hymn written in 1860 could not have touched the world any more profoundly than it did, and yet it remains one of the most simply stated interpretations of the Gospel known to our world today. Mark 10:16 tells us in the Bible: "And He [Jesus] took the children in His arms, put His hands on them, and blessed them" (NIV, brackets added).

Anna Bartlett Warner simply restated this truth for all of God's children: "Jesus loves me, this I know."   ☐

We have no 'fragrance' of our own
August 3, 1985

Several years ago I read about a plant that, by its very nature, had no fragrance of its own. However, during its stay in the greenhouse, this non-fragrant plant lived near a heliotrope plant. The heliotrope is noted for its fragrant clusters of flowers. During the time the odorless plant was beside the heliotrope, it absorbed the fragrance of the heliotrope.

One day the plant that now smelled like the heliotrope left the greenhouse to be delivered to a lady in her home. She was pleased with its lovely fragrance. But as time went on, the plant began to emit less and less of the sweet perfume until it gradually lost all fragrance and returned to its natural state.

The plant was once again odorless.

As Christians, you and I are like that non-fragrant plant. The effectiveness of our lives is nonexistent unless we keep ourselves near to the Source of fragrance and beauty — unless we spend time in the presence of the One who is "the way, the truth, and the life" (John 14:6, KJV).

An example of this is found in the Bible in Acts 4. Here Peter and John are being questioned by the religious leaders as to where they got the power to heal the man who had been lame since birth. Peter and John respond with boldness that this man has been healed by the Name of Jesus.

"Now as they [the council of religious leaders] observed the confidence of Peter and John, and understood that they were uneducated and untrained men, they were marveling, and began to recognize them as having been with Jesus" (v. 13, NASB, brackets added).

Peter and John had no "fragrance" of their own. But it was evident to those present: they had been with Jesus Christ. They were strong, effective and bold because they had been near Him. They had absorbed His power like the odorless plant in the greenhouse had absorbed the fragrance of the heliotrope.

How about you and me? Do we live close enough to Jesus that we have absorbed the fragrance of His presence? Or have we lost that sweet perfume because we have been separated from Him too long?

Whatever our state or condition, we can do something about it. We can resolve to stay by Our Lord's side until it's obvious that we have been with Him.   □

Bible goes from wall to child's heart

January 11, 1992

He will keep in perfect peace all those who trust in Him, whose thoughts turn often to the Lord! (Isaiah 26:3, TLB).

We, meaning my husband, daughters and I, tried to memorize it while we brushed our teeth. We glanced at it several times when we combed our hair. We couldn't avoid it each time we washed and dried our hands.

"It" was a hand-printed sign about the size of a three-by-five index card — often it *was* an index card — taped to the downstairs bathroom mirror.

On the card was a Bible verse we thought was a good one to focus on at the start of the day, or late at night before going to bed or any time throughout the day when we stopped off in the bathroom.

The card and the verse changed as often as we felt like changing them. Sometimes that meant weekly, monthly or only after the sign in place was water-spotted beyond readability.

Copying Bible verses on cards or small pieces of paper and displaying them in the bathroom, on the kitchen windowsill or on the refrigerator door was a substitute for what we had originally planned.

For a number of years we had longed to build a log house. We even traveled to Vermont one fall to select the type of logs we wanted and to design the exact style and layout of the home we "just knew" we were going to live in.

It's hard to believe that our desire for the log house spanned two decades and never became a reality. But we're glad we didn't wait for a "dream to come true" before doing things that really mattered to us. However small and insignificant it may seem, one of those "things that mattered" was the displaying of Bible verses on the "walls" of our home.

It all started back in the mid-1970s when we read one of the passages of Scripture in Deuteronomy where Moses is telling the people of Israel how important it is for them to obey The Commandments given by God:

"O Israel, listen: Jehovah is our God, Jehovah alone. You must love Him with all your heart, soul, and might. And you must think constantly about these commandments I am giving you today.

"You must teach them to your children and talk about them when you are at home or out for a walk; at bedtime and the first thing in the morning.

"Tie them on your finger, wear them on your forehead, and write them on the doorposts of your house!" (Deuteronomy 6:4-9, TLB).

Write them on the doorposts of your house!

After reading that, my husband and I decided if ever we built our log house we would literally carve, not only The Commandments, but also many other Scripture verses from the Bible into the log walls and posts of our home.

Seeing as how the log house for us was never anything more than a dream, it's a good thing we didn't wait to start writing God's Word on the walls of our home.

A few weeks ago our 21-year-old daughter Lori told us how much those Bible-verse signs meant to her as she was growing up. The impact she described let us know that, indeed, our dream of living in a log house was nothing compared to the benefits of providing a way for God's Word to be written in a child's heart.

That is certainly a dream come true.   ☐

What controls the world around and within each of us today?

September 7, 1991

Do you ever let the weather or the calendar or the clock dictate how you ought to feel?

Probably most of us, at one time or another, have had the blahs because the weather was damp and gray, or we got depressed three months before winter ever arrived just thinking about the long, cold, dreary, months ahead. And how many of us get ticked off because the clock is ticking too fast or too slow to suit our lifestyle or our deadlines?

It's normal to react to the world around us, but should we or should we not let the world around us control the world within us?

If the stability of the world within us depends on the weather or the season or the time of day, what's going to happen when the wind and the rain and the storms and the interruptions come?

Jesus said (in Matthew 7:24-27) we should build upon the rock and not upon the sand. I think that means not only building our homes on a solid foundation, but also our lives: our spiritual lives, our minds, our emotions, our attitudes, our expectations, our hopes, our dreams.

That solid foundation is Jesus Christ Himself. Often we need reminded that He is what we need when we start to waver like the wind because our perspective gets a little warped.

A few weeks ago, I pulled into a parking space at work, feeling sluggish from the humidity, drained from working long hours the day before and wishing I had the energy of an earlier season of my life.

Then I spotted something: one word, one name, hanging from the rear-view mirror in the car parked on my left.

The word, the name, was "JESUS."

It was only a needlepoint-type sign made of white and brown yarn, but it perked me right up.

The Name of Jesus on my lips and in my heart put a smile on my face. I forgot about the weather, the day, the time, the deadline ahead of me and I remembered. I remembered that Jesus is all I need to get me through any day, any season, any task, because He is my rock, my foundation.

Is He yours?

If not, He can be. Simply ask Him to become Lord of your life and let Him take control of the world within you.   □

Sharing faith at a yard sale?

September 28, 1991

If you've ever wondered how many things in and around your house came from yard sales, garage sales or flea markets, count them. That's what I did the other day. Not only did I count everything in every room, I also wrote them down:

"Double gooseneck lamp on desk in my office; two table lamps in Jim's office; steamer trunk in dining room as room divider; two strawberry crates in living room as coffee table and end table; upholstered chair in Lori's room; rocking chair in April's room; set of 12 matching glasses in kitchen...."

My list filled three pages.

I itemized everything I could see throughout the house that we had found over the years at bargain prices. All were things that were passed on because someone else didn't want or need them anymore and put them out for sale for a quarter, two dollars or otherwise a fraction of what the price would be for a new one of this or that.

The items I listed totaled 72. And that only included things visible in and about our house and yard without opening drawers, cupboards or closets. If I would have listed sweaters, jackets, pots and pans, books and dishes and everything else behind closed doors and in drawers, you would think I was trying to inventory the world's biggest indoor yard sale clearance sale.

But inventory is not my intent. I wrote things down to illustrate how people pass things on to other people — things that continue to be useful even after the original owners have no more use for these things. Even so, such an illustration is secondary to the real intent.

My primary motivation for all of this is to pose a question: *Do we pass on our Christian faith to others and see it bear fruit in someone else's life as it has in our own?*

Unlike yard sale items that are only passed on when they have outgrown their usefulness, we can witness faith being passed on through talking about faith, through sharing faith, through experiencing a living, growing faith in Jesus Christ.

If I can buy an object from you at your garage sale and have it work in my life for perhaps many years, why can't I "sell" someone on the idea of trying to put his or her faith in Jesus Christ.

It seems to me, that much like roaming around at yard sales looking for things we can use over and over, we can be encouraged to examine our faith and see how much of it we've shared with someone else lately.

Maybe the next flea market you or I attend would be the perfect place to start. Helping another person discover a workable faith in Jesus Christ could be the most valuable heirloom that person will ever find.   □

Holding on to 'the vision' often requires teamwork, and more

July 13, 1991

W hen God speaks, people listen. Or do we?

God may not be an E.F. Hutton, but He does have valuable things to say. Things that can keep us on track and spare us a lot of frustration and discouragement, even when we are about to be overwhelmed. Often He says them through earthly mouthpieces — well-known ones, as well as those quietly serving right around us.

Sometimes God speaks so softly we can miss His words if we aren't "looking" for them. Other times, because God surely feels our deepest agonies and sees our hidden burdens, He puts His reassuring messages directly in front of us as though these messages are already circled in red.

Such was the case in my own life this week as I performed my duties as religion editor of the *Press Enterprise* [a position I held from March 1988 to December 1993]. Wednesday evening, while sorting the mail, I opened a letter from a Berwick pastor announcing upcoming events at his church.

Opening piles of mail is nothing unusual; I do it every week. Press releases come in from local pastors, church secretaries, publicity volunteers and others who provide the newspaper with the bulk of local church news.

But, as you may already know, God doesn't always wait until Sunday morning to "preach" a sermon. This time, however, God didn't actually hit me with a sermon. He gently "touched" me at my point of need with a quote written by the above-mentioned pastor, Jim Winder, of Cornerstone Bible Church.

Pastor Winder had enclosed a church newsletter with the announcements he sent us at the newspaper office. The newsletter began with a greeting to his congregation written by Pastor Winder himself. It was through this greeting that the Lord "spoke" to me. I quote Jim Winder:

"While visiting in Florida in June, I spoke with a missionary who told me, 'Don't lose your vision.' Proverbs 29:18 tells us that without a vision we perish. We at Cornerstone Bible Church have a vision to reach the people in Berwick and the surrounding areas. That vision is to lead the lost to Christ. This folks, is our calling as Christians."

Only God knew how much I needed to hear these words. Only He knew what was going on behind the scenes in my personal life.

Clearly, God spoke to me right there under the fluorescent light in my cubicle in the newsroom. God touched the part of me that was tired. The part of me that wanted to go home and sleep. The part of me that was down and discouraged. The part of me that was engulfed by a swell of weariness plunging me toward the verge of "losing the vision."

Don't lose your vision. It was as though God reached down, lifted me up and placed me on a solid rock. I knew I wasn't carrying the load alone.

Do you ever feel like you're losing *your* vision? Have you ever spelled out your vision? If it includes serving the Lord, are you committed to serving Him only when things go well? Only when you're full of energy? Only when you have the necessary resources? Only when you feel like it? Only when people are responding?

Don't lose your vision means, under any and all circumstances, you must keep holding on. You are part of the team.

Lord, help us define our vision, just as clearly as Jim Winder did. Continue to reassure us that You will help us keep sight of the vision, especially at those times when we so need to hear You and know that You are there. That You are here. Thank You for speaking to us through others. Put us in positions where You can speak to others through us. In Jesus' Name. Amen.   □

CHAPTER TWENTY

Work

Preparation is important work

June 2, 2001

Memorial Day Monday dawned with my wanting to do only one thing: get outside to plant pepper plants, tomatoes and herbs. The day didn't go as I planned.

All morning long there was preparation for one thing after another. First, I helped my husband Jim prepare for *his* project of the day: cutting a hole in the wall to access shower pipes just in case there was ever a leak. Together we stripped the bathroom of all pictures, curtains and other accessories. Because I'm terribly allergic to drywall dust, this would aid in clean up later.

Then, as Jim began working on his hole-in-the-wall downstairs, I began another phase of necessary preparations up in the kitchen. Washing, chopping and assembling ingredients for a wild rice stir-fry and tossed salads, I took time to prepare food so we would have nourishment throughout the day and strength to accomplishment our goals.

Before I knew it, it was nearly noon and I still hadn't started my outside work. I was grumbling to myself that I was sick of preparing to get to work when all I wanted to do was get to work! I did take consolation in the fact that I had prepared plenty of food for the next couple of days and that Jim was essentially done with his project (he was very careful to vacuum up all the dust and build a "door" to cover the hole). Even so, I was frustrated.

Outside at last, ready to start gardening, there was yet more preparation. All my tools, buckets and plants had to be carried from under the deck on the lower side of our house to the upper side where the gardens are. Three wheelbarrows full of topsoil had to be screened and mixed with peat and "black gold" from the compost bin. Sod had to be dug up and hauled out of the way to prepare a new bed for my vegetables. Then the garden bed needed to be lined with thick layers of water-soaked newspapers before the soil mixture could be shoveled onto the bed and raked smooth.

Preparation was taking so much time, it was becoming my whole day. It was 3:30 p.m. before I actually started to do the one thing I wanted to do: plant.

Down on my knees in the planting position, then I remembered. I remembered something Jim had read to me a few weeks earlier from *God Meant It for Good* (Copyright 1986, Morning Star Publications), a book he was reading at the time. R.T. Kendall, the author, wrote: "Most of us...don't wish for further preparation. [And yet, you have to] admire the statement of the great C.H. Spurgeon who said that if he had twenty-five years left to live, he would spend twenty of them in preparation" (brackets added).

Preparation is important work. Without proper preparation drywall dust will descend on bathroom towels, curtains, pictures and baskets of silk flowers. Without proper washing and handling of fresh organic ingredients, stir-fry vegetables and tossed salads might harbor e-coli bacteria. Without correctly preparing a garden bed, weeds and drought might eventually take over. Yes, preparation is often as significant as the final product. Recalling Spurgeon's theory helped relieve me of some of the tension from my seemingly delayed start.

Spurgeon's theory also brings to mind another spiritual giant's words. Actually this giant is Jesus, the King Himself.

He is the reason we prepare our hearts, hopefully, each day for His Spirit to speak to us and lead us. It was He who said: "In My Father's house are many mansions: if it were not so, I would have told you. I go to prepare a place for you. And if I go and prepare a place for you, I will come again, and receive you unto Myself; that where I am, there ye may be also" (John 14:2-3, KJV).

Preparation is what Jesus is doing right now. He is preparing a place for each of us. If we know Him and have accepted Him as our Savior, someday He will come for us and we will experience what He has prepared. Because He is involved in eternal preparations, who are we to think that we, too, should not be asked to practice a lifestyle of preparation readiness.

Suddenly, it seems obvious that you and I should view preparation as the bigger part of our life's agenda. The question is: What should we spend the greater part of our life preparing to do? We already know Who can shed light on this concern.

Dear Lord, please show us that lifelong preparation is not only required, it's also quite possibly the most important thing we'll ever do. Prepare us, then, now and evermore, to see the joy in preparation for all that You have planned. In Jesus' Name. Amen.   □

Remaining firm and steadfast

April 28, 2001

Therefore, my beloved brethren, be ye steadfast, unmovable, always abounding in the work of the Lord, forasmuch as ye know that your labor is not in vain in the Lord (1 Corinthians 15:58, KJV).

Circumstances often dictate actions, especially when the circumstance is the Holy Spirit of God moving in one's heart, commanding a response. This is a divine principle I did not set out to experience Tuesday morning when everything I tried to do snowballed.

The day dawned quite warm inside the house. No sooner had I started clearing off the kitchen counters and loading the dishwasher than I had to stop and open windows in every room. I even slid the patio door wide open in our kitchen/dining room. The air was refreshing until, all of a sudden, the wind began blowing hard and steady, scattering red petals and flowers everywhere. My geraniums and begonias! The lipstick red blooms were thriving on the plants I had brought indoors last fall. Now the flowers (thankfully blooms and petals only, not the pots and plants) were all over the vinyl floor in the kitchen and the oatmeal-color carpeting in the living room.

As you may already know, and now I do, too, you can't step on lipstick red petals without leaving a stain on both the floor and your shoe. The only way to pick up the flowers is one at a time (which in my case would have taken forever) or with the hose end of the vacuum cleaner. You can't use the power attachment because the flowers stain the brushes underneath, spreading the lipstick color where it isn't wanted.

Something else unwanted on this particular morning were more dead lady bugs. We thought we had vacuumed up all of them in the preceding weeks, but, with the wind blowing so hard, lady bugs were released from window tracks and corners only to mix themselves with my scattered red blooms.

Circumstances were certainly dictating my actions. But was the Holy Spirit involved? That remained to be seen.

Closing windows and the sliding door to slow down the scattering of petals and lady bugs, I forgot one high window above our TV. *Oh, well,* I thought when I noticed it from across the room, *that's OK. It's high enough that it won't affect what's already on the floor. Besides, I need air.*

All set to embark on my unplanned major vacuuming campaign, I realized this was the perfect opportunity to cut clippings from my begonias and put them in water. I knew from last year's successes that I could expect these clippings to take root and be ready to plant in our numerous flower beds and outdoor pots in a month or so. Cutting the clippings was a project I had intended to do before this, but now that circumstances were dictating, I couldn't justify putting it off any longer. It was going to make a mess, but, at this point that posed *no problem.*

Naturally, the dirty dishes were put on-hold through all of this. The counters were still piled high with extra dishes, juice glasses, casseroles, baking dishes, mixing bowls, Tupperware and sundry other cooking "heirlooms." The "piled high" extras were things of my mother's that I wanted to find places for in our kitchen. I had set aside this particular morning to merge my mother's kitchen things with my own. Of course, the other duties were now more pressing.

Assuming I couldn't have had a bigger mess, once again, I was proven wrong, this time by the wind blowing in the high window. It blew so hard that the curtain was now suddenly hanging by a thread. Not literally, but it *was* hanging from only one end of the now bent, drooping rod. The other end of the rod was blown clear off the bracket and a nail was missing from the dangling bracket. Even as I write, the nail is still missing. Did it fall inside the TV below or will we find it some night when, barefooted, we march off to bed?

Dead lady bugs, scattered red flowers, dozens of sticky clippings, piled-high kitchen counters and dangling, dusty curtains seemed like an unlikely place for the moving of the Holy Spirit. But, when the wind blows, where *does* it originate? The more I thought about it later on, the more convinced I became that the chain of events blowing my way earlier was not a coincidence. I honestly believe the Lord permits unpredicted circumstances to enter into our lives. How we act, or react, is a teaching session we might not have signed up for, but from which we, nevertheless, can learn and grow.

What did I learn and how did I grow from this experience? I learned that being steadfast and unmovable, even in the face of a strong wind, can require a lot of patience and hard work. When the unexpected threatens to blow us off course, which happens in *every* life, we can either struggle alone or we can acknowledge our need of the Lord to keep us abounding in His work, thus enabling us to know — that's right, *know*— that we are not laboring in vain.

The tricky part, if there is one, is to acknowledge His hand in *all* that comes our way.

That being said, there is yet another parallel here for all of us. If you and I are likely to respond with immediate action and hard work when circumstances require it in the world around us, should we not do likewise when the Holy Spirit of God moves in our life, commanding a willing response? If the work in our physical world warrants a positive, determined, logical approach even amid something as potentially upsetting as an unexpected chain of annoying events, should we not also remain steadfast and unmovable in doing the work of the Lord?

I think the answers are as obvious as the visible results of a strong wind blowing.   □

Using God's tools
October 26, 1985

M y father-in-law died in August following an eight-month battle with a rare, incurable cancer. After his father's death, my husband Jim "inherited" his dad's brown, quilted, cool-weather jacket.

Going through the pockets before putting the jacket in Jim's clothes closet, I found a nail, a screw and a rubber plug. Holding these objects in my hand, I wondered what Jim's dad had been doing when he put those things in his pocket.

As I thought about how much I miss him, I imagined Dick Moore laughing and saying, "Well, Dotty, my work on earth is finally finished. You now hold in your hand some of the tools I left behind. What will you do with them?"

I didn't know how to answer that. I could have thrown them out, I suppose. Or I could have tossed them into one of Jim's boxes of nuts and bolts on our utility shelf. Instead, I put the nail, the screw and the rubber plug into an empty paper clip box on my desk. Every now and then I hold them in my hands. When I do, I recall the bond between my father-in-law and me; I sense that these objects are in my hands for a purpose.

Something similar happens when I pick up the Bible. As I hold God's Word in my hands and try to listen to His "voice" as I read, it's as though God is saying, "Your work on earth will be impossible to finish unless you, My child, use the tools I have given you. You hold My instructions in your hands. What will you do with them?"

When it comes to making good use of what God has given us, you and me, where do we stand? Are we using His words and relying on His power to accomplish His work? When we are finally gone from this earth, will we have completed the work that God intended for us to do?

There's only one way to respond. We must pick up the tools He has given us and get busy.   ☐

CHAPTER TWENTY-ONE

Worry

Stopping the 'worry, worry syndrome'

August 18, 1990

We can't relive yesterday, but we try. We can't live tomorrow until it arrives, but we try. We can't take back or undo the things we've already said and done wrong, but we try.

Two words say it all: We worry.

We worry about everything from how to do our hair to what to wear. We lose sleep wondering how we're ever going to stay awake tomorrow if we don't get any sleep tonight. We worry about getting sick from worrying about all the things that cause us to worry.

So what *does* cause us to worry?

My theory about this is neither scientific nor medical: I think we worry because we can't turn off our minds and our thoughts.

We mentally live over and over what could have happened, but didn't; and what we want to happen, "knowing" it probably won't, all the while fretting that we can't make it happen.

So we rehash and rehearse, rehearse and rehash, until it seems the volume is turned up, full blast, on the TV-like images in our minds; and we can't turn down the sound, because the knob is broken.

Not many of us are like Lee Remley, a friend whose wife tells me, "Lee drops right off to sleep as soon as his head hits the pillow."

But perhaps we can learn something from Lee's technique. According to Lee's wife Carolyn his technique is quite simple. Lee says he just turns his mind off and that's that.

But *how* does he do it? I don't know, but I can tell you this: Ever since Carolyn told me how easy it is for Lee to turn off his thoughts, I often pray along these lines when I need to sleep and not worry:

Dear Lord, help me to pull the plug on thoughts that will only keep me awake and cause me to be tired before tomorrow ever dawns. Help me to drop off to sleep, trusting You are taking care of things I can do nothing about, even while I sleep.

As I write this, it's after midnight and I don't see how I can possibly get everything done on my list, unless I skip sleeping. But at the same time, I know the Lord wants me to rest because that's consistent with the words of Jesus:

"Come to Me, all who are weary and heavy-laden, and I will give you rest" (Matthew 11:28, NASB).

So I'm saying, "Good-night, sleep tight," and I'm turning off my next thought before...zzzzzzzzzzzzzz.

Good morning!

Now, where was I?

Oh, yes. It's a new day. It's not the tomorrow I worried about yesterday. It's today. Another day to say:

Lord, help me to live this day worry-free. Help me to trust You to help me not to worry about anything, but to do what I can, and let You worry about what I can't. Amen.

☐

If headaches were 'gone with the wind'

October 5, 1991

Headaches are much easier to acquire than they are to get rid of — especially tension headaches. Having to think about more than one thing at a time — and who doesn't these days? — can give a person a doozy. I, for one, wish I could be more like Scarlett O'Hara in her oft-quoted declaration, "I'll think of it all tomorrow.... After all, tomorrow is another day."

But so much of the time, thinking about today can't be separated from thinking about tomorrow. And before you know it, the pain is all you can see.

It's no fun, but I've discovered I can force myself to function with a headache of an 85-90 percent pain level. But when the pain gets up around 95 percent, it might as well be 195 percent.

If you've ever had the kind of headaches I'm talking about, you understand what I mean when I speak of the pain level in terms of percents. It's a way of coping by labeling the severity of the pain either to ourselves or to close family and friends around us at the time of the headache.

Headaches. Tension. Worry.

If only the cure was as simple as Scarlett's philosophy. But you know, it was neither Margaret Mitchell nor Scarlett O'Hara that first thought of not worrying about things.

Jesus was the first to propose the concept. He said in Matthew 6:34: "Therefore do not worry about tomorrow, for tomorrow will worry about itself. Each day has enough trouble of its own" (NIV).

Tomorrow will worry about itself?

Since a day is incapable of such a human action or reaction, I interpret what Jesus said this way: It's as absurd for us to worry as it is for a day to worry. "Absurd" as in a laughable impossibility. And if Jesus addressed the idea of worrying with a sense of humor, should we do otherwise?

Then why do we worry? Because we enjoy headaches? Hardly. Because it's so natural for humans? Probably.

Why, then, can't it be just as natural for us to do what Jesus said?

Lord, it all sounds so simple when You tell us what to do and what not to do. But often we are so good at making simple things complicated. Things such as headaches are so unpleasant that we pray You will show us how to get rid of them before they start. Show us how to obey You and how to stop worrying. Show us how to do it today so that today's headaches will no longer ruin our tomorrows. In Your Name. Amen. ☐

SECOND PART

'Joy ... in the Morning' Favorites

Seasonal
&
Holiday Life

To everything there is a season,
A time for every purpose under heaven.
Ecclesiastes 3:1 (NKJV)

CHAPTER TWENTY-TWO

New Year

Using a gift says 'thank you'

December 28, 2002

One of the most treasured gifts I ever received was a box of crayons. Although the crayons were given to me for my forty-sixth birthday in March 1991, I think of them most often around Christmas because that's when our daughter purchased the gift.

The year was 1990. April, who was then 22, was serving as a secretary at a Christian mission school on an island in the Caribbean. She flew home in time for the two of us to do some last-minute Christmas shopping together.

While April and I browsed our way up and down the isles of the former Pharmhouse discount store in Bloomsburg, a familiar scent from childhood drew me to the Crayola display. Unable to resist, I reached for a box and flipped open the lid. Inhaling the aroma of crayons, I was lost for a few moments in the faded pages of memories which grew more vivid the longer I inhaled.

Jolted back to the present by the sound of April's voice in a shouting whisper right over my shoulder, "Mum! Where are you," I smiled.

"Oh, Honey," I replied, "I just love the smell of crayons. I wish I were a kid again...some days."

And that was that. Except that April and I hugged each other tight and pulled tissues out of our pockets before we walked on behind the shopping cart.

Christmas came and went. So did April. She flew back to the Cayman Islands and life went on, here and there.

When my birthday rolled around in March, there was a small package for me at the post office in Benton. It was no secret who had sent it. April's return address was in plain sight. Ripping open the padded envelope, I knew instantly what was inside even before I unwrapped the present. I don't remember which was the most overpowering: the scent of crayons or the emotions welling up in my heart.

Unbeknownst to me that day at Pharmhouse, April had slipped back to the crayon display and had selected a box for her not-totally-grown mother. The only way I knew how to thank April was to draw her a picture with my new crayons. I captioned it by writing: "The best way to say thank you for a gift is to use it."

As each year behind us draws to a close, before us stretches a new year. Three hundred sixty-five days we've never yet seen. Each day of the coming year is a gift from God. The best way for you and me to show Him our appreciation for life is to use it for Him and for His glory. When we do, our days will be filled with the vivid aroma of His presence.

Happy New Year. May we all use it with wisdom and love.

☐

When we see ripples, we know God is near

December 30, 2000

A few years ago I read about a little boy who delighted in dropping pebbles into a pond because when he did, "The water smiles at me," he explained.

The new year ahead of you and me can be likened to the undisturbed water in a pond. The surface is still and calm. Then, one by one, day by day, we begin dropping pebbles. We create ripples. Will the ripples created by our words, our actions and our choices smile back at us, or will they chasten us as in a smile turned upside-down?

An ideal way to end a year and begin another is with a prayer. A prayer of forgiveness for past mistakes, past sins and negligence. A prayer asking the Lord for insight and direction for the road ahead. 2 Timothy 2:7 lets us know: "The Lord will give you insight" (NIV).

What insights do *you* need to keep you going in the new year? Perhaps you, like yours truly, need strength. You need courage. You need redefined purpose. You need a nudge. And you need comforted that you might comfort others around you (as in 2 Corinthians 1:4).

Pebbles and ripples, like successes and failures, begin with an act of throwing something into life. As for those of us who love the Lord, we try to let Him be our coach and oversee our aim.

Whether we are entering into a new year, a new millenium or simply opening our eyes each morning at the crack of dawn, we don't know what will happen in the next instant, let alone know what all will take place in the course of a year. But this much is certain: each thing we do or don't do and each word we say or don't say will leave its mark.

Ripples can go on for miles, days, years, even lifetimes. That's scary. But it's exciting. It's invigorating to think that on any given day, at any unplanned moment, you or I might contribute a little pebble here and there that might cause a stir in someone's heart.

Life is not easy — for anyone. Everyone has doubts and fears to conquer; obstacles to overcome. Everyone climbs personal mountains and everyone experiences valleys. Likewise, everyone needs encouragement. Even the toughest of us has needs.

Perhaps you remember a time when you were alone, afraid and about to lose hope. Maybe you were too frightened and worried to pray, but comforted by knowing others were praying for you. Perhaps you are there now. Perhaps you need to see a ripple. God knows where you are. He knows your need. He knows your heart. He knows what's best. He can be trusted. Put your hand in His and rest.

God's hand tosses pebbles everywhere you look. Oh, I know, you and I don't always see the pebble, but where we see ripples, we know He is near. Sometimes God wants *us* to do the pebble tossing, but sometimes He only wants us to look around for little signs that He cares, that He's listening, that He is smiling in our direction. It's a childish thought, perhaps, but like a reflection in a pool, it might just be worth looking into.

May the Lord bless you this new year. May He guide you into creating worthwhile, long-lasting ripples. And may He also send a few encouraging ones your way.   ☐

CHAPTER TWENTY-THREE

Valentine's Day

A four-word prayer? My, isn't that a 'funny' valentine!

February 13, 1993

Every now and then you run across a concept or a philosophy so profound that its application knows no limits.

A few years ago, one such rare gem was given to me in the form of four words spoken in a casual, albeit spiritually focused conversation with a woman who directs a local evangelism organization.

The woman is Elaine Dymond of Child Evangelism Fellowship of Columbia/Montour Counties. The words she spoke that have affected my life from head to toe are: "Lord, keep me faithful."

As a Valentine's Day greeting, I give you Elaine's words which she says she prays daily in her work of serving the Lord and, along with her prayer, I offer you this challenge:

If you will pray the same prayer — *Lord, keep me faithful* — as you try to do the work before you, you will not be the same person a year from now as you are today.

By that I don't mean to imply you are a bad person, or that you don't do a good job at what you do. Rather, I can tell you from personal experience, asking the Lord to keep you faithful will touch you when your head tells you, "It's no use, give it up, quit trying, you're getting nowhere!"

It will touch you when your shoulders slump into a too-tired-to-go-on posture. It will touch you when your heart and your eyes see nothing but defeat. It will touch you when your gut tells you something must be done but your stomach says, "I can't take anymore!"

It will touch you when you're tired sitting around doing nothing but waiting for the signal to move on or stay put. It will touch you when you're too weak in the knees to try again, but when the Lord tells you to go, the touch will set your feet on fire to march to His music.

Such astounding effects from such a simple prayer could lead some to believe the prayer is a magic formula for achieving success, personally as well as financially. Not so. The prayer is not magic. The words, in and of themselves, contain no power.

Ah, but the God to Whom the prayer is directed...that's a different story. The power to answer such a heartfelt request comes from Him, and from Him only. It's His power that can touch troubled marriages, rebellious children, crippled finances and tough decisions as He responds to the soul crying out, "Lord, keep me faithful!"

It's His power that can lift a life out of the muck and mire of doubting drudgery into a realm of belief that "All things are possible to him that believeth" (Mark 9:23, KJV).

There's not enough space for me to tell you all the times in my own life this prayer to the Lord has been answered with a supply of fresh courage and enthusiasm, but I can tell you this: The Lord knows where each of us is weak and He knows what is needed to keep us faithful to our calling, whether of a professional nature or a personal commitment. The Bible tells us He is ready, willing and able to keep us from falling (Jude 24).

All we have to do is ask, "Lord, keep me faithful."

It might seem like a "funny" valentine, but this prayer can fill us so full of love for what God asks each of us to do, that it soon becomes a joy to pray the prayer for others, too, thus quietly, yet powerfully, passing on the life-changing concept.

(Elaine Dymond, director of Child Evangelism Fellowship of Columbia/ Montour Counties, Inc. from September 1988 to May 1996, is now missionary-at-large for CEF of Eastern Pennsylvania, Inc.)   □

Twelve batches of love

February 9, 1985

This year for St. Valentine's Day, why not give those you love a part of yourself? Why not give your time, your attention, your presence, your rice pudding.

Your rice pudding! Wherever did that thought come from? Oh, yes. How could I forget?

A few months ago, I set out to make a triple batch of rice pudding — the perfect amount for two nice-size dishes: one for my own family and one for our new minister's family who had moved into Benton that day.

While I was breaking the eggs into the mixing bowl, five chattering, giggling teen-age girls (two of them mine) and one of the girls' mothers were welcomed into my kitchen. At that moment I forgot to remind myself that I can't talk and work at the same time.

"OK, everybody, listen up. I'm ready to add the sugar to my recipe. So everybody help me count the cups — 1, 2, 3...6, 7, 7½ ...".

One of the girls interrupted. "Mrs. Moore, that's a lot of sugar. What are you making?"

As I glanced up to answer her, I also glanced at the recipe card in my hand.

"Oh, no! It was supposed to be 7½ cups of *milk* and only 1½ of sugar! Now what'll I do?"

Before it all dissolved into the beaten eggs, I scooped two cups of the sugar off the top of my mistake.

Everyone but I exited the kitchen, the house, the premises.

Five hours, 36 eggs (18 of them borrowed), three pots of rice, a whole box of raisins and 7½ quarts of milk later, there were 12 batches of rice pudding — enough to share with six other households besides our own.

When my husband arrived home from his graduate class at 11 p.m. I greeted him with, "Don't lock the door. I'm leaving."

"Leaving?" he asked as he quickly surveyed what was in the oven, on the table, on the kitchen counter.

"Yeh, Dad," our then-15-year-old offered, "don't you know, Mom has to deliver rice pudding before people go to bed?"

Many of those people still laugh at the words "rice pudding" and some of them even wanted the recipe.

So why don't you get out your own recipe files. Don't forget your calculators and your 15-quart kettles.

See what 12 batches of love you can create.

If I can do it by mistake, you can do it out of love.   ☐

Heart-shaped memory recurs every year about now

February 8, 1992

But now abide faith, hope, love, these three; but the greatest of these is love (1 Corinthians 13:13, NASB).

The other day when my husband and I walked hurriedly past the valentine candy display in Rea & Derrick at the Columbia Mall, I asked him if he was planning to buy me one of the heart-shaped boxes this year.

"One with a little doll dressed in red?" I teased.

He and I both knew what he would say, but he said it anyway — "Definitely not!" — as he cleverly quickened his stride toward the exit. Even though I couldn't see his face because he was a few paces ahead of me, I knew he was smiling, but then, so was I.

It's a question I ask him nearly every year around this time, knowing full well the answer never changes. You see, the first time Jim gave me a heart-shaped box of chocolates in the traditional red satin packaging, it cost him more than he bargained for. That was 18 years ago. Since then he has given me one or two boxes of valentine candy, but not red ones and definitely not with a doll attached.

It all started in February 1974. We had been married nine-and-a-half years and Jim, deciding it was about time he gave me more than a card and a kiss for Valentine's Day, presented me with the now-notorious box with the little doll attached.

Oo-ing and ah-ing over the red velvet and satin dress on the doll, I surprised Jim with, "Oh, Hon! That's exactly the shade of red I'd like in our bedroom!"

"On the walls?" he queried, his tone of voice saying, *I certainly hope not.*

"No, not the walls. A carpet...and drapes...and a bedspread!" I emphatically stressed. "Thank you. Thank you, very much!" I exclaimed as I hugged him, kissed him, and wondered when to start my redecorating scheme.

As Jim helped himself to a cream-filled chocolate out of my box, I was on my way down the hall toward the bedroom with a tape measure in my hand, a chewy chocolate in my mouth and visions of a new room in my head.

The next week, while I was out shopping alone, I "just happened upon" a Washington's Birthday Sale going on at a furniture store in downtown Chambersburg. (We were living outside Shippensburg at the time.)

Seeing carpet remnants featured in the window, I entered the store as soon as I spotted a bright red remnant that, from outside, looked perfect.

Not only was it perfect, within five minutes, it was also ours.

The plush red carpet measured almost exactly the dimensions of our bedroom and, better yet, because of the one-day sale, it was only $80.

I knew Jim would be tickled with the half-price bargain I had found. I also knew he would ask about installation charges and "how much for padding?"

Knowing what his reaction would be, I was ready with all the answers. When he asked one more question, "How is that carpet going to look with our yucky green walls?" I had the answer for that, too.

"We've not had time to paint our bedroom since we moved here [which was three years earlier], but now is as good a time as any. Of course, we have to paint before they install the carpet. I don't want any white paint spatters on our new red carpet ... don't you agree, Hon?" I pleaded with my words, my hug and my eyes.

"I suppose you're right," Jim sighed as he returned my hug.

And so it was. White walls. Red carpet. And yards and yards of red antique-satin drapery material.

I don't remember what happened to prevent my making the drapes and matching bedspread. I got the material out often enough and dreamed and measured, but for some reason I never cut it, so we never saw the completed results.

We enjoyed the wall-to-wall carpeting for a little more than a year, vacuuming it often because we liked the look of it right after it was vacuumed, all plush and smooth with no footprints.

But then, in the summer of 1975, we put the house up for sale and moved to Benton.

Along with the things we moved was the big bolt of red drapery material. Of course, the carpeting had to stay behind, and we commented more than once, "If only we would have had the carpet bound instead of having it installed wall to wall."

But what's done is done. When we got settled into our house in Benton, we painted the master bedroom white, I made pleated, red antique-satin drapes and planned to make the matching bedspread.

We fully expected to someday get another plush red carpet and "my vision" would at last be complete.

Well, the red drapes faded from the sun and eventually fell apart in the wash. We never found another red carpet at the right price. And the material designated for the bedspread was used for other things, although I think there's still a fairly good-size piece of it in one of our closets.

The moral of the story is: Our love has endured. Our love has not faded nor has it fallen apart through some pretty rough times. I guess that's way Jim never seems to tire of my asking him every year about now, "So, when am I going to get another red satin box of valentine candy? One with a little doll dressed in red." □

CHAPTER TWENTY-FOUR

Lent

Seeking the proper attitude
March 7, 1992

*W*ell, *here we are, Lord, at the beginning of the Lenten season. If there's something You want me to do to get ready for Easter, now's the time to tell me. I'm really focused and will continue to be for the next six weeks.*

Of course, You know, Lord, once Easter is here and gone, You can't expect as much from me, so You'd better take advantage of my willingness while You can. I'm giving up a lot of things for You between now and Easter, and I hope You realize how hard it is for me to discipline myself and ....

Before going any further with this disrespectful prayer — albeit hypothetical — allow me to explain: this *isn't* my prayer. However, if it reflects my attitude, I'm in trouble, even if I'm not verbalizing such words. Now, for what's really on my heart:

Dear Lord, I certainly hope my attitude toward serving You, obeying You and loving You has not even a trace of disrespect and arrogance. If it does, even to the slightest degree, please forgive me and remove such a tendency from me as far as the east is from the west.

When I was a child, I thought getting ready for Easter meant getting the spring cleaning done, finding a new Easter dress and Easter bonnet along with getting the Easter baskets out of the attic. I didn't think these things because anyone told me these things, it's just that these things accompanied the season, and I drew childish conclusions.

But these things have passed away and, now, getting ready for Easter is a lifelong process of trying to stay close to My Lord every day, day after day.

Oh, Lord, if only I were successful at my feeble attempts to honor You, to love You, to serve You, to obey You to the fullest of my potential. But I have absolutely no idea how to always be successful in these attempts; and I have even less of an idea as to the extent of my potential.

Thank You for not grading me on the success or failure of my efforts. I know that without Your help I couldn't do anything.

Does this make me sound weak and foolish and vulnerable? You bet it does. Not only do I sound weak, foolish and vulnerable — I am. Without the Lord, without Jesus Christ, without His sacrifice of Himself on the cross, I would be nothing.

Just think of it. Without the events of Christ's death, burial and resurrection, my life, your life, our efforts, our words, our being would count for nothing at all.

If you and I can ever begin to fathom this thought, we may be close to beginning, in a small way, to ever so slightly appreciate the days of preparation leading up to the remembrance of what Our Lord did for us.

Precious Lord, please, with Your help, show me how to begin, anew, remembering, loving, serving and worshiping You. In Jesus' Name. Amen. □

CHAPTER TWENTY-FIVE

Spring

Flowering moments guaranteed
May 18, 1991

W*atching a child awaken is like seeing a flower bloom.*

I remember having that thought many years ago when my now-grown daughters were babies, then little girls, waking up from their afternoon naps. They would begin to move ever so slightly, unfolding their little arms that had been clutching a favorite doll or stuffed toy.

Their little curled-up legs, often scraped and bruised from learning to skate or ride bicycles or simply being too busy to watch where they were going, would stretch straight out, and right before my eyes, their eyes would open — and the nap was over.

Each precious child was off and running to spread sunshine and blossoms throughout the house and around the neighborhood.

True, there was sometimes rain in the form of bad moods and angry temperaments, even squabbles and misbehavior. Sometimes that kind of "rain" lasted all day long, just like an all-day thunderstorm.

But did you ever notice how much prettier and brighter everything is after a rain? The grass is greener. The dust is washed off the sidewalks and cars. The air is clean and fresh.

So it often is in life. Quite simply, there are times when bad days and bad moods, in children and adults, are inevitable. However, as long as the bad is outweighed by the good, flowering moments are practically guaranteed.

The season of spring, with its showers and flowers, is a good time to cherish that thought. ☐

Life: To enjoy or not to enjoy

April 20, 1991

Spring. A time for new growth.

With so much to see and do this time of the year, and not knowing where to begin, I take a drive. Seeing forsythia, daffodils and dandelions blooming, I decide the Lord must surely like the color yellow. It's everywhere.

Suddenly, however, red appears.

There's construction on a bridge, and everyone stops. The sign is red. The cone-shape markers outlining one-lane traffic are red. Red warning flags wave in the wind. Traffic stands still.

When cars and trucks begin moving again, it's not long before another construction tie-up is visible up ahead with more red signs and flags. Ah, but this time, there's a side road to the left. I can avoid further delay by taking a route that's only slightly longer than the one under construction.

So I do just that.

No more obstacles until, less than a mile later, I see three utility trucks at one intersection. Workers are doing something up in the air, but the only thing their presence creates is a slight slowing down of traffic. After nothing more than a little pause,

I'm on the move again.

Spring. A time for new growth. A time to move on.

The thought reminds me that construction is a sign of new growth, too. Just like buds and blossoms and robins and green leaves, construction and reconstruction mean the same thing: newness and change. In other words, a new season.

Construction improvements often create roadblocks. Sometimes there's no way around these roadblocks, giving us no choice but to wait. Other times there are detours that keep us moving.

Life is like that in all seasons.

We can choose to appreciate change and growth, or we can refuse to enjoy anything until everything is perfect and remains unchanged.

If the latter is true, we'll not enjoy anything. Not spring. Not summer. Not fall. Not winter. Not life.   □

CHAPTER TWENTY-SIX

Palm Sunday

Palm Sunday: A good day to pray

April 7, 2001

I pray also that the eyes of your heart may be enlightened in order that you may know the hope to which He [God] has called you (Ephesians 1:18, NIV, brackets added).

Coming upon the above verse in Ephesians the other day, my eyes were reopened to a bit of insight someone pointed out years ago: a lot of Scripture can be viewed as a prayer.

If ever there was a prayer appropriate for all, Ephesians 1:18 is it. It's a prayer to be prayed for ourselves along with the names of others we know and love:

Dear Lord, please open the eyes of my heart so that I might know, anew, daily, the hope of Your calling. Please enlighten the eyes of So-and-So and So-and-So's heart that he, she and they might know, anew, daily, mightily, the hope of Your calling.

Palm Sunday is an excellent time to reflect on the Hope of our calling. Our Hope is Jesus Christ. When we acknowledge Jesus and His triumphal entry into our lives and circumstances, we have something in common with long-ago worshipers in

Jerusalem who carpeted Jesus' pathway with "their cloaks" and "spread branches they had cut in the fields." We share in the opportunity to direct all eyes toward Him just as the crowds did centuries ago when they proclaimed Jesus as "Hosanna in the highest!" (see Mark 11:8-10, NIV).

With our eyes focused on Jesus, it's easier to go down our prayer list and ask the Lord to open our eyes and the eyes of others to a renewed sense of His calling. We need not try to describe in minute detail what we perceive to be the greatest need in each life that comes to mind. Instead, as we name loved ones and friends, even a few "enemies," we are placing each life and each set of circumstances in the Lord's hands. Placing them in His will, trusting Him for His knowledge of what is best for each and for all.

It isn't necessary for you and me to pray for everyone and everything under the sun. We aren't that strong and we aren't that wise. However, in naming a limited number of people whose lives and whose witness concern us, we have a way of saying, *Lord, these are but a few. You know all the rest. We entrust them, also, to You.*

Giving ourselves, and others, over to the Lord, laying our offerings at His feet, sounds simple enough. But often it takes years of heartache before we actually do it. Thank God, He understands and has prepared the way through Jesus Christ for us to come to Him any time, any place, for any reason. Whether it's to entrust ourselves to Him or to pray on the behalf of others for the awakening and renewing He offers, He is always available.

Jesus continues to respond to our individual and collective cries of "Hosanna! Blessed is He who comes in the name of the Lord!"(v.9).

Indeed, Palm Sunday is a prime opportunity for us to pray that the eyes of many hearts will be enlightened.   □

CHAPTER TWENTY-SEVEN

Easter

Seed testifies to rebirth

April 13, 2002

The sound of the "peepers" was faintly in the air, so I thought. I couldn't be certain until I crossed the room to the open window. Cupping my hand around my ear, I aimed it toward the valley. Sure enough, what I thought was the sound of peepers, was.

"Hallelujah!" my heart rejoiced. "Spring truly *is* here!"

Although worth noting, such an observation is just that — an observation. However, when one is speaking of something profound, such as documentation of a biblical concept standing strong when there's no denying the truth, now that's a different story.

Never is such a conviction more solidly grounded than when one realizes, again and again, that Jesus knew what He was talking about when He spoke in parables. Take, for instance, Jesus' mustard-seed story in Matthew 13:31-32:

"The kingdom of heaven is like a mustard seed, which a man took and sowed in his field, which indeed is the least of all the seeds; but when it is grown it is greater than the herbs and becomes a tree, so that the birds of the air come and nest in its branches" (NKJV).

Arguably, one might conclude that the kingdom of heaven isn't very significant if it is no more powerful than a seed. But then you come across a piece of history like what I'm about to share, and it confirms what the Bible affirms: God's Word is Truth, and It will not be mocked.

The recorded story in point is one I came across recently in *Our Daily Bread* devotional booklet circulated around the world by Radio Bible Class Ministries of Grand Rapids, Michigan. The setting, of all places, is a cemetery. A place for nothing more than burying the dead. Or is it?

According to the *Our Daily Bread* entry for Easter Day, March 31, 2002, an out-of-the-ordinary gravestone stands in a cemetery in Hanover, Germany. The gravestone is there because a particular "woman who didn't believe in the resurrection directed in her will that her burial place be made so secure that just in case there was a resurrection it couldn't touch her."

In order to adhere to the woman's wishes, when she died, "huge slabs of granite were fastened together with heavy steel clamps and placed over her grave. Engraved on the marker were these words: 'This burial place must never be opened.'"

As time passed, a tiny seed germinated and sprouted "just beneath the edge of the stone." Eventually the seed "grew into a tree and [as] its trunk got bigger, the heavy [granite] slabs were gradually shifted and the steel clamps were wrenched from their sockets. Those massive pieces of granite could not withstand the dynamic life-force within that small seed," states the author of the account.

Now, of course, those of us who believe in the strength and power of God the Creator, Redeemer and Lord of all, know where the power of any seed originates. Nothing is strong enough to withstand the force, the might, the resurrection glory of the kingdom of God.

No grave, no heart, no soul can, nor ever will, escape the inevitable awakening to the resurrection power of Christ. Each and every one of us will one day be called forth at the sound of

His voice. We will either "come forth...unto the resurrection of life" or "unto the resurrection" of judgment (John 5:28-29).

There will be no second guessing the sound of Christ's return. It will happen! The seeds of heaven's kingdom will leave no room for doubt. What a day that will be!

(*Our Daily Bread* entry quoted above, copyright 2002, Radio Bible Class Ministries.) ☐

CHAPTER TWENTY-EIGHT

Mother's Day

A mother must know when to let go

May 11, 1985

When our daughters were in elementary school, I used to sing them awake every morning. For years I would stand at the bottom of the stairs and cheerfully announce it was a brand new day with original little tunes, like:

"Good morning, good morning, good morning,
It's time to rise and shine.
Good morning, good morning, good morning,
Be glad that you are mine."
or:
"It's time to have a wake up;
Wake up, get out of bed.
It's time to have a wake up;
Wake up, you sleepy head."

It made me feel good to wake them up this way and I always assumed they enjoyed my morning wake-up songs as much as I did. Then one night a few years ago they said to me, "Mom, do us a favor. Please, don't sing us awake anymore. Just tell us to get up."

I was crushed.

The next morning I honored their request. I yelled up the stairs, "Hey, you guys, it's time to get up ... so get up!"

One said, "OK, Mom. I'm up."

The other one said, "Thanks, Mom. Thanks for not singing."

They felt great. They came to breakfast as chipper as ever. But me? I felt terrible every morning for days. I had enjoyed the old routine. Now, I felt mean and grumpy because I wasn't singing to awaken my little girls.

Every morning I yelled, "It's seven o'clock — time to get up!"

No music in my voice. No cheer. Just a plain old, "Get up, girls!"

Then one morning a couple of months later, I woke up thinking, "What bothers me the most — the fact that I'm not singing them awake anymore or the fact that they're not 'little girls' any longer?"

I had to admit it was a lot of both. What could I do about it? After all this time, I finally prayed about it.

An idea occurred that I thought might solve the problem — and it did.

My husband and I bought each of the girls her own digital alarm-clock radio. Now they could wake up without my yelling up the stairs. At the same time, they could feel grown-up and independent by setting their own alarms and selecting their own music (within reason, of course).

It was just a natural ordering of a healthy parent/child relationship — I was letting go to let them grow.   ☐

Mothers: Can we overlook mistakes?

May 11, 1991

While emptying the dishwasher the other day, I discovered the first four-out-of-four "clean" dishes I picked up weren't clean at all. A dinner plate, a glass casserole dish, a saucer and a pan lid were much in need of being run through the dishwasher a second time. However, from that point on, everything else I lifted from the dishwasher's racks was spotlessly clean and shiny.

Just because four of the items had to be washed again, I could have chosen to get upset and perhaps declare the dishwasher "a no good, worthless machine." Quite honestly, it would take a lot more than four dirty dishes for me to discredit my dishwasher. I dislike hand washing dishes very much because it's one of the household chores that literally gives me a pain in the neck, as well as in the back. Crazy as it may sound, I can't stand to stand very long at a sink without getting knots in my neck and back muscles. So, for me, occasionally running a few dishes through the dishwasher a second or even a third time is no big deal.

Wouldn't it be nice if we, as mothers, gave our family members as much room for occasional errors as I willingly give my favorite kitchen appliance? If a dishwasher isn't a failure because a few dishes need redone every now and then, why do we yell and scream at loved-ones simply because they make mistakes?

Even if these mistakes are repeated over and over again, the people making them are worth more than anything else in the whole world.

Yet it happens, all the time.

We get upset when one of the kids spills her milk at nearly every meal.

We get upset when our mate forgets to close the closet door. We get furious when a member of the family repeatedly neglects to put anything back where it belongs.

We get even more upset if someone we love gets upset because we're upset at some of these things.

Whether a family member's mistake is talking too much, being clumsy, being absentminded, even being thoughtless and inconsiderate, we can still find ways to let that person know we don't dislike him or her just because of bad habits.

It's true that sometimes — perhaps often — we have to express disappointment or dissatisfaction with a child's or mate's actions or habits, but let's try to do it in such a way that we aren't calling the person "stupid," "a failure," "a loser" or whatever else comes to mind, when we are in such a state as makes us prone to making a bigger mistake than the one we're addressing at that moment.   ☐

CHAPTER TWENTY-NINE

Memorial Day

Honoring those too precious to forget

May 26, 1990

All through life, there are some things better forgotten:

The day in first grade when a best friend said, "I hate you"; the broken dining room window from playing baseball in the front yard instead of listening to Mom and staying in the back yard; the broken heart from breaking up with our first, true love.

Hopefully, however, there are plenty of other things that are a joy to remember:

The thrill of finding three four-leaf clovers in one day; the wonder of seeing Niagara Falls for the first time; the happy sounds of our children at play.

Ah, yes, remembering. That's what Memorial Day is all about:

Remembering with appreciation all those who died in our nation's wars, sacrificing their tomorrows so that you and I might enjoy our todays.

Remembering with respect and honor the families whose loved ones died while preserving for us the freedom to celebrate freedom.

Remembering our family on a day that has become synonymous with the family in many of our memories.

Remembering to be thankful to and for a God Who has given us a heritage worth remembering and preserving.

And while we're remembering, why not call or write to a living veteran and personally say thank you for what he or she did by serving our country, especially going to war, not only for the U.S., but for us.

Dear Lord, help us forget what needs forgotten and to remember, instead, the people and events too precious to ever forget. Amen.   □

Naming others who've paved the way

May 23, 1992

As much as I love hanging clothes outside to dry, I don't understand how the sun makes white clothes whiter, while at the same time it makes light skin darker. Oh well, there are lots of things I don't understand, but I'm thankful for the few things I know. One thing about which I am absolutely certain is that many people who have lived and died have already paved the way for the rest of us to be who we are and where we are today.

Specifically, there are five people I'd like to remember this Memorial Day, one famous, the rest not-so-famous, but all precious nonetheless:

• Catherine Marshall — I am surely only one among millions who thanks God for Catherine Marshall LeSourd. Except for the Bible, her writings have probably touched my life more deeply than any other one person's written words. My favorite story of Catherine Marshall's is from *A Closer Walk*, and it tells how she learned to keep her eyes on Jesus instead of on her problems. Oh the countless times I have drawn strength from Catherine's struggles.

• Helen Shaffer Heffelfinger — This is one woman you've likely not heard of, but when you get to heaven, you'll want to meet her. She was my aunt (married to my father's brother), and although she lived on this earth only 49 years, she touched a lot of lives and fed a lot of hungry souls. Her silver-white hair was a well-deserved halo (I never thought of her as prematurely gray). Aunt Helen could feed her family of five, and even when called upon to add two, three, four or more unexpected guests, she could still feed them all with the same three-pound pot roast "just cut into smaller pieces." To her, prayer was not work; it was like salt on the potatoes.

• Hazel McNutt — Mrs. McNutt was my first grade teacher at Sherrett Elementary School about 12 miles from Kittanning, Pennsylvania. But she was more than a teacher who taught me to read and write. She volunteered after-school time for child evangelism, welcoming between 10 and 20 of us school children into her home. There she made it easy for us to understand salvation through Jesus Christ and to memorize Bible verses, many of which still spring to my mind at times when I'm too worried, too sick, too frightened or too tired to think.

• Richard Moore — Dick was my father-in-law and a man who didn't like being sick. He didn't very well handle having the flu or a cold or pneumonia. But when he battled a rare, terminal cancer, he dealt with the suffering like a man who didn't realize he was suffering. As a matter of fact, that's exactly how he viewed his final months in 1985. Whenever he learned of others he knew who were also fighting different forms of the disease, he would ask, "Are they suffering much?" and then add, "I hope they don't suffer. I'm glad I've not had to suffer and I don't want to see anyone else suffer."

• Basil Heffelfinger — Last but not least, I'm thankful for

my own father. He's the one who taught me to how to hit the bull's eye in target practice and always told me I had a better aim than he did, even when I nearly blew off his right foot with a double-barreled shotgun blast that luckily only dug a hole in the ground. He never scolded me for forgetting to put the safety on, on that gun. He trusted me to never let it happen again, and it didn't. But I still marvel, even now, 21 years after his death, that somehow he communicated his complete trust in me simply by saying, "Don't tell your mother."

Dear Lord, I can't help but praise You and thank You for countless numbers of people You've put in my life who have taught me valuable lessons that keep on being valuable. The few special people I've mentioned today deserve much more than flowers on their graves. In Jesus' Name. Amen.   □

CHAPTER THIRTY

Graduation &
Commencement

Who might be writing
'the next song'?
June 2, 1990

It's over! It's finished! It has just begun!

Graduation and commencement are used synonymously when referring to the ceremony that marks the completion of a high school, college or trade school education. While these terms imply the end of a certain level of achievement, they don't literally mean "The End." More appropriately they signal "The Beginning."

The beginning of the next step. The beginning of a new adventure. The beginning of new opportunities.

Opportunity.

A person named L.P. Jacks once said, "The pessimist sees the difficulty in every opportunity; the optimist, the opportunity in every difficulty."

Intense drama and inspiring song aren't born out of lives of ease and comfort, but rather out of the heart of one who succeeds despite just the opposite. That's success.

Success.

"Success is to be measured not so much by the position that one has reached in life as by the obstacles which he has overcome while trying to succeed," said Booker T. Washington.

Who knows how many songs of success are yet unsung because they are yet unwritten?

Graduate of this season, YOU might be the one to overcome an obstacle to write the next song that will inspire someone else to keep going when he or she would rather give up.

Years ago, on a day full of difficulties and frustrations, I summarized my feelings by writing in my journal: "If necessity is the mother of invention, adversity is the mother of song."

If you can believe that, you're on your way to accomplishing something that might otherwise go undone. You're on your way to solving problems that might get other people down. You're on your way to making a difference.

The difference you make might be big or small, but unless you try, you'll make no difference at all.

Dear Lord, please be near to all the young people who are setting out to explore a world of possibilities. Make Yourself known to them in such a way that they will seek Your guidance for each day of their lives. Help them to believe and expect that, together, You and they can make a difference. Amen. □

Graduates: Hold on to your dreams

May 30, 1992

Every spring I remember springtime as a child. It was a happy/sad time for me then. I was happy to run and play with my dog Skippy without having to wear a heavy winter coat, but I was sad to be alone — it was just "me and Skip" as I used to tell my mother when she would ask, "Who are you talking to, Dotty?"

As an only child, I was often a lonely little girl. I didn't mind being alone with my dog, my kittens, my dolls or my crayons and coloring books if I could pretend I wasn't alone. So pretend I did.

I pretended Skippy was my friend, my pal. I talked to him, I sang to him, I read books to him, I told stories to him. I did the same with my kittens Snowball and Blacky and their mother Midnight.

And my dolls, they were real. They sometimes acted up and had to sit with their faces in the corner. They spilled their tea and I had to clean it up. They cried when they fell down and got hurt and I comforted them.

Thus went the seasons of my childhood, with spring and summer being my favorites. When I could be outdoors in the warm sun and the country breeze, I could dream bigger dreams than during the cold, lonelier, more confining days of winter and fall.

I guess that's why spring reminds me of victory — the victory of having survived!

Spring also reminds me of unlimited possibilities. Of dreams coming true. Of new dreams to dream.

Yes, it's important to dream and pretend sometimes. Pretending helps us escape reality, and, as long as it's healthy imagining, it helps us cope with reality by bringing us back a little refreshed.

As graduation time draws near, I'd like to say congratulations to all those who have completed one phase of their lives as they prepare to enter the next.

May each of you recognize what you have learned thus far as a foundation upon which to build the rest of your lives. While you are building, pray for wisdom, pray for strength, pray for health, pray for opportunities to serve others—and especially pray for the ability to dream. ☐

CHAPTER THIRTY-ONE

Father's Day

Father's Day sentiments and such
June 15, 2002

Each year come Father's Day I recall that my dad, who was sparing with smiles and laughter, always grinned from ear to ear when it was meat-and-potato time. The fact that Dad loved to eat is further illustrated by how much he loved ice cream. He likely would have eaten it for breakfast, lunch and supper if it weren't that he was such a practical man. Dad's favorite words were, "Let's eat!"

Words are funny things. Some are worth more than others, and yet, it costs so little to speak words of endearment. Remembering my dad's fondness for food reminds me of one of the ways he expressed his love for me, not in words, but in a way that proves he was not swayed by the every-man-for-himself philosophy of selfish-hearted souls.

When I was a young girl at home, Dad, on more than one occasion, opened the freezer compartment above the refrigerator only to discover that the ice cream carton was nearly empty. He could have grabbed a spoon and devoured the last scoop for himself before either Mum or I protested. But he didn't. Instead of being selfish, Dad was self-less. He always offered the last spoonful to me. He did likewise with the last square of Mum's homemade chocolate fudge, any time he happened to be the one who discovered the last piece.

It's good that I have these memories of Dad's way of showing me he loved me. I see the tenderness in his gestures to give to me what he would have enjoyed for himself. Even so, there's a part of me that wishes there had been more. I wish I could remember Dad's saying, "Come here, Dotty, I want to tell you how precious you are to me. I want you to know how much I love you." I can't remember anything like that because nothing like that ever took place between my dad and me.

We all know that actions are supposed to speak louder than words, but who of us doesn't relish the sounds of music in our hearts from *hearing* tender, loving words spoken directly to us?

If Dad was alive, I'd like to think he and I could have grown to a point where we might have communicated more deeply. Perhaps it's only wishful thinking on my part, but like I said, I can't deny the part of me that wishes things could have been different. It was great to have a dad that could fix almost anything or make something out of nothing (like when he turned a junked truck seat into a porch swing), but I wish I could have had a dad who took time for listening to my heart.

Dad never asked about my friends at school. Seldom was he conversational with the young men I dated. And he never put his arms around me when I was big enough to wash dishes at the sink and tell me, "You're a good kid, Darlin'. " Matter of fact, Dad never called me a pet name of any kind.

Honestly, though, I should not be lamenting the dad I *did* have. Largely because Dad couldn't fulfill all my needs, I, at a young age, turned to the only Father who can: The Lord.

Dear Lord, it really is OK that Dad was like he was. Although he and I didn't talk much, I grew to appreciate talking to You. You are my Father, even more than any dad could ever be. I have a lot to thank You, and Dad, for giving to me. The irony is, You and Dad both contributed to the developing of my faith. Life with Dad wasn't so lacking after all. He gave to me of himself the only way he knew how, and You, Lord, continue to supply everything else.

Happy Father's Day, Lord. Tell Dad I expect he and I will have a lot to talk over, in the bye and bye. I can say that, because, not long before Dad died, he came to know You and Your Son Jesus as Lord and Savior of his life. It doesn't get any better than that. Not on this earth. In Jesus' Name. Amen.

☐

CHAPTER THIRTY-TWO

Summer

Card stack holds spirit of victory

July 28, 2001

This is the victory that has overcome the world — our faith (1 John 5:4, NKJV).

There's no time like the present to recycle, especially when sorting last year's Christmas cards in the middle of summer. That's precisely where I could be found a few days ago, shaking my head at this private little Christmas-in-July party, while separating the stack of cards into keepers and not-keepers.

The keepers are worthy of stashing not just because of whom they are from but because of something I call "inspiration potential." When you are an inspirational writer you never know what, where, when or through whom inspiration might strike. Thus, so and therefore any greeting card — Christmas or otherwise — conceivably can create a spark that is soon ablaze with possibilities.

It might be the picture on the front of a greeting card or the message inside that grabs my attention. It might be a specific blend of colors or design that calls out, "Save me, save me!" Or it might be the circumstances that brought this or that particular card into our home. For instance, there's the card from Carol and Bobby.

Bobby is a survivor of not one, but two liver transplants. It's been a long, hard-fought battle, and the card from him and Carol is a reminder to keep the faith and praise God for *all* victories. How can I possibly discard Carol and Bobby's card when simply seeing both of their names on it is a miracle!

Then there's the card from John and Arlene. This dedicated couple represents the epitome of faithfulness — faithfulness to God, to family and to friends both near and far. You just can't help but hold on to a card from them, knowing that every time you pick it up and look at it you'll be encouraged to stay the course.

Early into this sorting spree I can see that I am inclined to label every card I pick up "a keeper." How can I possibly *not* hang on to the one from Marmee and Arthur, seeing as how Marmee has been a staunch Christian influence on my life for more than 50 years! Not to mention her being a trusted friend to my mother when Dad died 30 years ago.

"OK," I sigh as I catch myself literally digging discarded cards out of the trash bag (yes, I *did* manage to toss a few), "this has got to stop. I can't save everything! But what can I do? I feel guilty if I throw away these meaningful cards, sentiments and signatures."

Suddenly, it is clear. These cards represent people I will never forget. I don't need a pile of recycled Christmas cards to remember the day more than 20 years ago when Dave and Francine "rescued" our kids by taking them on a picnic to Lake Jean after I sprained my ankle in a garden rut. I don't need another storage box filled with keeper cards to bring names and faces to mind when counting my blessings at prayer time. For me and for you, too, there are people and circumstances in each of our lives that forever leave an imprint on one's heart, and for such as these we can all be grateful without piling up cards to gather dust.

Whether you and I are "celebrating" events and holidays, in season or out, a celebration of friendship, faithfulness and inspiration is timely any time we draw on a spirit of victory through thankfulness. As for me, as you now know, I found such a reminder among a stack of Christmas cards on a hot summer's day. But a find like this is not surprising for any of us when you consider:

It is a blessing to thank the Lord, not only for past victories, but also for the ones about to happen as you and I continue to experience life, especially a life of faith in the Lord. This is where we find more than "a spirit" of victory. This is where we overcome!   □

CHAPTER THIRTY-THREE

Fourth of July

No time to waste: Seeds must be planted

July 5, 2003

W eeks ago, I remarked to my husband that I hoped to get a packet of zucchini seeds into the ground by the Fourth of July. You guessed it! The Fourth has come and gone, and the seal on the packet remains unbroken.

But hold on a minute, the planting info on the back of the packet says "harvest in 50 days." Great! Even if it takes me another week to get the seeds in the soil, I can still expect to have floured and fried zucchini slices by Labor Day.

Isn't it a thrill to be a gardener and feast on the results of our labors so quickly? It gives us added motivation when we know it won't take but a couple of months to go from dry seed to steaming platter.

Conversely, there are other "seeds" that need to be planted which come with no such guarantee of fast results. And yet they *must be planted*; otherwise a more precious harvest will be compromised with much more devastating certainty than either an abundance or lack of zucchini.

The must-be-planted seeds are the ones we plant in the very hearts, minds and souls of the next generation, especially the very young, while they are still receptive to Christian beliefs and sound morals. Call it what you like — indoctrination, role modeling, a legacy of faith or lifestyle education — it must be done, and it must be done early.

Why early? Because the older a child or any person gets, the harder it is to break through the "crust" of habits, notions and preferences. Whether in casual conversation or fun-and-games playtime, we must make the best use of opportunities to instill a love for God in the tender, sprouting generation. Our children and youth need to see us reading the Bible, hear us talking to the Lord in prayer, and witness our living in our daily walk what we profess in the church pews on Sunday morning.

Thank the Lord we live in a land where we are free to teach and train our young people openly and without restraint when it comes to singing "Jesus" songs and acting out Bible character dramas. And although it's grand to do these things in a big way, it's also absolutely necessary to incorporate biblical truths and examples of godly character in our home life and in our social activities.

It's not enough to sing along with the congregation in the sanctuary during a weekly worship service; we must also live and act along with and according to God's will and His way. The only way to discern His will and His way is to "know" Him by living close to Him, seeking Him for each decision and circumstance we face. Then we can and should "make Him known" to the little ones entrusted to our care, especially within the sphere of our influence.

As adults we need to take stock of our behavior. How are the young and impressionable among us processing the way we act, both in public and private? Are we sending mixed or confusing messages? Is it clear on any given day, in any given circle of work, play or other activity that we do or do not have double standards? We have got to get our own act together so the kids will know what is true, what is honest, what is reliable, what is faith, what is false, what is deception, what is commitment, what is honor and what is honorable.

We can't put off planting the seeds that will offer the next generation its best shot at living abundant lives. Adults are always saying we want our kids and grandchildren to have it better than we did, but "the best" any generation can pass on to the next is a desire to please the Lord. This desire is contagious only if it is consistently displayed in real time, day after day. Around the supper table. In front of the TV. And on the playing fields of family gatherings.

Not that we have to be perfect. We can't be. But we need to be consistent. We need to speak with actions and words that have originated from a willingness to be led and to be forgiven by the Lord Himself. When we live close to Him, He will help us make wise choices which are, in and of themselves, seeds of promise for the future.

Whether today is a holiday weekend or tomorrow is just another day, it's the right time to care about what we and our lives are sowing. The harvest of young souls is living and breathing in our midst. We must communicate to them: "Oh, taste and see that the Lord is good" (Psalm 34:8, NKJV).   □

CHAPTER THIRTY-FOUR

Woman's faith reaps 'amazing' harvest

July 25, 1992

When my husband remembered something I asked him to do this week without my reminding him, I, too, remembered something: I recalled the significance of information I had read earlier about John Newton, the man who wrote the world-famous hymn "Amazing Grace."

Shortly before his death at age 82, London-born John Newton (1725-1807) loudly stated while preaching a sermon, "My memory is nearly gone, but I remember two things: that I am a great sinner, and that Christ is a great Savior!"

It seems the seed for Newton's bold conviction was planted deep in his mind by his mother when he was a little boy. Even so, history books about the background of famous hymns and their authors tell us Mrs. Newton didn't have a long planting season in young John's life: She died while John was only six years old.

Although John Newton's mother dedicated him to the ministry before she died, the seeds she had planted within him lay dormant for so long it appeared they had been snatched away.

Nonetheless, memory and the Lord's intervention revealed otherwise many years later.

John, by age four, could recite passages from the Westminster Catechism and the children's hymns of Isaac Watts (another writer of hymns such as "When I Survey the Wondrous Cross"). Sadly, by age 17, Newton "laid aside every religious principle and abandoned himself to the service of the devil," according to the book *Living Stories of Famous Hymns* by Ernest K. Emurian (copyright 1955, Baker Book House Company).

Living for the devil included Newton's eventually becoming captain of his own slave-trading ship accompanied by "one continuous round of rebellion and debauchery" lasting for a number of years.*

It took a violent storm at sea and Newton's simultaneous reading of the book *Imitation of Christ* by Thomas a Kempis (a Dutch monk, 1380-1471) for the seeds planted earlier by Newton's mother to begin to sprout, still hidden, deep within his wretched soul.

Although history says Newton regarded the day of the raging storm, March 10, 1748, as his "spiritual birthday," it was not until nearly six-and-a-half years later in August 1754 that he came to "consider himself a regenerated Christian."

For John Newton, seeds planted deep within his memory, a mother's prayers and a severe storm all played a part in his eventual trading his life of being a slave to sin to becoming a servant of Jesus Christ. Such service, leading him into becoming "a strong and effective crusader against slavery" and an ordained minister, often attracted "large crowds gathered to hear the 'Old Converted Sea Captain.' "

Kind of gives a person something worth remembering any time we ourselves partake of the harvest of someone else's planting, someone else's nurturing, someone else's faithfulness so we can be fed. Rather amazing, isn't it?

*(Additional resource used in preparing above column: *101 Hymn Stories* by Kenneth W. Osbeck, 1982, Kregel Publications.)   □

CHAPTER THIRTY-FIVE

Grandparents' Day

Watering family tree on Grandparents' Day

September 6, 2003

Grandparents' Day in the U.S.A. is observed annually. This year it falls on September 7, a date that also happens to be the birthday of my mother's sister Lodema M. Hull. Aunt Lodema is a wonderful grandparent to her three grandsons and a great-grandson — Matthew, David, Jonathan and little Logan.

Aunt Lodema is a lot like a lot of us: she prizes her family and is proud of whom they are. She's a prime example of what it means to be a "grand" parent. Oh, to be as grand in the eyes of my grandchildren as I know she is in the eyes of hers.

What is it to be a grandparent? I guess the "grand" part is a station we arrive at after we've done our best at being a parent. We get a chance to really shine. In many ways being a grandparent is a little easier than being a parent. It seems we have more opportunities to play with the grandchildren than we did with our own kids. But I think it's supposed to be that way, don't you?

Grandparenting is similar to being a kid in reverse. Although we lack the energy of the very young, often, like the kids, we do have insights into what really matters, without having to take the time to actually think about it. It's as though we suddenly awaken to the notion that parenting is grand because we are no longer just the parent. We are free to have fun with the grandkids without having to be the only one to encourage them to eat their vegetables, brush their teeth and make their beds.

Of course, there's more to grandparenting than fun. There's cookie-baking and finger-painting and storytelling, yes, but there's a bond even when we have to say no to the horsing around in the house or no to the idea that candy is better than meat and potatoes.

But of all the blessings of being a grandparent or of remembering my own Grandma (Margaret) and Granddad (Carl) Heckler who lived on Grant Street directly across from the former East Brady High School in East Brady, Pennsylvania, there is one word that probably defines the whole scene more vividly than any other: hospitality.

Hospitality. As in open arms and a full refrigerator. I surely hope my grandchildren remember my special treats as much as I remember my grandma's pecan tarts, colorful and crunchy Jell-O salads and mouth-watering apple pie.

You know, when I think about it this way, I wish I could go back for a day. I wish I could tell Grandma and Granddad Heckler how calming it was to come into their quiet, neat, clean house and enjoy whatever they had to offer. Even when they didn't know I was coming, they made me feel like they were expecting me. They stopped what they were doing and visited. They acted as though I was their pride and joy.

Now that I'm a grandparent, I know why my grandparents acted the way they did. There is nothing quite like grandchildren. It's really the grandchildren that make Grandparents' Day worth celebrating. *Isn't that right, Aunt Lodema?*

Dear Lord, thank You for grandparents and grandchildren. Help us to use the bonds between the generations to fill in the gaps of our comprehension regarding things You would have us learn from one another. Concepts such as character building and nurturing are invaluable extensions of the inheritance of Your Love on all branches of the family tree. In Jesus' Name. Amen. □

CHAPTER THIRTY-SIX

Autumn

In all four seasons, 'press on'

September 24, 1988

Whether we like it or not, it's here: the season of autumn. With it are certain indicators that have to be reckoned with:

Leaves are beginning to turn colors and commence falling. Sniffles and scratchy throats are becoming more common on the chilly, damp mornings. And it was only last week I wondered why I encountered three spiders in one day, until I remembered that they're coming indoors out of the cold. That's not something that makes me happy — neither the cold *nor* the spiders.

Yes, very definitely, "fall is in the air."

There's something else in the air, too. I think it's a touch of melancholy for the season just ended.

If you're like me, you're thinking of all the things you had planned to do this summer but never got around to, and now they're over: the summer *and* the opportunities that came and went with it.

It's too late to plant the petunias that never even got bought. Too late to go on the picnics that never got packed. Too late to go to the beach for fun in the sun.

For those of us who failed to do something memorable in the season just ended, perhaps we're feeling cheated because that season is now gone.

But wait a minute.

Just because we didn't accomplish some of the things we had planned for this summer, it doesn't necessarily mean that we didn't do anything.

What about the things we did do?

If we take the time to name a few, maybe we'll surprise ourselves. I think sometimes many of us are guilty of only looking at all the things that are undone instead of at the things that are done.

For instance, how many times do the kids clean their rooms, rearrange posters and maybe even move the furniture around, and yet the first thing we notice and comment on is: "You didn't get your bed made, did you?"

So let's take a second look, not only at some of our accomplishments of this past summer, but also at the many things our family members do that go unnoticed or without due praise.

Why not try to focus on all the good things that have been done instead of drawing everyone's attention to what isn't done?

Now, I'm not suggesting that we never require anyone to do his best or that we promote leaving important tasks unfinished. But let's recondition ourselves to see that someone polished the living room furniture — and let's praise that effort — before we hastily comment about the pair of shoes left in the middle of the floor. Maybe later will be soon enough to comment on the less-than-perfect appearance of the room. Perhaps *never* will sometimes be even more appropriate.

However, before I wander too far away from the melancholy fall scene, I think our backward glances at any season's passing need to be balanced with hopeful glimpses into the approaching season.

Therefore, if we discover that very little of any memorable

value happened in the season behind us — without wasting too much time lamenting on that perception — let's resolve right here and now to make sure we create something memorable in the season immediately in front of us.

The Apostle Paul said something similar in regard to being in the race of the Christian life: "... forgetting what lies behind and reaching forward to what lies ahead, I press on toward the goal for the prize of the upward call of God in Christ Jesus" (Philippians 3:13,14, NASB).

Spring, summer, fall or winter. One season is as appropriate as any other to do just that.   □

Maintaining the 'evergreen quality' in the Christian life
September 23, 1989

It's official: Fall is here. But we don't need a calendar telling us what we already know.

We already know things are not as green as they were a few weeks ago. We see the browns and yellows appearing in the fields and on the hills. The falling leaves sprinkling the lawns are replacing the very same green lushness we walked barefoot in, only a few yesterdays ago.

It won't be long, and green will be a thing of the past season, except for indoor plants and evergreens.

Evergreen.

Somewhere, someone in my past once suggested that a Christian should be like an evergreen: always green, always fresh.

But why would a Christian want to be "green"?

Since green symbolizes life and freshness, the question answers itself.

How, then, does a Christian acquire the evergreen quality? What gives us our "green leaves" throughout every season of the year?

In June, when I participated in the press conferences at Creation '89 (the Christian music festival at Mt. Union, Pennsylvania, where 40,000 Christians gathered for inspiration and teaching), an interviewer in the press tent asked one of the featured singers, "How do you keep your walk with the Lord fresh?"

The singer/songwriter Carman who is based in Tulsa, Oklahoma, thoughtfully answered, "The Word of God is always fresh...so I go to the Word."

Time was too short for Carman to expand on his response, but it's fairly easy to draw our own conclusions from his statement: God's Word is always fresh because it's alive. It's alive because it's full of Jesus, and Jesus is the Living Word of God.

Through Him we can "lie down in green pastures" and be refreshed (Psalm 23:2).

Through Him we can be "like a tree planted by the rivers of water...[where our] leaf...shall not wither; and whatsoever [we] doeth shall prosper" (Psalm 1:3, KJV, brackets added).

A couple of years ago in Minneapolis, Minnesota, I heard Jill Briscoe (Christian writer, speaker) refer to the freshness found in God's Word. Jill said something along these lines:

"No matter how often we [like sheep] graze on a particular verse or passage of Scripture, it's never depleted as a source of freshness and nourishment. It's always there for us to feed on ...time after time, after time."

Jill suggested there's always something new to discover and taste in God's Word. In this context, she used the word evergreen in her talk to more than 300 Christian writers that day, and maybe that's where I was first exposed to the concept of Christians being like evergreens.

Regardless of where or by whom the seed was planted, I desire the evergreen quality in my life more and more every day.

None of us has to wither and turn brown like vegetation in the fall. Our witness can stay fresh and green if we expose ourselves to the Son and drink of the Living Water found in Him and in His Word.

Be planted. Drink. Swallow. Grow.

It doesn't sound that hard to be an evergreen after all, does it?   □

God equips wild geese...and us

September 12, 1992

"Ready or not, here we go!" the wild geese flying over our roof top seemed to be saying long before dawn last Saturday. I wasn't sure whether they were real or whether I was dreaming. When I woke up a few hours later, my husband said he had heard them, too.

If I had my choice, I wouldn't be ready for the geese to fly south for quite a while yet. Actually, I probably wouldn't mind if we just skipped fall and winter altogether this year. Perhaps you, too, find yourself lamenting that we haven't had much of a summer.

Nonetheless, to paraphrase the wild geese, "Ready or not, fall is on its way!"

It's just one more reminder that we often have to do things whether we want to or not — whether we feel qualified or not — whether we feel prepared or not — whether we're scared or confident — whether we've had years of experience or whether we haven't the foggiest idea of what we're doing.

For example, how many of us feel ready for morning to come *every* morning? Well, we certainly can't stop it any more than we can slow it down once it gets here. So what else is new? Perhaps that's the point. Nothing is new. Yet everything is new.

The wild geese have flown south before. But it's the first and only time, this year, that fall is on its way. Ready or not, we can't stop it. Ready or not, we shouldn't even try.

Even if it were possible, trying to stop all the things we're not ready for might mean we would never, ever experience some things that are essential to growing, productive lives.

If we have the slightest tendency to procrastinate doing everything from the smallest to the largest task, can you imagine what catastrophic events we might precipitate if we suddenly had a choice about moving on or standing still?

Some of us would destroy ourselves and our reputations because we weren't ready to care about being responsible witnesses of how Christians are supposed to look and act.

Just how are we supposed to look and act? We'll probably never know unless we're ready to open our Bibles and our hearts to fund out.

A good place to start might be with 2 Timothy 3:16-17 which says:

"The whole Bible was given to us by inspiration from God and is useful...to make us realize what is wrong in our lives; it straightens us out and helps us do what is right. It is God's way of making us well prepared at every point, fully equipped to do good to everyone" (TLB).

Well prepared... fully equipped.

Ready or not, the answers to life's questions can be as near as God's Word. If we're not ready to look for them there, then perhaps we'll never be, unless we're willing to take the risk and start looking before we're ready.

Maybe that's why the geese do so much honking as they fly. They're simply voicing their unwillingness to move on, but the Lord has created something within them that equips them to do it anyway.   □

Where does it come from, the courage to take risks?

September 9, 1989

There's one sure thing about taking a risk: Things could go either way. Either we'll be glad we did it...or wish we hadn't.

Some days, simply getting out of bed is a risk. This seems to be the way a lot of us are feeling about the changing of the present season. Many of us don't want to leave the security and familiarity of summer. We don't want to face the uncertainties and the unknowns of the approaching season.

But the fact is: Summer is over!

Maybe it's not official until September 22, but it's a fact that the kids are back in school. It's a fact that the nights are cooler and the sights and sounds of fall are in the air. It's a fact that we can't stop the fall season from creeping into our lives, unless we move to a climate that is summer-like all year 'round.

The reality of fall's approaching reminds me of the reality of risk-taking. Facing either of them requires a letting go, a step of faith, blind courage, sheer ignorance or whatever else we might call the ability to go forward.

This ability came to my mind when I read the following item in the "Today" box in the *Press Enterprise* on Wednesday: "On this date (September 6): In 1620, the Pilgrims set sail from Plymouth, England, on the Mayflower to settle in the New World."

"Isn't that something," I thought. "Here we are — wishing that summer wasn't over yet — and it was at this very point in the summer/fall season more than three centuries ago that the Pilgrims faced much more than a change of season."

There I was, comfortably seated at my Formica-topped kitchen table, sipping a cup of tea heated up in a microwave, reading a newspaper delivered to my front door, wishing that things didn't have to change.

It made me feel pretty small and petty to think how nice I have it when I might not even be here if it weren't for the risks those emigrants took, many of them losing their very lives.

"Where did they get the courage? The Pilgrims? The explorers? The pioneers?" I wondered as I briefly recalled some of the hardship stories we all learned as early as first grade when our teachers taught us about the first Thanksgiving.

And then I knew.

Their courage came from the same place — or places — we get ours today. We get our courage either from God or from self. Either from being forced or from choosing. Either from an abundance of preparation or from sheer ignorance.

I also knew something else: I knew — or rather, I know — that I want my courage to come from God, not me. That I want to choose His way and not the world's. That I want to better understand the deception and mind-control tactics of humanistic thinking so I'm neither deceived nor controlled by it.

I want to focus on learning, being prepared and having the courage to do whatever God asks of me — no matter what the season.

How about you?   □

CHAPTER THIRTY-SEVEN

Thanksgiving

'I'm only going to be here today'
November 20, 1999

One Saturday last month, as I was coming out of the Bloomsburg Wal-Mart, a small boy touched my heart with the wisdom of his innocence. He represented a young scout troop selling candy in the store's lobby, and as I headed toward the exit door with a shopping cart full of purchases, the boy in his crisp uniform politely approached me.

"Would you like to buy a candy bar for a dollar?" he asked in a respectful tone, subtly conveying a pure and hopeful assumption that I was a very nice lady who would likely say yes.

But instead, with a sigh and half a smile, my response was, "Oh, I guess not today."

Naturally, this precious little fellow had no idea why I didn't want to be bothered with digging out a dollar and stopping long enough to pick out a candy bar. He had no clue I had just endured a 25-minute wait in the check-out line because there were only two lines open; and now I was overdue in getting home to fix supper and relieve my husband who had stayed home to look after my mother. The boy was unaware, and rightfully so, that I was physically and emotionally spent from the night-and-day care my dear mother had been requiring lately.

Beyond that, this well-mannered boy did not know I had only come to the store in the first place because I needed numerous items to make caring for my mother easier. Items like a nursery monitor to enable my husband and me to hear Mum's every move from throughout the house so we might assist her when necessary.

Hopefully, it will be nearly a lifetime from now before this little candy-selling scout has to experience the heartache of becoming a parent to one of his parents. Fortunately, however, that day in Wal-Mart, this young boy's response to my weariness not only changed the focus of my day, but also created, for me, one of the highpoints of the entire year.

For when I said, *Oh, I guess not today*, he looked up with the most angelic expression and said, "But I'm only going to be here today."

In a moment of humility, I understood completely what he meant and my heart melted on the spot. He was saying with his eyes and with his unspoiled posture of reason, If you don't buy a candy bar today, tomorrow will be too late. I won't be here then. I'll be gone. Please reconsider. There's not much time left.

Of course, he didn't speak all of that with his voice. When he had said, *But I'm only going to be here today,* that was all the more he said.

It was all I needed to hear. A smile arose from deep within me and spread across my face. With a flood of joy I reached into my pocket for my car keys. Attached to my keys was my change purse. I dumped the contents of my change purse, first into my own hand, and then into his.

"I'll tell you what," I said to him as I laughed away a big knot of stress in my chest. "You can have everything in here...all my change. And I won't need a candy bar for it...I'm not supposed to eat them anyway. I'm sorry there's not much money in my change purse, but it's all yours...except for this paper clip."

The boy's beaming face and his sincere thank you revived within me an attitude of appreciation for each today I have faced since that day. The message of the young boy's words was spoken as if straight from the mouth of the Lord:

"Today, your mother is with you. Give her your all and it will be blessed. You might be inclined to think it's not much, but that's not the point. The point is making the most of the opportunities of today."

How can I be so sure that the Lord was "speaking" that particular message to me? Because I recognized it as such. Furthermore, within two weeks of the Wal-Mart episode, my mother now has moved from our home into a nursing center where she can receive 'round-the-clock care from a whole staff.

The days of saying today she is here with us are past. The final weeks with her in our home not only were some of the most difficult of the past three years, they were also some of the best. I think I looked upon her more tenderly and fondly than I ever had, all because of one little boy's comment:

But I'm only going to be here today.

Happy Thanksgiving, Little Scout. You have made mine complete.   ☐

Counting blessings
November 23, 1985

I knew it was going to be "one of those days" when it started off with the toaster eating the toast and refusing to cough it up. With breakfast over and the toaster slammed onto the fix-it shelf in the utility room, it was time for a shower.

The shower revealed another problem: a ripped-beyond-repair, mildewed shower curtain. A decision to buy a new one required no thought. It was as automatic as puddles on a rainy day.

The hard part came in the housewares department at the store: Which shower curtain do I buy? Do I get the blue one to match the bathroom walls or the gray one to match the duct tape holding our loose shower tiles in place?

The blue one made the bathroom look and smell new and I was thankful — when I pulled the new curtain the full length of the rod — that I couldn't see the gray tape on the shower walls.

Being thankful over this simple touch of newness, I was reminded of Thanksgiving Day at our house a couple of years ago.

We had just finished eating a traditional dinner of turkey with all the trimmings. We remained at the table to read something from the Bible: the story in John 21:1-13 where the disciples were unsuccessful at catching any fish — unsuccessful, that is, until Jesus told them to throw their net out on the right side of the boat. When they did as He told them, their net became so full they couldn't draw it in because of the weight of the fish.

"So Simon Peter went out and dragged the net ashore. By his count there were 153 large fish..." (v. 11, TLB).

We stopped reading and I asked my family a few questions: Why do you suppose Peter counted all those fish? Could this story be suggesting to us that we count our blessings as Peter counted fish? Why don't we do that? Why not literally list and count some of our blessings?

That's exactly what we did. Each of us numbered a piece of paper from "1" through "153."

We began to write down all the things we could think of for which we were thankful: Jesus, the Bible, food, water, friends, ice cream, sunshine, doctors, smiles, trees, houses, cheese, laughter.

It took time to list 153 items. As a matter of fact, we didn't finish our lists on Thanksgiving Day.

For the next month, we each worked off-and-on at counting our blessings. On Christmas Day, we pulled out our lists and read them to each other. Listening to what each person was thankful for brought tears to our eyes and joy to our hearts. My mother laughed because she discovered she had recorded "bread and butter" seven or eight times.

When we were all finished reading our lists, each of us had 153 thank yous to give to Jesus on His birthday. Why not try this idea with your family this Thanksgiving? It could turn out to be one of the biggest blessings of all.   □

Thanksgiving is confidence in God
November 23, 2002

It's one thing to praise and thank the Lord for all He has done in the past. It's another to thank and praise Him for all that is yet to come. The first is gratitude, and we owe it to God Our Father who blesses us so richly. The latter is an expression of our faith and trust in God's eternal lovingkindness toward us.

Really, though, it's impossible to separate what God *has* done from what He *is* doing and what He *will* do. Along this vein, we are reminded that God never changes. He is steadfast, dependable, constant, rock-solid. He "is the same yesterday, today, and forever" (Hebrews 13:8, NKJV).

Why, then, do we find it so difficult to be thankful for the unanswered prayers in our lives? Do we not realize that the prayers and needs God has already answered and met are testimonials to what we can rightfully expect in days and years to come? Past answered prayers let us in on a secret: The same God will provide what's best for us in the future, just as He did earlier in our lives.

For the most part, the real test of our faith in God is not so much about *will* He or *won't* He answer our prayers. More than likely the test is summed up in the word "when!"

This leads us to muse: What would we be thankful for if every prayer we have ever prayed, to date, was yet unanswered?

That's a toughie because no one likes to go on and on indefinitely without so much as an arsenal of answered prayers to fall back on when times are hard and hope and faith are weak. Thankfully, perpetually unanswered prayer is not the norm. God does hear and He does respond.

Nevertheless, when you and I really think about it, the unanswered prayers in our lives have contributed more to our dependence on the Lord than the prayers that were answered in short order. When our ongoing prayers and concerns seem to meet with nothing but resistance, at least from a human perspective, we are forced to acknowledge that without the Lord we are nothing. Without His hand on our lives we are empty and lost.

Even so, it's not normal for us to jump up and down with joyful enthusiasm at the suggestion we are better off with unanswered prayers. That's just not so; but there is merit in the idea that God simply wants us to wait upon Him (Isaiah 40:31) and believe that, because He is eternal, the future is as secure as though it were already clear, as though it were already revealed.

In other words, unanswered prayers, as we see them here and now, are really already answered in God's timeless perspective. If this is so, we can truly thank Him for what we don't yet know or see, because He knows, He sees and He has everything, absolutely everything, under control.

We can thank Him. We can trust Him. We can believe what can't be seen because God is faithful. Thanksgiving Day is only one opportunity out of countless opportunities to let Him know our complete confidence is in Him.   □

Giving and living our thanks
November 17, 1990

Learning from our mistakes is not a new concept. But every time it happens, a light of understanding gets a little brighter. It's like the sunrise of a new day. The concept has been around since God said it would be so. But each new day is new territory to explore, new minutes and hours to fill or leave empty, whichever we choose.

When we gather around our Thanksgiving Day tables, will we include in our lists of blessings some of the things we've learned from our mistakes?

I've got one that came from a misspelled word. Actually, it's more of a mental typographical error.

Recently, while reflecting on some of the things I want to give thanks for, I saw the word "Thanksgiving" in my head. Except when I "looked" at it more closely, it was spelled wrong. The word I saw was "Thanks*living*."

Oh well, being a writer does strange things to a person sometimes. But because I'm a writer, the incident prompted me to play around with a couple of Webster's definitions.

Webster says that Thanksgiving Day is "a day appointed for giving thanks for divine goodness." Could we not also say that *Thanksliving Day* is a day appointed for *living* thanks for divine goodness?

Thanksgiving without the capital "T" is defined as "an act of giving thanks." With our new word, we could say it's "the act of *living* thanks."

The concept of living our thanks doesn't need a lot of explanation, does it? It may only require some creative thinking about how to implement it. Or it may require nothing more than smiles on our faces, twinkles in our eyes and thankfulness in our hearts. For when we are truly thankful, nothing expresses our thanksgiving more accurately than our thanksliving.

Dear Lord, sometimes we're simply too busy and too tired to look or act thankful. Help us to see ourselves as You see us, and if we don't appear very thankful, help us to change. In Jesus' Name. Amen.   □

Looking toward Advent with eyes opened by thanksgiving

November 28, 1992

Usually, life presents us with a lot of options. Take this past Thursday, for instance. Since it was Thanksgiving Day, it wasn't just another day of the week, or was it?

In our region, the day couldn't have been grayer or gloomier. Waking up to a day like that makes a strong case for staying in bed, or at the very least, moping around all day — two options, I imagine, more than a few of us considered when we first opened our eyes to no sunshine, no blue sky, no promise of a beautiful day.

And yet, speaking strictly from a personal circumstance, the first thing that came to my mind on Thanksgiving morning was not the color of the day, but instead was a silent shout of joy: "My headache is gone! Thank You, thank You, Lord!"

However, I have to be honest. If Thursday morning hadn't been preceded by 18 hours of a horrible migraine, I'm sure I wouldn't have been as readily thankful to greet a gray day.

The moral of my little story is best spelled out, not in my words, but in a paraphrase of the words of a radio preacher I heard recently on my car radio when I tuned in, in the middle of a broadcast on WPGM out of Danville.

I didn't catch the preacher's name or the name of the program, but I did catch the theme of his message: the results of an attitude of thankfulness compared to the results of an attitude of unthankfulness.

What he said was something like this (I jotted it down before I got out of the car when I pulled into the parking lot at Wal-Mart in Bloomsburg):

"Thankfulness opens our eyes to see the goodness of God and all His blessings. Unthankfulness closes our eyes to all that God has done and is doing."

Because I was thankful to wake up free of excruciating pain on Thanksgiving, I saw the light of joy before the gray of day. My eyes were glad to be open. Had not the pain preceded the gray dawn, my eyes may have remained closed to other blessings throughout the day. Oh yes, the sky remained dreary all day long, but I saw God's hand at work. No amount of gray could make the day just another gloomy day.

Thankfulness opens our eyes to see the goodness of God and all His blessings. Unthankfulness closes our eyes to all that God has done and is doing.

Nothing compares to what God can do, if only we will let Him enter our circumstances. A thankful attitude is one way to let Him in.

Seems like Thanksgiving is the perfect prelude to Advent — the season in which we begin to prepare for Christmas celebrations commemorating the coming of Jesus.

The coming of Jesus. A great place to begin giving thanks, if we haven't already done so. □

Being thankful for our mistakes

November 26, 1994

As I sit at my dumputer keyboard — oops, the computer is not the dumb one, but the mistake makes me smile — Thanksgiving is two days away.

Even so, preparations of the usual nature are not what's on my mind. Instead, I'm trying to think of what I might mention when we go around the table asking each person at our family gathering to name one thing he or she is most thankful for.

Many things come to mind: God, His Son Jesus, my husband Jim, our daughters April and Lori and their husbands Allen and Scott, our mothers, friends, health, eyesight, a home and all the things in it.

Home and all the things in it. Here I pause. Once again I smile. I'll bet you'll never guess what "things" in our house I'm going to say I'm thankful for.

Well, here goes: I'm thankful for all the holes in our walls.

No, I didn't say in my head, I said "in our walls." But don't worry, they're not big holes, they simply represent years' and years' worth of several families' decisions of where to hang this picture or that plaque.

Many of the holes were here when we moved into the house in 1975. We painted over them without knowing then how to fill them in properly. Once we learned what we should have done, we figured we'd do it right the next time we painted, and in a few rooms we did. But, years have a way of going by, and holes in the walls have a way of multiplying. The easiest thing to do is what we've been doing: hang pictures, mirrors, baskets, plates, lights and plants over the holes.

Yes, this is how the number of holes has multiplied, because, in order to achieve a pleasing arrangement of groupings on a wall, we (meaning I) have often made two or three *more* holes in order to hide one.

Ah-ha, but it's not been destructive hole-making. I prefer lots of things on the walls anyway; but I suspect placing many of our collected "junk and treasures" in clusters and groupings would not have come about if our walls were perfectly smooth and free of all those unsightly holes.

Therefore, the moral of my "what to be thankful for" tale is quite simple: Mistakes that make us smile, perhaps are not mistakes at all, for just like nail holes in the walls, they can serve to enlighten our lives and brighten our homes.

Thank You, Lord, for allowing us to grow and make choices and decisions based on all that we have learned from our mistakes. In Jesus' Name. Amen.   □

Thankfulness: Better late than never

December 7, 1991

There is less time this year between Thanksgiving and Christmas than usual. Thanksgiving was late and it just threw everything off.

Hm-m-m-m. Could we apply this calander fact to our spiritual lives? What are the ramifications of being late with our thanksgiving, our giving thanks to our Lord?

It sort of just throws everything off, doesn't it?

When we delay acknowledging the goodness of God's blessings and thanking Him for them, we delay a whole series of things:

- Peace escapes us.
- Finding joy in little things becomes a forgotten art.

- Smiling is replaced with worrying about creating our own blessings, and other impossible, unrealistic goals.
- Sighs of relief disappear and are replaced by sighs of stress and exhaustion.

How do I know this?

Because there have been times in my life when I forgot to thank God for today before today became yesterday.

There have been times when I forgot how to laugh, and, along with those times, there was not only the absence of laughter but also a temporary loss of a sense of humor.

There have been times when I complained more than my share, because I thought I had more than my share to complain about, only because I allowed an over-extended lifestyle to rob me of time for offering proper thanks.

Praise the Lord and thank Him, the above described conditions, whether excerpted from my life or yours, don't have to be permanent.

Thank You, Lord, for accepting our thanks, even when it's belated.   □

CHAPTER THIRTY-EIGHT

Christmas

'The Baby' changes us all

December 4, 1993

There's nothing in life more precious than life itself. You see it when you look upon the face of a newborn baby. You feel it when you caress a baby's soft hand. You hear it when an infant coos.

A baby is the beginning of a promise. A promise of untold possibilities. A promise of surprises and changed lives. No shape, no form, no concept could be more perfect than that of a baby for sending God to the earth.

And yet God's coming to earth in the being of a baby would never have been dreamed of by mere man. It took a wise God to orchestrate such a masterful plan, a plan so brilliant it appears foolish to the human heart. And yet, God surely knew: What appears foolish to man is often the only thing that softens his hardened heart.

Walk with me for a moment down a hospital corridor. Your mind is not on the coming of Christmas. It's not on the season of Advent. It's on getting where you have to go and getting what you have to do over with.

You're in the hospital helping a loved one find the lab for some routine testing. Your mind kicks into "automatic waiting mode" until you can leave the setting and get on with your plans for the rest of the day.

You sit down and shut off thoughts of whatever could conceivably make you impatient. You don't know how long the wait will be, but there's no sense making it harder on yourself by tapping your watch.

Then, without flashing lights or a marching band, a young mother enters the waiting area and sits near you. The bundle she is holding is fast asleep, and yet it stirs something within you.

By now you aren't thinking about much of anything, and yet, all of a sudden, you're smiling. All of a sudden you have to stand up and walk over where you can get a closer look. All of a sudden you hear yourself speak the words, "He's so precious. So very precious."

And all of a sudden everything is changed. You feel refreshed. You're hopeful. You're thankful. Thoughts and plans begin to dance around in your head. You don't get out your pocket calendar and circle December 25, but your renewed spirit knows Christmas is just around the corner.

That night in your home you find a quiet spot before bedtime and ponder the wonder of a God who created babies. For a moment, everything makes sense as you remember the baby in the hospital and how its presence changed your day. And all of a sudden, you're filled anew with awe at "The Baby" God sent to change the world. □

Receiving with open arms, hearts

December 24, 1994

What is the best way to receive a gift?

Anyone who wonders how to answer such a question needs

only to watch a child on Christmas morning.

With outstretched arms and eyes as big as footballs, a little boy responds to a package heading his direction with the patience of a hungry puppy. A giggling little girl, dancing up and down and clapping her hands together, can't wait for the go-ahead signal to start ripping

Ah, but we adults, too often we become so poised and proper over the years that we show little or no enthusiasm when someone hands us a gift. Life has a way of teaching us to hide our emotions so well for so long, we can lose the ability to receive joy — the kind of joy that can brighten our lives and lighten our loads.

Surely this is not the way to receive. I prefer to think that an open, spontaneous willingness to accept a gift, is a gift we can graciously give back to the giver.

I'm reminded of a time when our daughters were quite small. April is the older of the two, so she did this thing first. I can see her yet in the part of my mind that fondly recalls such things.

"Here I come, Daddy!" she would announce from across the room. "Here I come!" And off she flew.

Running into her daddy's open arms delighted April and her daddy over and over again. Never once did she expect her daddy to be disinterested. Never once did Jim stand or sit there with his arms behind his back, unwilling to participate. Always, always, always, the daddy gladly received what the excited little girl wanted to give.

April gave her all in the playful gesture of love and trust. Daddy gave love and trust right back to her by instinctively receiving with an attitude and posture of sheer joy.

This is how, I believe, we are to accept what others have devised to give us. This is how, I trust, God would have us receive the Gift He sent when He presented His Son Jesus Christ to the world.

On this Christmas Eve, are our heads downcast and our hearts so distracted it's as though we're standing hopelessly with our hands behind our backs, without any thought of being blessed?

Or are our arms, hearts, spirits and attitudes open to receive the miracle of Christmas in the form of the Son of God?

For me, expecting is part of the joy of the surprise. That doesn't mean I expect a lot of gifts. It doesn't mean I expect any gifts. It does mean I want to be properly prepared to receive what God has surely put so much thought into giving.

Dear Lord, help us this Christmas season, in the Name of Jesus, to receive the Presence of Jesus with open arms — especially with expectant hearts. Amen.   □

When Jesus was born, we were there

December 17, 1994

Where were you the night Jesus Christ, the Son of God, was born?

Silly question!

Unless you secretly have been sipping waters from a private fountain of youth for nearly 2,000 years, you and I both know: No human alive today was alive when The Baby Jesus was born.

And yet we were there — every last one of us. At least that's how I see it.

As the Christian world prepares to celebrate the historically and spiritually significant event we call The Birth of Christ, we gain insight surrounding truth and victory if we consider how we fit into the time frame of Christ's coming to earth.

First, however, a necessary disclaimer: In my opinion, it matters not whether the actual day of Christ's birth falls on the actual day we celebrate it. What matters is, He came and He is worthy of our worshipful observations of the remembrance of His coming.

Now, back to where we all were when He *did* come.

As Jesus lay cradled in a Bethlehem manger that pivotal night—the night when The Baby bridged the gap between heaven and earth, when His coming put into motion the plan for a future battle to win our very souls — you and I were there. At the very moment when Baby Jesus drew His first breath as a God-Man, I repeat, we were there.

No, we weren't walking around anywhere on the earth or standing around taking pictures of the shepherds and other visitors who came to see Jesus. But there is reason to believe we existed in Jesus' heart that night. Furthermore, if He came for the purpose of making a difference in our lives, then we can relate to the time frame of His birth from the perspective of Jesus' knowing us before anyone ever laid eyes on us.

To me, it's this simple: Biblical passages tell us we were created by the Lord, in His heart and mind, even before our time on earth began.

One such Bible reference from Jeremiah 1:4-5 tells us: "The Lord said to [Jeremiah], 'I knew you before you were formed within your mother's womb; before you were born I sanctified you and appointed you as my spokesman to the world' " (TLB, brackets added).

Another passage from Psalm 139:13-16 says: "You [Lord] made all the delicate, inner parts of my body, and knit them together in my mother's womb. ...You were there while I was being formed in utter seclusion! You saw me before I was born and scheduled each day of my life before I began to breathe. Every day was recorded in your Book!" (TLB, brackets added).

Because of these and other Bible references, I believe there was never a time when we were isolated from the Lord's personal plan for each of us.

In light of this, I choose to believe you and I were in Our Lord's heart when He was delivered into our world nearly 2,000 years ago. If we were there in His heart, then we *were* there when He came for the sole purpose of winning the ultimate battle — the battle He fought and won 33 years later when He died on the Cross, later to arise from the Grave to provide Eternal Victory for all who believe in Him, to all who repent of their sins and acknowledge Him as their Lord and Savior.

Since He came to earth with each of us in mind, perhaps this Christmas is as good a time as any to invite the Lord to show us how we can know Him, in the way He intended right from the start.

To me, His coming, and all He brings with Him, is a time frame relevant to every last one of us.   □

A gift 'fore given' is often the best

December 21, 1991

Attention, last-minute Christmas shoppers! You are not alone!

Even if you've been thinking for weeks and months about what to give So-and-So on your gift list, if you're like me, you're still not done shopping.

However, if we already know what we want to give the last few people on our list, the pressure of actually going out and buying these gifts is minimal. The knowing-what-to-give part of giving is sort of like a gift "fore given," isn't it?

A gift fore given. When the idea of what to give is born, part of the giving is already done. We could call it: fore giveness.

Fore giveness.

Something about this thought has a familiar ring to it! It sounds like something I jotted down on the bulletin in church one Sunday not too long ago. Wonder if it's still folded up in my purse? Yes, here it is.

On November 17, Pastor Howard West said is his sermon at Waller United Methodist Church: "God's grace, given *before* we need it, is forgiveness."

That means forgiveness is *fore* given. God planned to forgive us even before we sinned; even before we were born. God created the concept of forgiveness before any of us knew what it was. He lovingly devised the way to send us forgiveness through His Son Jesus, before He sent Jesus to deliver the gift.

The gift existed before anyone knew anything about it. And God, the Greatest Giver of all time, cared enough to wrap the Greatest Gift of all time in a surprise package.

Only a clever God could have thought to put forgiveness in a tiny bundle in a manger of straw. And, today, while children and adults look under the tree for gifts on Christmas, the best gift is the one *fore given* 2,000 years ago.

Is there someone on our gift list we need to forgive? Before we give a "boughten" gift, perhaps we need to give, and receive, forgiveness.

No one can say it any better than Jesus Himself in Matthew, chapter 6, verses 14 and 15:

"For if you forgive men when they sin against you, your Heavenly Father will also forgive you. But if you do not forgive men their sins, your Father will not forgive your sins" (NIV).

The greatest part of forgiveness is how freely God intends it to be given. There really is no better gift, is there?   □

Christmas found shining in likely places

December 19, 1992

By the looks of our house, inside and out, you'd think the Moores aren't celebrating Christmas this year, and you'd be partly right.

This is the season of weddings in our family, with the second one in five weeks taking place the day this column runs. I think it's safe to assume that that's enough explanation as to why our Christmas lights and ornaments are still in the attic.

Oh, there's been a lot of decorating all right — decorating of churches and reception halls (there's a surprise ahead about this "category"), the making of three dozen table centerpieces, not to mention corsages, bouquets and boutonnieres (fortunately, a friend made all the corsages, boutonnieres and the bridal bouquet for the first wedding) — but, at our home, there's no Christmas tree in the bay window, no wreath on the front door, no lights on the shrubbery.

Even so, you know what? Although it's been hectic getting ready for two daughters' weddings during holiday time, it's been more of a joy than ever to see Christmas lights come on in the windows of neighbors' — and even strangers' — houses.

Each of these lightings has been a precious, quiet reminder that Christmas isn't on hold. It's happening all around us. And believe me, speaking personally, the lights of others have contributed greatly to helping turn on "the Christmas within."

Expanding on that thought, imagine my surprise when I slipped into the Benton United Methodist Church last Sunday afternoon to make mental notes on what was needed to decorate the sanctuary for today's wedding. The work was already done! The church was filled with poinsettias, greens, bows and candles — all in preparation for the congregation's celebration of Christmas.

What an unexpected blessing! For the first time in weeks, I sat down and relaxed for a few minutes, right there in a front pew, taking in the beauty and the worshipful atmosphere.

In those few moments alone, I realized I had just received a priceless gift: I was experiencing the joy of being the mother-of-the-brides and, at the same time, soaking up the glow of Christmas that shines from the lives and efforts of others.

My reason for sharing all of this with you? Well, the next time (whether it's Christmas time or *any* time) you wonder if anyone is ever blessed by the light you try to keep burning, stop wondering, and just keep your light shining. It may be exactly what someone needs to see.

May God bless all of you, and may You find Him all around you this Christmas season.   □

Giving the right gift to Jesus
December 22, 1990

If I were going to place a gift under the Christmas tree tagged, "To Jesus, From Me," what would that gift be?

Would it be a store-bought present? A homemade one?

Should it be something to eat? Something to wear?

How big? What color? What size?

How much should it cost?

What would Jesus like to have?

What would He like to have from me?

Hm-m-m-m.

If I knew how to make Jesus happy, if I knew what He wanted most in the whole-wide world, would I get it for Him?

If it meant working extra hard, extra long hours, would I do it? Or would I be too tired, too sleepy or too busy?

What if it were to cost more than I have? What if it were to cost more than I want to give?

What if I already know what Jesus wants from me, but I'm afraid to give it to Him?

What if He wants my heart, my life, my time, my talents?

What if I keep telling Him, "Later"?

What if I wait until it's too late?

What if I find out all He wants is me and all that I am, but I keep telling Him, and myself, that that's not enough?

What if all He wants is all of me, so He can make me into all He wants me to be?

If I don't give Him me, He doesn't have me.

If there's a chance that all He wants for Christmas is all of me, than I'd better start unwrapping all the excuses I've given Him in the past, and just give Him myself.

Merry Christmas, Jesus. I hope You like Your present. By the way, Lord, I'm nonreturnable. If I don't fit Your specifications, You're welcome to do whatever altering needs done. Amen.   □

Christmas memories: From tree, to train, to sunset

December 8, 1990

Sometimes Christmas makes me want to be a young girl again. Back then I couldn't wait for Dad to bring home the Christmas tree. Setting it up and decorating it were highpoints of the year for both of us.

Dad was always busy, often working 12 and even 18 hours a day as a self-employed coal stripper, so about the only things he and I did together with any regularity were small-game and deer hunting and putting up the Christmas tree.

Dad never told my mother about the time I accidentally fired the shotgun while he and I were talking out by the picnic table in our back yard, tearing up quite a hole in the ground beside Dad's insulated hunting boot — with his right foot in it — and I never told Mum that Dad made a big mess in the living room drilling holes in the trunk of the Christmas tree so he could insert extra branches where nature was negligent.

The reason Dad didn't tell Mum about the close call between my shotgun and his foot was because he didn't want her to worry. And the reason I didn't tell Mum about the Christmas tree mess was because I didn't see one.

All I saw was Dad, in his gray Montgomery Ward work clothes and scuffed-up, high-top work shoes, kneeling on the living room carpet, drilling, sawing and tying branches in place so that we could have the best looking, most perfectly shaped tree ever.

Unlike the shotgun incident that happened only once, the Christmas tree ritual of drilling and adding branches was a yearly occurrence. But if I was keeping a secret from Mum, I didn't realize it at the time. It never occurred to me, until I became "The Mom," what a mess putting up a tree really is.

There is one secret, however, I did keep from both Mum and Dad for a lot of years.

One December, when I was 10 or 12 years old, I was hiding some gifts I had just bought for Mum and Dad. Thinking I was putting these gifts in a bag with some other things I had hidden days earlier, I opened up a medium-size white paper bag, only to find something I wasn't supposed to see until Christmas morning: a box labeled "Lionel Bumper Car."

You see, being an only child, I was my dad's daughter — and his son. So having a Lionel train was a big deal to both of us. And each year Dad surprised me with "a new piece of equipment" for the train set for "us" to play with under the tree.

I knew he didn't want me to know about the bumper car, so I never let on I had seen it. But I didn't know what to do when Christmas morning came, and after all of the packages were opened, there was no Lionel box among them. Dad had forgotten, and how was I going to let him know without letting him know I knew?

"Well ... sure looks like we got a lot of gifts this year," I said as Mum and Dad and I hugged each other and said our thank-yous and you're-welcomes.

"Sure looks like we got a lot," I repeated.

"That must be it. There's nothing else under the tree. All the packages are opened," I sighed extra loudly.

"Yep," Dad responded. (He always was a man of few words.)

And off the three of us went to the kitchen for our Christmas breakfast.

During breakfast, I suggested Dad and I play with the train while Mum did the dishes. (Poor Mum, but I was desperate. I didn't want Dad to miss out on surprising me because he always got such big kick of it.)

"Sounds good to me," Dad said, and so after breakfast, that's what we did.

Nothing. He didn't remember.

Actually, he didn't remember all day, even with countless hints from me.

It wasn't until Christmas night, when my aunt, uncle and cousins arrived and began to tell what all they got for Christmas, that I saw Dad's eyes light up and heard him whisper to himself as he slipped out of the living room, "Oh, I almost forgot."

"Almost forgot! Oh, Dad," I laughed inside.

When Dad re-entered the room, he gave me the medium-size white paper bag right in front of everybody and said, "Dotty, here's one more present. Sorry it's not wrapped. I almost forgot."

Well, if Dad were alive, I'd tell him that I never forgot how happy I was to see him happy to have remembered.

I was reminded of that memory last Saturday when I looked out the window and saw a spectacular orange sunset.

"Oh, Lord," I sighed in awe of His masterpiece, "I've been so busy getting ready for Christmas, I almost forgot something. I forgot to praise You and thank You for a new day. Sorry I'm a little late. But thank You for being You and praise You for all You give me and all You do for me. Especially for sending me and the whole world a Savior. In His Name. Amen."

□

Show others Christ is in Christmas
December 18, 1993

During this final week before Christmas, suppose you were suddenly asked to play host to a group of people who know nothing of a Christmas holiday. People who know nothing of Christmas from a religious sense, from a traditional sense, not even from a commercial sense. In other words, what might you show and tell aliens from another planet about Christmas, if such a task were suddenly assigned to you?

OK, so the hypothetical situation is too farfetched for you to waste even a moment's thought, because, after all, this is the final week before Christmas and there simply isn't time for foolish supposition. Forget the remote possibility of entertaining creatures who've never heard of Christmas. Get back to the busyness at hand: decorating, shopping, cleaning, wrapping, cooking, baking.

Forget having to explain to anyone about the meaning of the season. Just rush on with getting it all done so you can get it over with.

That's right, *get it over with*. Isn't that what you want right now? For Christmas to be over with!

Oh, I see. That's what you're thinking, but you don't want anyone to know *that's what you're thinking*. You weren't planning on saying it out loud.

Well, in that case, you aren't the local Wal-Mart shopper I overheard one evening this week exclaiming, "I can't wait till Christmas is over!"

I'm so glad you aren't the stranger I heard clarifying what she had just said to her friend by adding, "I mean it! I hate Christmas!"

The outburst made me sad. It made me wonder just what some people are made of. Then, a little while later, on my way home in the car, I remembered. I recalled a Christmas past when I was one of those who wanted Christmas to be over and done with. Our girls were small and we had a house full of people coming for Christmas weekend.

There was so much to do. So much to get ready. So little time to sleep or rest before everyone arrived. Once they arrived there was so much going on. So many people all over the place. So much noise and confusion it was upsetting to me.

Silently, internally, I exploded, "I can't wait till Christmas is over!"

Like all "good" things, it did come to an end, but most of my memories of that Christmas are not good. It was awful. So awful, I vowed it would never happen again. And I don't think it did.

You see, no one but I seemed to feel that particular Christmas was so horrible. That's because no one but I was miserable. Why? I guess because I was the only one trying too hard to make everything perfect.

Since then, I've had my share of hectic Christmases, and I've gotten myself into some Christmas messes. But none of them have been so awful I couldn't wait until they were over.

So what changed things? What made other Christmases more enjoyable than the "awful" one?

I changed. My attitude changed.

Instead of thinking and preparing and perfecting every little detail, I came up with a new plan. Where once I had reasoned, "If anything is out of place, what will people think of me?" I now asked myself, "What will people think of Christmas because of me?"

Today, after giving it years of more thought, I've amended my own thinking, hopefully with an even better question to set me straight, not just at Christmas time, but all the time: What will people think of *Christ* because of me?   □

Why celebrate Christmas?

December 17, 1988

This week as I read an article called "Why I Celebrate Christmas" published in the current issue of *Christianity Today* magazine, I added one word and a question mark to that title and asked myself, "Why *do* I celebrate Christmas?"

The first response that comes to my mind is not the same one that I might have had when I was younger. Years ago I likely would have said: "I celebrate Christmas because it's a Christian holiday, a family tradition ... it's the day we remember the birth of Jesus. I celebrate Christmas because it's my favorite holiday ... I LOVE CHRISTMAS! I love the lights, the sparkle, the magic. I love red and green, the Christmas carols, and the scent of pine."

Today, my answer is every bit as exciting as all that, just a lot shorter and hopefully more focused: "I celebrate Christmas because I LOVE JESUS!"

It's not that I didn't love Jesus all along, but it's only been in recent years that I've begun celebrating Christmas as a form of worshiping Him.

I never intended to worship *Christmas* and I don't think I did. But it's more clear to me now that it's Jesus, and Jesus only, that should be celebrated, decorated, made room for and proclaimed.

Nowadays, when I look at a bare, undecorated Christmas tree in my living room, I fill up with love and adoration for Jesus who willingly came into the world as a naked Baby. Although He was and is the King of Kings, He was born without kingly robes and royal decorations. And He was beautiful. Because the bare Christmas tree reminds me to love Him more, I leave it undecorated for nearly a week.

When I finally begin to put the lights on my tree, I think of how only one light, one star, was used to point the way to the place where the Light of the World was born in Bethlehem. And I love Him. I begin to worship Jesus for His humble birth when He could have demanded a royal carriage instead of a manger.

The unadorned Baby Jesus who came with no crown and no golden scepter deserves more lights, more tinsel and more ornaments than my tree could ever hold. As I add each light and each ornament to my tree, I do it for Him, to proclaim His coming, His presence, His glory and His right to be worshiped.

During His life on earth, Jesus did not receive the recognition and place of honor due Him. When I think of all He should have had but didn't, I'm glad for decorated Christmas trees around the world that proclaim His Royal Majesty. It's true that not everyone puts up a tree for Jesus. But that doesn't mean that every Christmas light shining inside our homes and up and down the landscape of our world isn't silently showing the way to Bethlehem.

After all, you can't stop a glowing light from shining unless you turn off or eliminate the power source. That, of course, can never happen to the Light of the World, the Bright and Morning Star. Jesus and His Presence will never stop shining. I celebrate Christmas because it's a glorious way to say, "I have seen the Star, and have come to worship Him."   □

Finding a place for Christmas
December 15, 2001

A few years ago, a friend, Linda Cox, from Colorado sent me a handmade bookmarker that recently resurfaced in the general vicinity of my infamously cluttered desk. The woven bookmarker adorned with a golden cross and pink needlepoint flowers states in colorful lettering: "My place with God."

The bookmarker is actually a Bible marker, but instead of using it in the way it was intended to serve, I have needed it in a different way. Each day since I re-found it, the marker's message has served to usher my pulled-in-every-direction self into a quiet, reflective corner of my thoughts, there to be alone with God.

Time alone with the Lord seems never to be more desperately coveted than during the Christmas season. It's true for me and I imagine it's true for you, too. Why is it, in the midst of the time we set aside for drawing near to the Lord and to the memory of His coming to earth, we suddenly get lost in the place where we can't find Him? This season becomes a dreaded treadmill of frustration instead of a worshipful shelter of stability.

One reason is that life must go on despite Christmas. Normal routines don't cease. Sickness, heartaches, jobs, bills, worries, work and burdens don't take a holiday. Instead they often multiply and intensify. All through the Christmas season it can be difficult if not nearly impossible to breathe a sigh of relief that everything is under control, when, in reality, it is not.

But I'll tell you this, seeing as how reality at times is too real to be comfortably tolerated, I'm thankful that the reality of Jesus Christ overshadows all else. Do you agree? If you will join me in a resounding "Amen," we can, together, be reminded that Christmastime is indeed our "Place with God."

Christmas is a place in our heart. A place for the Christ Child. A place for the Son of God, the Savior of the world. A place for God crucified. A place for God resurrected. A place readied for His return.

Christ came into a cluttered, sin-filled, dark, desperate world. He ministered to the world, and still does. He lived and died for us. He arose again for us. He lives now and for all eternity for us. And He *is* coming again for us.

As you and I look around — you in your home, in your life, and I in mine — quite possibly we are deep in lament that there is no way we'll ever be "ready for Christmas." Well, even this is quite acceptable as long as your heart and my heart are ready for receiving Christ. That's all there is to it.

In His Name. Amen.   □

Filling the void

December 22, 2001

Christmas is a time for reflection. Not just a reflection and dancing shadows on the ceiling from the lights on the Christmas tree, but especially for reflections of the heart.

The child within each of us reflects on some of our earliest memories. You can go back to a Christmas Eve of your childhood in an instant. I know I can. I'm there, even as I write. The one thing I wished for more than any other was for someone to share my life with. I had a mother and a father — and a big empty spot in my heart.

For years and years the spot remained empty until I was sure it would never be filled. There were times I would cry alone under the tree because I knew something was missing. There was a longing I could not describe.

Finally I grew up, fell in love, got married and had children. More years went by and now our children are grown and I'm a grandmother, but there is still an empty spot in my heart that often baffles me.

Why do I still have this spot that can't be filled? My life is filled to overflowing with loved ones, responsibilities, plans, dreams, commitments and tasks. Why is there yet an ache for something more? Something that seems so close and yet so far from fulfillment and understanding?

As I reflect on this, again, right here and now, I perceive a tiny speck of realization that might qualify as a revelation, at least on a personal level. The revelation is more a rhetorical question than a brilliant flash of insight. Nonetheless, it might be significant enough to warrant putting into words. At least I'll try.

Could it be, I ask, that the longing, the emptiness, the spot that never seems to be filled is a homesickness for my eternal home...my eternal destiny...my eternal family?

The Bible confirms in Hebrews 11:13 that this earth is not our real home. We, like generations before us, are strangers here, visiting for a spell, until we reach our home in heaven. Believing in Jesus Christ as our Savior and Lord, confessing and repenting of our sins and receiving His free gift of salvation are the steps we must take to know we are heaven-bound. The emptiness of our earthly world can not, and never will, fill the void in our hearts and lives for the place where we will, at last, reside.

This year, as in countless Christmases past, you, like yours truly, might acknowledge a loneliness, a longing, an empty spot that can only be filled when we reach the heavenly city prepared for us by the Lord (Hebrews 11:16). That's as it should be, because nothing here on earth is supposed to take the place of eternity with God.

Reflecting on this is quite a gift — a gift wrapped up in the swaddling clothes of a Babe in a manger. May you all have a blessed Christmas as you reflect on the Eternal Christ — and an eternity with Him.   □